The Biblical Seminar
5

ANCIENT
ISRAEL

ANCIENT ISRAEL

A NEW HISTORY OF ISRAELITE SOCIETY

Niels Peter Lemche

Sheffield Academic Press

Translated by Fred Cryer
from the Danish original, *Det Gamle Israel*
Det israelitiske samfund fra sammenbruddet
af bronzealderkulturen til hellenistisk tid
(Aarhus: ANIS, 1984)

Published with support from the Danish Council of Research in the Humanities

First published 1988
Reprinted 1990, 1995

Published by Sheffield Academic Press Ltd
Mansion House
19 Kingfield Road
Sheffield, S11 9AS
England

Printed on acid-free paper in Great Britain
by The Cromwell Press
Melksham, Wiltshire

British Library Cataloguing in Publication Data

A catalogue record for this book is available
from the British Library

ISBN 1-85075-017-3

CONTENTS

Preface   7
Table of Chronology   9

Chapter 1
GEOGRAPHY, DEMOGRAPHY, ECONOMY   11
  1. Introduction   11
  2. The Geography of Palestine   11
  3. Demography and Economy   17
  4. Concluding Remarks   27

Chapter 2
TEXT AND HISTORY   29
  1. The Old Testament as History   29
  2. The Old Testament Regarded as a Text   34
  3. The Old Testament as a Historical Source   45
  4. Methods of Reading the Texts   60
  5. Other Sources   69

Chapter 3
THE PRE-MONARCHICAL PERIOD   75
  1. Palestine Between 3000 and 1500   75
  2. The Late Bronze Age   77
  3. Israelite Tribal Society   88
  4. The Pre-national Period in
    Earlier Academic Discussion   104
  5. Concluding Remarks   116

Chapter 4
THE PERIOD OF THE MONARCHY   119
  1. The Deuteronomistic History   119
  2. The Political History of the Monarchy   122
  3. Israelite Society During the Monarchy   130
  4. History as Intellectual Experience:
    the Development of a National Identity   155

Chapter 5
THE EXILE AND THE POST-EXILIC PERIOD   173
   1. The Sources   173
   2. The Babylonian Exile   175
   3. The Post-exilic Period   186

Chapter 6
ISRAELITE RELIGION   197
   1. Presuppositions for Writing a History of
      Israelite Religion   197
   2. West Semitic Religion in the Second Half
      of the Second Millennium   198
   3. Monotheistic Yahwism   209
   4. Pre-exilic Israelite Religion   223
   5. The Transformation of Pre-exilic Religion   238
   6. The Origins of Yahwism   252
   7. Concluding Remarks   256

A Guide to Relevant Literature   259
Index of Biblical References   271
Index of Authors   275

PREFACE

In the last generation or so literally scores of histories of Israel and introductions to the study of the Old Testament or of Israelite religion have appeared. Why, then, should anyone take the trouble to either write or edit yet another addition to this prodigious list? The reason why this writer has chosen to do so is that a fundamentally new approach to the study of Israelite history and religion is more needed now than at any time in the past. Until the present, most scholars have offered in the guise of research efforts which are by no means independent scholarly interpretations of the history of Israel, but more or less rationalistic paraphrases of the biblical version of the history of Israel and its religion. This approach is becoming increasingly unsatisfactory, especially when it is considered in the light of the ongoing discussion of the earliest history of the Israelite people.

In presenting this new attempt at a synthesis I have been able to build on the results of the research which was set out in detail in my previous volume, *Early Israel. Anthropological and Historical Studies on the Israelite Society Before the Monarchy* (Leiden, 1985). Here I argued that it is absurd to speak of historical recollections in the Old Testament which date from before the introduction of the monarchy. It is accordingly methodologically wrong to base one's reconstruction of the emergence of Israel in the late second millennium BCE on the Old Testament itself. This being the case, a broader socio-historical approach will be essential if we are to replace the usual efforts to rewrite the Old Testament.

A corollary of this insight is the acknowledgment of the necessity also of abandoning the usual interpretations of the history of Israelite religion, as such interpretations have invariably been based on the usual reconstruction of the profane history of the nation. It should be obvious that a radical re-evaluation of Israel's profane history must inevitably lead to a new synthesis as far as her religious history is concerned.

The form of this work has been purposely chosen so as to present my versions of the histories of Israel and Israelite religion as a kind of introduction to a renewed debate on these topics, rather than as a definitive synthesis. I can only hope that this project will be received in the spirit in which it was conceived.

Copenhagen, 24th February 1987

This book is, apart from minor corrections, reprinted as it appeared in 1988. The author is aware of the changes in the field which have happened over the last ten years and which would perhaps warrant an almost totally new version rather than a revision of the original version. Nevertheless, from a methodological point of view the volume may still be considered the most coherent and up-to-date version of a History of Israel, and for that reason it was decided to change as little as possible

Copenhagen, 12th May 1995

TABLE OF CHRONOLOGY

The Late Bronze Age	c. 1500-1200 BCE
The Iron Age	c. 1200-500 BCE
The Persian Period	c. 538-331 BCE

The Kings of Israel and Judah
The following chronological outline is based on K.T. Andersen, 'Die Chronologie der Könige von Israel und Juda', *Studia Theologica* 29 (1969), pp. 69-114.

Saul	before 1000 BCE
David	c. 1000-960
Solomon	c. 960-925

The Kingdom of Israel		*The Kingdom of Judah*	
Jeroboam	c. 925-911	Rehoboam	c. 925-916
Nadab	911-910	Abijam	916-914
Baasha	910-887	Asa	914-874
Elah	887-886	Jehoshaphat	874-850
Zimri	886	Jehoram	850-843
Omri	886-875	Ahaziah	843-842
Ahab	875-854	Athaliah	842-837
Ahaziah	854-853	Joash	837-797
Jehoram	853-842	Amaziah	797-769
Jehu	842-815	Uzziah	769-741
Jehoahaz	815-799	Jotham	741-734
Jehoash	799-784	Ahaz	734-715
Jeroboam	784-753	Hezekiah	715-697
Zechariah	753-752	Manasseh	697-642
Shallum	752-751	Amon	642-640
Menahem	751-742	Josiah	640-609
Pekahiah	742-741	Jehoahaz	609
Pekah	741-730	Jehoiakim	609-598
Hoshea	730-722	Jehoiakin	598
		Zedekiah	598-587

Chapter 1

GEOGRAPHY, DEMOGRAPHY, ECONOMY

1. *Introduction*

The historical Israel was the single society which more than any other left its mark on the southwestern part of the 'Fertile Crescent' in the first millennium BCE. By 'Fertile Crescent' is meant that part of the Near East which has agricultural potential, and which therefore also makes possible the emergence of urban societies. The area in question, which comprises less than fifty percent of the total area of the Middle East, extends from the Persian Gulf on the southeast in a bow up through the Mesopotamian (Iraqi) river valley, through northern Syria, and then down along the Mediterranean on the western side. Here it exhausts itself in the unfertile sandy deserts in the northern part of the Sinai Peninsula. The Nile Valley is also included in the Fertile Crescent. This region exercised an influence upon events and developments in the neighbouring regions of the Middle East and received in turn impulses from them.

In geographical terms the Israelite territory, or, more correctly, the region of Palestine, which was the Greco-Roman name for the area, is regarded as a part of the greater Syrian region. With respect to geography, topology, ethnic composition, and ecology, Palestine is merely a continuation of this greater Syria, and between the two there are no actual natural borders, but only occasional, historically conditioned political divisions.

2. *The Geography of Palestine*

2.1 *The Geo-Physical Structure of the Country*
2.1.1 *Delimitation of the Region*
Palestine is insignificant in area. In the Old Testament it is often elliptically referred to by the expression 'from Dan to Beer-Sheba'. In

Ancient Israel

other words, it includes the territory stretching from Dan, at the sources of the Jordan to the north down to Beer-Sheba in the northern part of the Negeb Desert in the south, a distance of only about 250 to 300 kilometres. From the western boundary, that is, the Mediterranean, to the traditional eastern one, the river Jordan, the distance is about 50 km in the northern part of the country, and about 120 km in the southern part. All told, this area is about 25,000 km² (in European terms corresponding to the area of, say, Jutland). Shifting political circumstances have occasionally permitted other regions to be included, such as the stretch passing down through the depression of the Arabah to Aqaba and Elath at the northern end of the Red Sea, or the region east of Jordan to the verge of the desert, a little strip of land less than fifty kilometres wide.

Under ordinary circumstances one would expect such an insignificant geographical area to be politically organized under some central authority. However, this has not often been the case, or rather, it has only exceptionally occurred that such political unity has existed. There are a number of reasons for this, some of which are to be sought in the nature of the country itself. One reason is the lack of natural boundaries against the surrounding countries. Admittedly, Palestine has the natural border of the Mediterranean on the west, which has historically meant that influences from the Mediterranean world only reached the country to a limited extent; it has also meant that sizable groups of intruders have only rarely come from that direction. Examples would include the arrival of the Philistines around 1200 BCE and that of the Crusaders around 1100 CE. Palestine is separated on the southwest from Egypt by a sandy desert about 100 km across, and the Sinai desert may accordingly be regarded as a natural boundary towards Egypt. This fact has not, however, prevented Egypt from exerting both cultural and political influences on Palestine which have sometimes played a major part in developments there.

Towards the south there is a gradual transition in the Negeb region into the desert regions of the Sinai Peninsula (mainly stony desert) and, as we move towards the east and upwards along the depression of the Arabah there is a transition into the Great Arabian Desert. Historically, this borderline was never impenetrable, as numerous examples demonstrate. Farther up in the eastern reaches we find a similar fluid boundary between the arable land which at times belongs within the sphere of Israelite political influence and the

Syro-Arabian Desert. At various times the river Jordan has served as a natural border; this was made possible by the peculiar character of the Jordan itself, as this river is not navigable by reason of its winding course and sharp descent (the riverbed declines on an average of 3-4m per km). On the other hand, the river itself is not really an insurmountable obstacle, in part because it is fordable at numerous spots, but also because it is only modest in breadth (at its widest the Jordan is more a riverlet than an actual river). Farther to the north the border between Palestine and Syria is completely fluid. When one ascends from the Sea of Chinnereth to the north one finds an elevation eastwards which ends in a great plateau, but this continues onwards far into Syria, mostly in the form of a flat range of heights known as the Golan Heights. However, in the far north Mt Hermon must be regarded as a barrier towards the northeast.

The northern boundary facing the Lebanon is fluid in part. The lowlands continue naturally up into the valley which, running north to south as it does, comprises the central part of our contemporary Lebanon (the Beqa' Valley). Farther to the west the mountains of South Lebanon merge more or less without incident with the mountainous regions of northern Galilee, which extends to the west until they reach the Mediterranean.

2.1.2 *Physical Structure*

The physical structure of the region also serves to explain the historical lack of political unity, as it aided fragmentation into innumerable small or merely moderate regional enclaves. If we move from north to south in the territory west of the Jordan, the northwestern part consists mainly of a mountainous region which only occasionally (the exception being Mt Hermon, which approaches 3000m) exceeds 1000m in height, and which in the northern section is usually around 500m or less, declining as it moves southwards. However, the area is not an integral massif, as it is intersected by a number of lateral valleys, some of which are both deep and broad.

Towards the west and south this mountainous region is terminated by the Galilean lowlands, in part consisting of the plain at Acco, which extends from the border of Lebanon (Rosh Haniqra) in the north to Carmel in the south, and in part consisting of the Plain of Jezreel, an eastward-facing branch of the coastal plain which ends by gradually descending into the valley of the Jordan to the east. The Carmel chain and the central Palestinian massif terminate this valley

at the southern end and make up a border between the northern and
central parts of the country, since Carmel's tip extends as a
promontory out into the Mediterranean to the west and continues in
an unbroken chain until Mt Gilboa to the east at the edge of the
Valley of the Jordan.

South of this line the physical structure of the country becomes
more regular. If we start at the Mediterranean, we first encounter a
very narrow coastal plain, only about 20 to 25 km wide, which ends
in a chain of coastal mountains, or, more accurately, a hilly
landscape, called the Shephelah, which runs almost like a hem along
the actual mountainous region in the centre of the country. Even the
central mountainous area, however, scarcely attains to any impressive
altitude; it is mostly confined to between 500m and 1000m and only
exceptionally exceeds this mean, as, particularly, in the vicinity of
Hebron. Nor does this region make up a continuous massif, as the
mountains are interrupted by a number of greater or smaller
stretches of valley which are connected with one another by
negotiable passes.

The Jordan Valley is a peculiar phenomenon in its own right. The
Jordan runs from Mt Hermon in the north down through the two
freshwater lakes, Lake Huleh and the Sea of Chinnereth, to the salt
lake known as the Dead Sea, in the south. It is a rift valley which also
continues up through the Lebanon as the Beqa' Valley. As far as
Palestine is concerned, this depression is part and parcel of the
course of the river Jordan. By the same token, this part of the country
contains a remarkable natural phenomenon, in that the Jordan
descends from its sources at an altitude of about 200m above sea-
level, and then falls, sometimes quite sharply, to a depth of -200m at
the Sea of Chinnereth, only to end at more than -300m at the
northern end of the Dead Sea. The valley continues through the
Dead Sea and there attains a maximum depth of almost 800m below
sea level, after which it gradually rises all the way to Aqaba and Elath
at the Red Sea in the south.

The descent from the central highlands down to the Jordan Valley
is steep, and the ascent in the territory east of Jordan is no less so;
here in what was once ancient Israelite territory the maximum
altitude of 1000m is frequently approached. The region east of the
river differs from the area west of it, to the extent that we are
speaking of the region west of the desert, in that the eastern slope is
intersected by a number of deep laterally running riverbeds, the

valleys of the Yarmuk, Jabbok, and Arnon (in Moab). Towards the east the ascent includes a tableland, the western part of which is prairie which gradually turns into desert as it moves to the east.

2.2 Climate and Fertility
2.2.1 Water Supply
The climate is subtropical, with completely dry summers and a vital period of rain in the winter months. This rainy season begins with some light precipitation in September or October (the so-called 'early rain'), and diminishes in March or April (the 'late rain'). The actual rainy season extends from the months of November to February, the climax of this period usually being in January and February. In large parts of the country this winter rain is sufficient to enable the growth of vegetation, and thus permits agriculture. This does not, however, apply to the entire country. The western regions and particularly the regions in the northern mountains, are most favoured, while the Jordan Valley and the Negeb are least so; in the latter areas winter rain is a rarity, so that agriculture based on rainfall alone is quite impossible.

Another difficulty confronting the agricultural exploitation of the country is the uncertainty of the climate, which entails that it regularly occurs that the early and late rains simply do not come. In years like these, as in the drier regions, agriculture must accordingly be based on the existence of artificially collected rainwater (via cisterns), or on the aid derived from natural springs or rivers. However, many of the rivers dry out in the spring and are first resuscitated by the arrival of the rains in the autumn. On the other hand, since the first millennium in Palestine the technique of collecting rainwater was known and was in fact employed, particularly in the mountainous regions. However, exploitation of the few continuously serviceable rivers like the Jordan and the larger sources in the region east of the Jordan only occurred sporadically, since the technology of the time could not solve the problems of irrigation over any considerable distance. Major irrigation systems were first introduced to the region in Hellenistic times and first became common in the Roman era, when they were largely used to ensure the water-supply of the towns.

The final possibility the Palestinian peasant possessed for a stable source of water was the springs in which the land is quite rich, and which are the results of subterranean geological features which

permit water accumulation in natural reservoirs. We are informed by
numerous passages in the OT that the peasant's many tasks also
included well-digging, in the process of which the attempt was made
to reach the water-bearing subterranean strata in order to ensure a
constant water supply. However, we are also told that such wells
could easily become the objects of conflicts, since there were never
enough of them (cf. e.g. Gen. 26.12ff.). Finally, the natural springs
also played a part in regions which were otherwise infertile desert;
these are the small fertile enclaves known as oases. The most famous
oasis in Palestine is the one in Jericho, at the southern end of the
Jordan Valley, where abundant springwater enabled the construction
of a sizable village or even a town perhaps as early as 10,000 years
ago.

The uneven distribution of precipitation creates a correspondingly
uneven subdivision of the region into fertile and infertile areas. In
general, the plain valley regions in the western part of the country
were always the most favoured by nature, and so were intensively
exploited. In some valleys, however, settlement and agriculture were
hindered by a range of factors such as malaria, which flourished in
such relatively rainy places as the Valley of Huleh and the coastal
plains. The real 'breadbasket' of the country was Galilee, on the
plain near Acco and the plain of Jezreel. To the extent that the
necessary technology was present, it was also possible to exploit the
mountainous areas agriculturally. This was especially true of the
western slopes, including the Shephelah, where rain coming in off
the sea regularly visits the area; against this, the eastern slopes going
down to the Jordan Valley were so dry as to approach actual desert
conditions. In the land east of the Jordan, the cooling of the western
winds as they ascended from the Jordan Valley caused sufficient
precipitation in the mountainous areas that these regions, too, could
be exploited agriculturally.

*2.2.2 Indigenous Flora and Fauna and Man's Encroachments on
them*
On the other hand, already in antiquity this agricultural exploitation
entailed that the mountainous regions became an important source
of food production. The natural undergrowth in a region of this sort,
that is, one possessing a Mediterranean climate, would normally be
light forest. There are numerous indications, both in the Bible and in
archeological (palaeobotanical) sources which suggest that forestry

was not an unknown phenomenon in the mountainous regions of Palestine in historical times. However, the intervention of man entailed that already in antiquity such woody growth was seriously deforested in order to make room for cultivable fields. The consequence of this process is well known: if one removes undergrowth from moutainsides, in the course of a relatively short time topsoil will be eroded by rain, and all that will survive will be the naked rocky surfaces. One particular agricultural technique, namely the construction of terraces on the mountain slopes, is able to amend the unfortunate consequences of such deforestation. In what follows we shall see that the emergence of the Israelite tribal system in these mountainous areas towards the close of the second millennium BCE was very much connected with the introduction of the terrace system.

Among other obstacles to the exploitation of the mountainous regions in particular were the local fauna, which in those days included a variety of carnivores such as lions and leopards. These animals occasionally constituted a real danger for humans, as we see in a few passages in the OT (see e.g. 1 Kgs 13; 2 Kgs 2.23-24). In reality these fauna, which at least in part were of African origin, were survivals from a more favourable climatic period. This period goes back to prehistoric times, but around 3,000 BCE it gave way to that climate which has dominated—with regional and periodic variations— until our own times.

3. *Demography and Economy*

3.1 *Exploitation of the Resources of the Country*
3.1.1 *The Settlement Pattern*
Throughout the ages, the settlement pattern has tended to follow the varying fertility of the country, since the greatest population density has generally occurred in regions which were suitable for intensive cultivation. Regions which were less susceptible to cultivation, such as the mountainous areas, were also capable of supplying the needs of a peasant population, but hardly the same relative numbers of individuals as in the valleys or plains. Finally, the marginal regions, that is, those which have always been dry and where the annual precipitation is so sporadic as to be disregarded for agricultural purposes, also contained a population. However, such groups were invariably forced to supplement their rudimentary agriculture with some stockbreeding.

Of course, in historical times this picture has varied widely for a number of reasons. Above all, political conditions have sometimes entailed that fertile regions have been abandoned as primary settlement zones, whereas the highly situated regions, even in the mountains, were able to provide shelter and protection only to a somewhat reduced population, which attempted to survive a period of troubles. Furthermore, the over-exploitation of agricultural areas, particularly in the mountains, has also frequently led to the abandonment of populous and cultivated areas as the soil was gradually depleted. Finally, certain exceptional conditions have sometimes caused changes in the numerical and political weight between the various traditional occupational groups. For example, peasants have sometimes had to turn to stockbreeding, in the process frequently also becoming nomads (see below), while at other times nomads have sometimes been forcibly settled or have chosen themselves voluntarily to settle and convert into sedentary peasants.

The conditions which contributed to the fact that such easily cultivable regions as, for example, the Valley of Huleh or the coastal plains, have not always been fully exploited, are also reflected in the historically varying settlement patterns, as we discover that towns and villages are not nearly as numerous in these regions as we might otherwise expect. On the other hand, on the slopes of the Shephelah and along the border of the Valley of Huleh we find both larger and less sizable settlements, which suggest a certain exploitation of the neighbouring lowlands. Thus, for reasons of health, and possibly also with a view to defence, the inhabitants appear to have lived in the hinterlands where they farmed the ridges of the valleys, even if this entailed that the path from a village or a town to its fields was thus extended somewhat. In any case, the short distances within the confines of the country always ensured that it would be possible to reach the cultivable areas. Against this, the fertility of the Galilean plains is directly reflected in the construction of townships of a respectable size, by Palestinian standards, as well as in the numerous villages which have been present there throughout history.

The mountainous regions in northern and central Palestine ordinarily contained a population which could not be compared numerically with that of the plains regions. They were nevertheless far from waste regions. In the valleys in these mountainous regions we find dense collections of villages, and sometimes also an occasional town (more rarely even a town of some considerable size).

A number of the best-known localities in both the Old and New Testaments were situated in just such sites: Hebron, Jerusalem, Bethel, Shiloh, and Shechem. Also, the establishment of the Israelite society towards the close of the second millennium BCE itself entailed numerous innovations in the settlement pattern in the mountains.

Corresponding conditions applied (and still apply) to the region east of Jordan, where the large transverse-running rivers have, however, also influenced the establishment of human settlements. Against this, the settlements in such arid regions as large parts of the Jordan Valley or the Negeb Desert have been more than just sporadic. In the former, settlements were confined to oases like Jericho, while in the latter most settlements are situated in the northern part, on the border of the Judaean hill country (the southern part of the central Palestinian highlands). The reason for the establishment of the last-mentioned settlements is that they made possible a mixed economy, consisting of agriculture and stockbreeding.

3.1.2 *Agriculture and Stockbreeding. Nomadism*
In all parts of the country in which agriculture was feasible, the most important crops were cereals, particularly barley and wheat. However, there was also a considerable production of wine and olives which must have been rather profitable, and for which the mountain slopes were well suited. Other crops, such as dates, were also known, but these played no great rôle for the peasant in antiquity. One should note that the several varieties of citrus fruits for which the region is justly famous today were unknown in antiquity. They were first introduced at a rather late date. The wide assortment of fruits which are now grown in Palestine were also the results of much more recent importation. Thus, for example, the apple was then unknown, and the much less flourishing pomegranate (which is unrelated to the apple) was cultivated instead.

By far the majority of the population of the country have always engaged in the cultivation of the soil. Scholars have estimated that peasants composed about 90% of the population; this figure corresponds to that applicable to present conditions in other parts of the Near East which have not yet been industrialized. The peasant population ordinarily lived in villages which were scattered round the towns, on which they were dependent, and to which they paid taxes in the form of foodstuffs. But even in the towns people were generally engaged in the production of agricultural products for consumption in the towns themselves.

However, the special character of the country is such that many regions are not suited for agriculture as such. Such regions had then *faute de mieux* to be used for other purposes, such as stockbreeding, which was always important for the Palestinian peasant. In general, we may suppose that every village possessed a small herd of animals, especially goats and sheep (the so-called 'small cattle'), but also a few cows; these will either have been owned by the village in common or by the individual families. Sheep and goats are by nature herd animals, so that it was possible to shepherd them on a collective basis. We are not well informed about these processes in the Old Testament but if the evidence of later Near Eastern practices be admitted, it is likely that already in antiquity professional shepherds were employed to care for the village herd of small cattle. Use may also have been made of unemployed members of the family, such as adolescent boys, in this connexion. An obvious reflection of this practice is the narrative of the sons of Jacob, who looked after their father's small cattle away from home (Gen. 37.12-17), and, of course, there is also Jacob himself, who was employed by his uncle Laban to shepherd his animals (Gen. 29-30).

As far as the mountain villages are concerned, this possibility was especially appropriate, since both the climate and the topography of the mountainous regions may have motivated the inhabitants to make use of the altitudinal and consequent climatic differentials by the practice of some sort of *transhumance*. Following this practice, the small cattle were kept at home during the winter, that is, in the village or its environs, whereas in the summer after the conclusion of the harvest, herdsmen or even entire families led the herds up into the mountains.

A special variety of this type of husbandry is *nomadism*, in which entire families and family groups (i.e. clans or tribes) concentrate on the herding of animals to such an extent that other occupations become either wholly or partially excluded. Nomadism has manifested itself in countless forms. These range from mountain nomadism, whose practitioners can hardly be distinguished from the previous mentioned mountain peasants, and for whom a certain degree of agriculture is a significant side occupation during certain periods of the year, to the 'pure nomads', whose sole occupation is the raising of cattle. It is of vital importance for the understanding of the history of the Middle East, Israel included, to note that scholars are well aware that nomadism is not an occupation which is separate from all others, since in many respects it shares both tasks and strategies with other parts of the economic life of society. It is likewise important to acknowledge that the nomads in the ancient Near East did not come from the desert, even though this is frequently asserted; it is utterly fallacious. This type of nomadism, which had its origins in the Syro-Arabian Desert, the Sahara, and other, similar locations was first made possible by the use of the camel as a beast of burden. There was no possibility of this sort of nomadism before around 1000 BCE, when the camel was domesticated. In fact, a number of modern ethnographers maintain that the actual *bedouin* first appeared some time after the beginning of the Common Era, in the first or second century.

The nomads of antiquity were to be found in countries which also possessed peasant populations, or else the nomads inhabited the peripheries of such societies. Thus the nomads contributed to a significant degree to the peculiar economic and political structures which were dominant in the Middle East in pre-industrial times. In this manner stockbreeding and agriculture complemented each other in such a way that—at least in theory—the resources of the regions in question were invariably exploited to their utmost. The reason for using the phrase 'in theory' in the preceding sentence is that the Near East, and Palestine in particular is, compared to European conditions, a rather problematic agricultural area. Not least among the problems of the region is the irregularity of the annual precipitation, since only a season or two without rain can easily entail the destruction of the agricultural basis and so threaten both animals and humans with famine. From the hand of Nature, Palestine is a marginal area. Throughout its history, the country has been exploited to the limit and beyond. This has in turn exerted a constant pressure on the available resources and led to competition between population groups and different economic sectors which has often resulted in hostilities. The topographically fragmented character of the region has also played a rôle, and, taken together, these factors have historically meant that Palestine has usually consisted of small competing enclaves.

3.2 *The Differentiated Society and its Way of Life*
3.2.1 *The Emergence of the Differentiated Society*
One would expect the fundamental agricultural structure in Palestine
to produce a society which is broadly speaking homogeneous, that is,
without significant class distinctions. Scholars who have been
inspired by evolutionist thinking, including some who advocate a
materialist understanding of history, often maintain that an
agricultural society in which the peasants own their own land, dwell
in villages, and have no contact with urban culture, tends to develop
an *egalitarian* ideology. According to such an ideology, all the
members of such a society are in principle equal.

Whether these sorts of conditions have ever existed anywhere or
are merely a *fata morgana* of the academic imagination, it is at least
possible to say that no egalitarian socio-economic structure has
characterized Palestine within the last 5,000 years or so. The reasons
for this are numerous, and it would be impossible to say just which
factors were decisive in individual cases. However, we pointed above
to the fierce competition for the available resources and the
geographical subdivision of the country into small enclaves. A
competitive relationship exists between stockbreeding and agriculture,
since the interests of these two ways of life do not always coincide
(for example, the livestock may tend to graze on crops, if not kept
under control). But competition also exists between the various local
communities (e.g. the farmers in one mountain valley vs. those in
another), and may be exacerbated by such factors as local harvest
failures, droughts affecting the entire region which only permit the
strongest units to survive, or periodic overpopulation, to mention
only a few quite banal and obvious possibilities.

Social integration is a probationary measure intended to reduce
the risk of losing out in the competition for resources. This means
that individuals decide to live together in order to protect each
other's—and hence their own—interests reciprocally. For this
reason, we find, quite literally, no isolated farms in Palestine; they
are invariably collected in villages. Such integration is capable of
intensification as necessity dictates, for example by the fortification
of one or more of the villages in a given region. In this event, we
discover that the course of development tends towards the formation
of a town properly considered, since it speedily becomes evident that
it will be necessary to locate certain common functions in the
fortified village. Reasons for doing so include the necessity to

coordinate the common defence against external enemies, the convenience, of having a common leader who resides at the fortified site, and the need to create an adequate administrative apparatus to help such a leader perform his functions. In this way a differentiated society comes about, since it would be unreasonable to expect that such individuals would be able to perform their necessary functions if they also had to produce their own foodstuffs; thus it is essential for them to be supplied from without by the peasantry in general.

Of course, this evolution is purely theoretical. However, the fact of the matter is that since the Bronze Age Palestine was dominated by a system of greater and smaller towns, all of which were surrounded by villages which were dependent on them. These conditions created that material basis for the emergence of a number of mini-states of which we are informed already by the first (written) historical sources describing conditions in the country. Thus the differentiated society had already arisen; in it the fundamental social distinction was that between those individuals who produced their own foodstuffs and those who were dependent on others to supply their needs. Here the towns served as centres which absorbed a part of the production of the rural districts and which also coordinated the work in those districts.

The emergence of the town led immediately to the further subdivision of society into occupational groups localized on the towns. In addition to a military staff at the disposal of the leader of the society—and this meant in practice the king—the leader also presided over a number of civil servants who assisted him in the control of the rural districts and the other sources of supply which arose and defined themselves within the context of the establishment of such mini-states. At the same time, various crafts in which all members of society had previously participated, such as pottery making, tool production, and so forth, became the province of specialists. And these specialists, too, had necessarily to live off the foodstuff production of the rural districts.

All of these features characterized the emergence of the differentiated society which has been present in Palestine and the Near East throughout their history. However, there were numerous possible ways of organizing the economy of such societies. One of these was the establishment of free markets in which the peasants themselves sold their surplus production to the towns. Another system entailed that the state absorbed the surplus via taxes which were paid to the central authorities, whose power base lay in the towns. In general it would be wise to assume that these practices may have existed side by side. Thus it was possible for the king to redistribute the taxed commodities among his employees, artisans, and civil servants, but it was equally possible for him to allow them to provide for themselves by barter exchanges on the free market in which they exchanged their own products for services of the necessary foodstuffs. Contrariwise, the individual peasants and villages were in a position to secure for themselves an external source of income, which in good times might be employed in new investments.

3.2.2 Trade

It should be noted that the town was more than just a place where surplus production was concentrated, as it became at an early date the centre of regional trade. We noted previously that the town contained markets for the exchange of agricultural products which originated in the rural districts surrounding them. Of course, such markets were also useful for the populace of the surrounding areas, since in them it will have been possible for people to buy those products which they either could not produce themselves, or perhaps not expertly, such as tools, pottery, textiles, or even such luxury commodities as jewellery. In other words, in historical times Palestine was dominated by a mixed economy which extended all the way down to the small enclaves which even at an early date had developed into states.

Archeological excavations have shown that certain of the urban societies developed into what were, the prevailing conditions taken into account, sizable settlements. Obviously, some special conditions must have obtained which allowed some such societies to develop faster than others. The basic agricultural production and local trade will scarcely have been sufficient to account for this development. No doubt the geographical situation of certain towns enhanced their magnetism on the surrounding districts and their inhabitants because they made possible larger profits through trade. The type of trade in question was probably not the barter exchange that existed at the local level, but long distance trade with other societies. In Palestine the possibilities for obtaining goods which would serve the purpose of international trade were few and limited, since precisely the same products were available to other corresponding societies.

For example, every town in the countryside produced pottery which, in spite of local variations was only rarely of such exceptional quality as to be able to serve as tradegoods. Foodstuffs were not ordinarily traded over considerable distances since both the means of conveyance available and the techniques of preservation were inadequate for the purpose. Thus the most commonly traded goods were such specialities as rare metals and gemstones which, although not present among the natural resources of the country, were sufficiently attractive as to be tradeable in exchanges which ranged beyond the local borders.

Although Palestine was poorly supplied with raw materials, the region did possess a considerable advantage in that geographically considered it serves as a bridge between two parts of the world which in antiquity contained great civilizations, namely the Egyptian and Syro-Mesopotamian regions. The flourishing trade which was conducted between these two regions in historical times ordinarily passed through Palestine, usually in the form of trading caravans (there is, however, evidence from several periods that the Egyptians conducted a not inconsiderable trade by sea with the trading centres on the northern coast).

This international trade followed a variety of courses or *trade routes*. The best known and probably most exploited of these routes (the so-called 'via maris', or 'sea route') took its point of departure in the Nile Delta in Lower Egypt (the northern part of the country), crossed the Sinai Desert by a route which ran close to the sea, and then continued up through the Palestinian coastal plains to the Carmel chain. Here, by means of the narrow pass at Megiddo the route arrived at the Plain of Jezreel, where it branched off onto a number of courses. Of these, one led towards the north along the coast and up into the Lebanon, a second passed through the Beqa' Valley to the north, while the third and most important followed the Plain of Jezreel to Beth-Shan in the Jordan Valley, crossed the Jordan, and continued eastward to Damascus, from where there were numerous accesses to the great urban cultures of northern Syria and ultimately those of Mesopotamia as well.

A second, though less exploited route departed from the *via maris* in the southern part of Palestine, crossed the Negeb and proceeded into the region east of the Jordan, from where it ran northwards via the tableland east of the major river valleys which intersect with this area transversely. This route then passed through what is now modern Amman (the Rabbat Ammon of antiquity) and on to

Damascus in the north. This was the so-called 'royal route', or *via
regis*. Finally, there was also a third north-to-south-running route in
Palestine, which, however, was not ordinarily of significance for
international trade. This route started at Beer-sheba in the south and
continued on through the central Palestinian heights via Hebron,
Jerusalem, Bethel, Shechem, and ultimately to the Plain of Jezreel.
This route offered numerous possibilities for taking detours across
the fords of the Jordan.

These trade routes, in particular the coastal route, or *via maris*,
offered the local societies the possibility of economic gain by means
of taxation of the occasional caravans, and in this connexion it is
perhaps symptomatic that several of the more sizable Palestinian
towns lay right along the caravan routes: from the south and
proceeding northwards there were Gaza, Ashcalon, Ashdod, Megiddo,
which controlled the important pass through the Carmel chain, and
Beth-Shan. Other towns connected themselves either with the
ramifications of this main route to the north, as did, Hazor in Upper
Galilee for example, or with the routes leading to the region east of
the Jordan, or that passing through the central heights.

By the same token, these trade routes also ensured that external
influences, both of a positive and a negative character, achieved some
importance for Palestine. Among the positive aspects was the
importation of wares from the neighbouring cultures to the north
and south, which was advantageous for all the societies involved.
Such imports may have consisted of material goods; in this
connection it should be noted that we have found evidence of
considerable importation of pottery. There were also some cultural
loans, which entailed that the Palestinians made the acquaintance of
the types of organization which obtained in the surrounding great
cultures. It also meant that the Palestinians encountered the
literature of these cultures, as well as religious and ideological views
(which in antiquity were identical). In short, the foreign trade
ensured that Palestine became part of the general culture of the
ancient Near East.

The negative side of the international trade lay in the desire of the
primary producers of the goods in question to control the trade
routes themselves. If a foreign producer, particularly one of the great
powers, could control Palestine, it would in the process also achieve
decisive influence on trade and so increase its own profits. This is not
merely a speculative thesis, as the history of Palestine bears out, for

ever since antiquity the region has been subject to the political influence of its neighbours to the north and south, and for considerable periods of time it has proved difficult for it to assert any claims to regional independence. Palestine has often been reduced to the status of a province of a foreign power, and it has sometimes been part of a sizable empire, that is, a very small and insignificant part, aside from its rôle in international trade. Moreover, although the routes leading through Palestine were primarily trade routes, they have repeatedly served as military lines for the foreign armies which sometimes met in order to determine the question of hegemony over the region. Thus Palestine was frequently both a field of confrontation and of battle for foreign powers, very much to the detriment of the local population.

4. *Concluding Remarks*

When we attempt to describe the history and culture of Israel in the following pages, these features are to be seen in the light of the geo-political situation described above. The scarcity of natural resources in the region entailed that it was rarely in a position of economic strength. In fact, this occurred only when the region was politically independent, so that the local rulers were in a position to be able to control the entire territory, or most of it. It was much more often the case that Palestine was a cat's-paw for forces vastly greater than itself. The very geographical position of Palestine makes it obvious that it would be extremely unlikely for the region to have the opportunity to develop an independent culture, so that we should expect the society to have been greatly influenced by the foreign impulses and cultural features which permeated it. Nevertheless, in the course of time a peculiar local culture, that of the Jews, did arise in the country, and it is perhaps our most important task to attempt to explain the emergence of this specifically Jewish culture.

Chapter 2

TEXT AND HISTORY

1. *The Old Testament as History*

1.1 *Biblical History*

The Old Testament contains an uninterrupted narrative of the history and religious history of Israel from the dawn of time until a few centuries before the birth of Christ. This historical account fills roughly the first half of the entire work, and thus unavoidably dominates the reader's impression of the work as a whole.

In what follows, I shall present only a brief sketch of the contents for the reader's orientation. In earlier works, such a sketch would have been completely superfluous, since the biblical history was generally known by almost every schoolchild; today, however, such thorough familiarity can no longer be presupposed to the same extent. It will therefore hopefully 'facilitate' the understanding of the following sections if the reader is by way of introduction briefly informed as to the traditional scheme of biblical history.

Above all, we should note that the Old Testament contains a chronological skeleton on which the various periods of Israelite history are mounted. It also contains a clear subdivision into periods. If we follow both the biblical chronology and its historical narrative and attempt to relate them to our own chronology, we arrive at the following results.

The earliest history of Israel was identical with the era of the three patriarchs, Abraham, Isaac, and Jacob, who according to the biblical figures are to be dated to somewhere between 2200 and 1900 BCE. This period was followed by the Israelite sojourn in Egypt, which lasted slightly more than 400 years, that is, from around 1900 to around 1500. Israel's exodus from Egypt took place around 1500 and was followed by a period of wandering in the desert which lasted c. 40 years; thus the Israelites are supposed to have arrived in the land of Canaan sometime around the year 1450 BCE. During the following

centuries leading up to the introduction of the monarchy around the
year 1000 Israel consolidated her grip on the country under the
direction of a number of so-called 'Judges' (for which reason this
period is usually called the 'period of the Judges'). The monarchy
lasted for about the first 400 years of the first millennium BCE, and
ended with the 'Babylonian Exile', when Israel had to abandon the
land of Canaan. The Exile proved to be the nadir of the history of the
Israelites, but it gave way to a new existence in Palestine after the
release from Babylon in 538 BCE. The Old Testament offers no more
chronological information as to Israel's subsequent history; scholars
generally subdivide the following centuries into a number of epochs:
the Persian period (538—331 BCE), the Hellenistic period (331—63
BCE), and the Roman period (63 BCE—135 CE). Of couse, it is
possible to suggest additional subdivisions, as it is to discuss the
legitimacy of those previously mentioned, but to do so would have no
consequences for the study of Israel in 'Old Testament times'.

The history of the people of Israel is thus depicted as identical with
that of the fortunes of a single family, namely the descendants of
Abraham: Abraham 'begat' Isaac, who in turn 'begat' Jacob, who
'begat' the ancestral fathers of all the tribes of Israel, and so forth. As
far as the patriarchal age is concerned, the entire narrative is
concentrated on the three patriarchs and their immediate families; it
is first with the sojourn in Egypt that the perspective broadens, and it
is from this point onwards that the 'history' that is related is that of
the entire people. From Egypt onwards, the texts speak continuously
of the people of Israel.

However, it is important to acknowledge that this is not a
description of profane, but of religious, history. The central and
thoroughgoing theme is not that of, for example, the fate of the
Israelites in relation to that of one of Israel's neighbours; rather, the
narratives have to do with the relationship between Israel and the
god, Yahweh, who elected them to be his own. In the Old Testament
the fortunes of the Israelite people are always depicted in terms of
varying relationships to Yahweh. It is this Yahweh who chooses
Abraham, leads Israel down into Egypt, releases her from Egypt,
enters into a covenant with Israel on Mt Sinai in the desert, leads her
to the land of Canaan, and so on. In this fashion the Old Testament
account of the history of Israel is also a narrative about how Israel
sinned against the god to whom she owed everything because Israel
was unable to live up to the covenant to which she was herself a

partner. Thus the individual events which are mentioned are not related for their own sake, but because they illustrate the ways the relationship between god and the people changed, just as they also illustrate the consequences of apostasy from the right way of worshipping god.

1.2 *The Problems of the Biblical Account*

It would be extremely easy simply to adopt this account of the history of Israel as one's own, and in fact throughout the history of Christianity and Judaism people have in fact tended simply to follow this history uncritically. Moreover, one should not forget that there are still significant elements in our own culture who would still prefer to accept this description without question. Some familiarity with the efforts of earlier Old Testament scholars will also serve to illustrate how they attempted for several centuries to make the history of Israel conform in some measure to 'reality'. This 'reality', however, became increasingly problematic for the notion of the 'absolute truth' of the Bible, once our knowledge of the history and culture of the ancient Orient in antiquity was extended through the decipherment of Egyptian hieroglyphics and Mesopotamian cuneiform writing in the beginning of the nineteenth century.

It soon became evident that there was a multitude of problems connected with the biblical account. The very first mention of Abraham is problematic, since we are there informed (Gen. 11.28-31) that Abraham came from Ur in Chaldaea. Ur presents no difficulties, particularly because excavations at the site have demonstrated the existence of a culture which was far older than the biblical date for Abraham. However, the 'Ur' which Abraham left was not situated in *Chaldaea*, but in *Sumer*. The area in question was first called 'Chaldaea' when the Chaldaeans gave their name to the region, and this did not take place prior to the eighth or seventh centuries BCE. Later on scholars discovered that the silence in the Egyptian sources as to the presence of Israel in the country was an obstacle to the notion of Israel's 400 year sojourn in exile. On the other hand, archeological excavations in Palestine have required that both the biblical account of the conquest of Canaan and the date assigned to this event have had to be seriously revised, to mention but a few examples of the difficulties with which scholarship has had to deal.

The general scholarly approach has been relentlessly conservative.

Researchers have preferred to retain the biblical version of events as far as this was at all possible, and in spite of insights gained into the textual tradition. For example, virtually all scholars are today agreed that with only one or two exceptions all the texts in the Old Testament derive from the first millennium BCE; thus, as far as the pre-monarchical period is concerned, the texts are significantly younger than the events they depict.

When scholars have recognized the necessity of abandoning the biblical account, they have often done so in favour of a rationalizing version of it. This approach will be more closely explored in connection with the traditions dealing with the settlement in Canaan, since quite a number of scholars have not regarded this settlement as occurring through a collective conquest of the country at a particular point in time, but rather as the result of the infiltration of nomads from the desert-like borders of Palestine. This infiltration of foreign (i.e. Israelite) elements is thought to have taken place over a considerable span of time, perhaps even over several centuries.

Corresponding problems arose in connection with the history of Israelite religion as scholars began to gain more insight into Canaanite society and its religion. It became increasingly clear that Israelite religion in the Psalms, for example, displays a close kinship to Canaanite religion; it is also clear that Israelite pre-exilic religious conceptions were closely related to their counterparts in Canaan. In general, however, scholars have been even more reluctant to alter the biblical account of the origins, earliest contents and development of the worship of Yahweh than they have been to quarrel with the Old Testament historical narratives.

1.3 *The Study of Israel's History*
In the following chapters these problems and numerous others will be examined. We shall make an attempt to evaluate the possibility of using the Old Testament as a source for the history and religious history of Israel in the period prior to the emergence of the texts. Secondly, these deliberations will form the point of departure for an attempt at a reconstruction of Israel's history and religious history. From a methodological and logical point of view it is impossible to reconstruct the history of Israel and its religion in pre-exilic times. However, we must try to reconstruct it, knowing that our endeavour is presenting nothing more than a working hypothesis.

Some might object that the only legitimate subject for such a study would be the analysis of the period in which the Old Testament traditions were collected or committed to writing. According to such a procedure, one could describe the understanding of the development of the religion and the earlier history of the nation, which was current in this age, and one could stratify this understanding according to its different layers. It is correct that this is really the only legitimate subject of research, particularly for the scholar who insists on certain or 'objective' conclusions. However, such an approach runs the risk of limiting insights into the development of the Old Testament to such an extent that they would be one-dimensional and lacking in depth. The historical reconstruction of the Old Testament is not merely an attempt to reconstruct the understanding of the history of a particular epoch, as that understanding is itself the result of the prehistory of that epoch. It is paradoxical that while the Old Testament reconstruction of the past is a hypothesis or a working model, this model is itself the result of the history which the Israelite society had experienced; it expresses the life-experience and message to posterity of that society. There is therefore always a dialectical relationship between the reconstructed (or, if you will, the constructed) past and the society which was behind such a reconstruction. Moreover, this is true even if the reconstruction in question was only a fictional creation, the representation of a past which never was.

It is the task of the modern historian to investigate this reconstruction and to explain it, that is, to interpret it on the basis of the society in which it came into being. At the same time, it is also the obligation of the scholar to enquire as to those factors which ensured that the society in question arrived at the conclusions it did. In other words, it is the duty of the scholar to investigate the previously mentioned dialectical relationship between past and present, which in this case means Israel's history in pre-exilic times and the same society in exilic times, in order better to understand the society in which the traditions about the past were fixed in written form. In such a process the historian cannot avoid 'recreating' this past. To this end he or she must make use of the whole range of available methods, which include new ways of reading the biblical texts, historical procedures, and insights. The historian must make the attempt to determine the relationship between primary and secondary sources and to 'weight' their respective evidential values accordingly. Nevertheless, the result of such efforts, that is, the actual historical reconstruction, will only be a tool (or 'heuristic model', as such hypotheses are popularly called today). The practical result of this way of posing the problem is therefore not the study of the relationship between Israel's history 'as it was' and the Old Testament, but of the relationship between the reconstructed model and the Old Testament historical tradition. The result of such an investigation can never be 'true', but only 'probable', and we shall allow readers to determine for themselves *the degree of such probability*.[1]

2. The Old Testament Regarded as a Text

2.1 The Structure of the Old Testament

Even only a cursory reading of the Old Testament reveals that we have to do with a work which is not homogeneous. Although it is an ancient literary work it is impossible to compare it with other more or less contemporary works from the ancient Orient or the classical world. This is so because the Old Testament does not consist of just a single integral text which, for example, describes Israel's history from the earliest times to the Macedonian conquest of the country in 331 BCE. Rather, it is a collection of individual writings of widely divergent character and, in part, of varying degrees of antiquity, each of which has its own peculiar prehistory and special function within the compass of the work as a whole.

In fact, Jewish tradition does not know of an Old Testament, as the term is a Christian designation which arose from the association of the work with the New Testament. For Jews the term is simply the Bible or the 'law', that is, the *Torah*, a term which frequently serves as a comprehensive designation for the entire work.

On reading the *Torah*, however, we soon discover that only certain sections are legal texts. Thus, the Jewish designation is a way of emphasizing those sections which have played such an important

---

1. The attentive reader will not fail to note that the word *ideology* plays an important rôle in this account. By 'ideology' I intend that set of opinions which dominated Israelite society and which made up the 'system' of values with which the Israelites actions corresponded. In an Oriental society like Israel's one should furthermore be aware that *ideology*, *religion*, and *theology* are to a large extent synonyms, since the separation between the sacral and the profane realms which characterizes our contemporary European culture was unknown in antiquity.

part in Jewish tradition that the work has been popularly named after
them. One ought in this connexion to note that the word 'law'
actually bears a wider meaning than usually imagined, in that it also
signifies such features as instruction and general rules for the
conduct of life. We should also note that the Jewish designation
indicates that as far as the *canon* (that is, as a religious guideline or
vade mecum, which is the actual meaning of the term 'canon') is
concerned, some parts of the work are of more importance than
others.

But Jewish tradition has yet another way of defining the Old
Testament, namely by means of the trifocal designation 'the Law, the
Prophets, and the Writings'. These are normally literary genre
designations, but in this context they are employed to describe the
Old Testament as a trilogy composed of three different groups of
texts. In this connection 'the law' refers to Genesis, Exodus,
Leviticus, Numbers, and Deuteronomy. These books are also the
'Pentateuch', and their being termed 'the Law' in Jewish tradition
shows the importance that tradition attached to this part of the Old
Testament. In reality 'the Prophets' consists of two sections, namely
a series of historical books which describe the history of Israel from
the time the Israelites are supposed to have immigrated into the land
of Canaan to the time when it ceased to be an independent country,
plus a series of writings which have been assigned to, and which
derive at least in part from, a number of important individual
personalities, that is, the so called 'prophets'. Finally, the 'Writings'
make up a sort of catch-all category, containing as they do a variety
of individual works of a widely varying nature, including some of the
most famous and valuable texts in the Old Testament, such as the
Psalms, the book of Job, and the Song of Songs.

The tripartite division of the texts in question corresponds to their
order in the Jewish Bible, almost all of which is written in Hebrew.
This sequence, however, is not the same as that to be found in the
Bible of the Church of England, or any other European Church. The
main difference lies in the subdivision of the 'Prophets' into two
distinct sections, so that the historical texts are associated with the
Pentateuch, while the prophetic writings as such follow the 'Writings'.
This organizational practice is a continuation of the arrangement
which was already present in the ancient Jewish translation of the
Old Testament into Greek, known as the *Septuagint* (LXX).

2.2 *The Forms of Old Testament Literature*
2.2.1 *The 'Historical' Writings*

If we turn to the Law, that is, the Pentateuch, we see immediately that these works are heterogeneous in character. Narrative texts alternate with list-like sequences, censuses, genealogies, and so forth; or else we encounter legal sections of considerable length, since the whole of the middle part of the Pentateuch consists in the main of religio-cultic regulations or 'laws'. It is not difficult, within the compass of the narrative materials, to distinguish such sections as the Primeval History (Gen. 1–11), which tells of the creation of the world and of the first people; the Patriarchal History (Gen. 12–36), which deals with Israel's tribal ancestors; the so-called Joseph Novella (Gen. 37–50), or the Exodus narrative (Exod. 1–15), the last two of which inform us, respectively, of how it came about that Israel migrated to Egypt and escaped from there. There is also the Sinai Narrative (Exod. 19–24), which speaks of Israel's encounter with her God, Yahweh, on Mt Sinai during the flight from Egypt, and the narratives of the Desert Wanderings (Exod. 16–18; Num. 10–36), which follow the Israelite fugitives from Sinai to the borders of the land of Canaan.

There is much which suggests that these and similar sections originated and were collected without reference to other parts of the Pentateuch. In other words, they had their own literary prehistories before they were incorporated into the whole at a date later than their composition.

Finally, the book of Deuteronomy is clearly independent of the four works which precede it (for which reason the latter are sometimes called the Tetrateuch) since it contains no narrative at all except for the brief account of the death of Moses in Deut. 34; rather, the book is mainly a record of a speech which Moses is supposed to have given on the border of the Promised Land, which he himself never entered.

The 'Laws' have been worked into this complex of narratives in a variety of connections, several times in the form of sizable collections, or 'codices'. Thus scholars speak of the *Book of the Covenant* (Exod. 21.2–23.16), which is the codex of laws that has been inserted into the account of the revelation on Mt Sinai (Exod. 19–24). It is one of the most important sources for the understanding of Israelite society, since it contains a number of laws which regulate the relationships in an Israelite community. Yet another legal collection is the *Holiness*

Code (Lev. 17-26), which, as its title suggests, is largely concerned with cultic and religious affairs, but which also contains some sections dealing with social conditions (such as the law of the *year of the Jubilee* in Lev. 25).

The so-called 'Former Prophets', that is, the writings from Joshua to 2 Kings, inclusive, actually present a collected historical account of the history of Israel from the days of Joshua to those of Nebuchadnezzar II. This collection bears numerous signs of homogeneity which suggest that it received its present form through a significant redaction. Scholars ordinarily term these writings the *Deuteronomistic History*, where the expression 'Deuteronomistic' refers to the circle of authors who are thought to have composed it. The term itself derives from Deuteronomy, which is usually held to form the introduction to the history. Nevertheless, this work, too, contains, a considerable number of individual narrative complexes which may well have existed independently prior to their incorporation into the work as a whole. The tradition of the Settlement in the book of Joshua (Josh. 1-12), which consists of a series of aetiological legends (see below), gives way to a lengthy list-section which details the settlement areas of the individual Israelite tribes (Josh. 13-21). In a similar fashion, the narratives of Israel's early heroes (the 'Judges', Judg. 1-12) are succeeded by a cycle of narratives about an Israelite 'superman', Samson (Judg. 13-16). The books of Samuel consist mainly of two writings about David, the first of which is a narrative, exhibiting features of the classical romance, and dealing with David's rise to power (1 Sam. 16-2 Sam. 6), while the second is an account of the days of his reign and particularly of the struggles to find a successor for him (the so-called *Succession Narrative*, 2 Sam. 7-1 Kgs 2). Such mixtures of literary types continues on into the books of the Kings, in which a central part is occupied by a number of legends dealing with two early North Israelite prophets, Elijah and Elisha (1 Kgs 16-2 Kgs 9). Furthermore, the historical account is constantly interrupted by sermon-like sections inserted by the author in order to inform us of his interpretation of the events in question. Thus, considered as a work of history, the Deuteronomistic History differs considerably from what we ordinarily take history writing to be. This fact is, of course, significant when we attempt to utilize the work as a source for understanding the history of Israel.

2.2.2 *The Poetic Materials*

The Pentateuch and the Deuteronomistic History consist largely of prose texts. There are some passages which are actually in poetic form within the prose texts; indeed, they are frequently older than their prose settings. Examples of such poetic inserts include the 'Blessing of Jacob' (Gen. 49), the 'Songs of Balaam' (Num. 23–24), and the 'Song of Deborah' (Judg. 5); the last-mentioned of which is the poetic counterpart to the prose narrative immediately preceding it (Judg. 4). If we proceed to the prophetic books as such, or to the 'Writings', we discover that these are largely poetic works, and that prose played only a modest rôle in them (although Ruth, Esther, Chronicles, Ezra and Nehemiah are prose compositions). In the prophetic writings prose and poetry sometimes alternate with one another. However, among the 'writings' there are some collections of a homogeneous character in which a single type of literature dominates the entire piece.

This feature is most obviously true of the Psalms, which consists of 150 religious poems of varying lengths. The main body of these are texts which were employed in worship, primarily in the Temple in Jerusalem. It would not be appropriate here to list the various types of psalms, but examples would include those which praise Yahweh as 'the King', as well as some others which praise the earthly (Judaean) king. Some seem to be concerned with the well-being of the entire nation (the so-called 'collective' psalms), while others have to do with individuals. Some psalms express the thanksgiving of the society or of a single individual to the deity in the Temple, while others complain of the misfortunes which have afflicted the individual, and so forth. Finally, there are a very few psalms with no obvious cultic associations; one such is Psalm 137, which recollects the destruction of Jerusalem and the Babylonian captivity; others include such historical 'didactic' poems as Psalms 104–106.

A considerable number of works within the 'Writings' may be termed 'Wisdom Literature'. Most import of these is the book of Proverbs, a long collection of rules of a more or less practical nature for conducting one's life. Another is the book of Job, a lengthy poem dealing with the 'problem of the righteous sufferer', which theologians call the problem of theodicy, that is, the question of the righteousness of God in the face of human suffering. Wisdom literature is, however, also represented to some extent in other writings. In particular, some of the Psalms are 'Wisdom poems' (e.g. Pss. 1 and 36) which express

the same understanding of life and its significance as that present in
the book of Proverbs. But also some prose texts in the Pentateuch
and the Deuteronomistic History contain sections which scholars
have held to reflect an understanding of existence influenced by this
sort of Wisdom.

The Prophetic writings are a quite distinct phenomenon. They
usually contain a number of more or less connected materials
bearing on specific historical situations in the history of Israel, or
they may address specific social conditions within Israelite society.
They are generally characterized by a basic religious attitude which,
although varying in some degree from book to book, nevertheless
relates the more important of these writings to one another. This
attitude concerns the idea that Israel has violated the relationship
between herself and her God, which is to say that she has done things
in defiance of Yahweh's will, or she has worshipped other gods than
Yahweh, for which reason the land will be punished (although in
some cases it is held that she will be spared an annihilating final
punishment). We shall return later to the prophetic literature, since it
provides us with the most important witness to the religious attitudes
which arose in the latter part of the monarchical period.

2.3 *The Developmental History of the Old Testament*
A conscious redactional process led to the selection of the individual
writings which were incorporated into the Jewish Bible and which
now form part of the Christian Bible (in all its variety). The fact that
such a process of selection has taken place is evident when we
consider that the LXX contains a number of works which were not
included in the later canonical Bible and which were instead
relegated to the collection known as the Apocrypha (the 'hidden'
writings). In many Western Bibles, these writings are to be found
sandwiched into a section between the Old and New Testaments. It is
clear that the Jewish scholars who were responsible for the formation
of the canon did not find these works worthy of inclusion. But in
addition to these there are also quite a number of writings dating
from the period, that is, from the centuries around the time of the
birth of Christ, which were neither included in the LXX nor in the
Jewish Bible. These are the so-called 'pseudepigraphic writings' (the
'lying writings'). The pseudepigraphic works contain numerous
examples of one particular genre, the apocalypse or 'revelation', akin
to the Revelation to John in the New Testament. These works claim

to be able to inform us about the last days, that is, about the end of the world and the imminent judgment of God. The rejection of such writings in conjunction with the establishment of the canon must have been dictated by pressing theological motives, and it is to be supposed that equally cogent grounds led to the selection of the rest of the writings within the canon.

The establishment of the Jewish canon was begun in the post-exilic period and concluded in the time after the death of Christ. It is not possible to follow this process in detail, but in general it may be supposed that the Pentateuch was the first part to achieve canonical status. It was followed by the prophetic books, and the catch-all collection known as the 'Writings' was finally fixed a few generations after the time of Jesus. A number of clues for the understanding of the canonical process might be mentioned. Thus it is conceivable that the relationship between the Pentateuch and the prophetic writings is to be seen in the light of the fact that the Jewish sectarian society known as the Samaritans only acknowledges the Pentateuch as their sacred scripture. Unfortunately, it is not possible to date with any precision the schism between the early Jews and the Samaritans, although it is known that this took place in the post-exilic period. The break may have occurred during the transition from the fourth to the third centuries BCE, or even later. Moreover, it is possible that dogmatic considerations prevented the Samaritans from incorporating the prophetic books into their canon, since these works were to a high degree associated with the Jerusalem Temple, whereas the Samaritans were specifically concerned to dissociate themselves from that Temple and even founded their own on Mt Garizim, in the vicinity of ancient Shechem.

The fact that the 'Writings' achieved canonical status later than the 'Prophets' is illustrated by the Septuagint, which was translated into Greek during the last few centuries prior to the birth of Christ. While the Septuagint version of the Pentateuch is virtually unchanged from its Hebrew original, the Prophets differ only occasionally from the original, and as for the Writings, some were included in the Septuagint which were, as we have seen, omitted from the Jewish canon. In other words, the formation of the canon, and in particular the selection of the Writings, was first completed after the Jewish Bible had been translated into Greek.

2.4 *The Redaction of the Old Testament Text*
2.4.1 *Strata of Tradition in the Pentateuch*

As we have seen, the books of the Pentateuch seem to be a collection of originally independent traditions or groups of traditions which were preserved for some time and were subjected to a variety of reworkings, expansions, and revisions in the process. Scholarship has in this connection pointed to a variety of strata; *Yahwistic*, *Elohistic*, and *Priestly*, to use the conventional terminology. Each of these designations represents a phase of the process by which these materials were woven together, or redacted, and each has its own specific characteristics, since the oldest stratum was reworked by the author(s) of the younger strata on the basis of different theological premises. The discussion as to the nature of the redactional process has been long and somewhat complicated, and it will be impossible to describe it here in detail. However, it is clear that there is so little internal coherence in the Pentateuch that there is no question of a single author or group of authors having composed this part of the Old Testament.

Let us take a single example which may demonstrate that there are a number of strata present in the Pentateuch. In a reading of the biblical account of the Flood (Gen. 6-9), even a casual reader cannot help but notice that the narrative contains a considerable number of discordant features. In one passage we are told that the Flood is the result of forty days of constant rain, while in another we read that the waters rose for 150 days. In one passage Noah, the hero of the narrative, brings the animals into the Ark by pairs, while in another a distinction is made between clean and unclean animals (in accordance with Jewish sacrificial practice) in such a way that Noah brings seven pairs of the clean animals, but only one pair each of the unclean ones, into the Ark. The text also records differing dates for the onset and cessation of the Flood, and so forth. If one reads the text fairly closely, one will with relative ease be able to distinguish two narratives, each with its own chronological scheme. These have been worked together by a redactor who has attempted to harmonize their divergent features, although his success in this respect has not been complete.

But in addition to the disagreements in the text, we also discover that the two versions agree to a large extent, which shows that a common tradition underlies both versions; this common tradition was then recorded by two authors independently of each other. In the text in question, scholars distinguish between a 'Yahwistic' and a 'Priestly' layer.

It is assumed that the 'Yahwistic' layer, so-called because it makes use of the divine name Yahweh, represents the oldest version of the Pentateuch. The dating of the Yahwist is controversial; scholars have proposed dates ranging from as far back as the days of Solomon, that is, in the latter part of the tenth century BCE, to the seventh century or even the sixth. A date in the tenth or ninth centuries has generally been preferred because of the wish to regard this stratum as containing reliable historical evidence, on the theory that the older the text is, the more dependable it is as a source (we shall return to this below). Scholars have in the same vein attempted to reconstruct the milieu in which the Yahwistic stratum came into being, and have concluded that its background was in the earliest days of the monarchy. Furthermore, the attempts at dating have been character- ized by evolutionary views; thus scholars have maintained that the Yahwist represents an early and primitive stage (with respect to, among other things, its understanding of God) in relation to the other strata.

However, in the last ten years an increasing number of scholars have opposed this early date and have instead preferred to demonstrate connections between the Yahwistic tradition and, for example, the prophetic literature, meaning that the Yahwistic materials have been influenced by the prophetic proclamations. But if there are connections between the Yahwistic literature and the prophets, then the earliest stratum of the Pentateuch cannot be dated to the beginning of the monarchy, but rather to the latter part of the monarchical period at the earliest, which is to say, E to the eighth or seventh centuries BCE. Indeed, certain scholars have pointed to some aspects of the Yahwistic tradition which suggest that it may reflect the situation of the Babylonian exile. They have also pointed out that the tradition contains connections with the Deuteronomistic literature and with the intellectual climate of the Deuteronomistic period. Such scholars are accordingly prepared to claim that even the oldest layer of traditions in the Pentateuch does not derive from the pre-exilic period, but from the sixth century BCE.

The next stratum is called *Elohistic* since it utilizes the usual Hebrew word for 'God', *Elohim*, instead of Yahweh. This stratum has usually been held to be younger than the Yahwistic layer. On the other hand, scholars have thought to identify unambiguous connections between the Elohistic layer and prophetism, and even with the Deuteronomistic materials. For this reason, this layer has always been held to be considerably later than the Yahwistic one, that is, on the assumption that the latter is to be assigned to the tenth or ninth centuries BCE. But if, as previously suggested, the Yahwistic stratum is to be assigned to the seventh or sixth century, then the Elohistic layer cannot be much younger. It should also be noted that a number of scholars, in particular some from Scandinavia, have denied the existence of an Elohistic 'source' at all. Unlike the Yahwistic tradition, which is represented in all parts of the Pentateuch with the possible exception of the legal materials, the Elohist tradition is much more sporadic. Thus, for example, it does not appear at all in the Primeval History. There is accordingly reason to regard the Elohistic layer as a redactional reworking of the Yahwistic stratum, which it both supplements and wages polemic against.

The youngest stratum in the Pentateuch is the *Priestly* tradition, which a broad consensus assigns to the late exilic or even post-exilic period. This layer, which is present in the Flood narrative and formed one of the original versions of it, is present throughout the entire Pentateuch. Indeed, it is possible that this stratum is identical with the final phase of redaction which created the present collection of the books of Moses. The circle of redactors responsible for this stratum presuppose the earlier strata, which they were to comment on and supplement, not least by means of the inclusion of an extensive body of cultic laws which bear the earmarks of this circle (a feature which, among others, has given this stratum its name).

2.4.2 *Other Witnesses to the Reworking of the Tradition*
Other parts of the Old Testament have been subjected to a similar process of redaction, although it is not always possible to demonstrate these as clearly as is the case with the Pentateuch. For example, the previously mentioned Deuteronomistic History is the result of a redactional activity which has joined and commented on pre-existent materials; in so doing, the editors left their own indelible imprint on the materials. It is clear that the Deuteronomistic circles were working under the influence of the disasters which had affected Israel towards the end of the monarchical period, the chief of these being the destruction of Jerusalem in 587 BCE and the subsequent exile of the Jews in Babylon. The Deuteronomists were therefore concerned to interpret these events in such a way as to explain why Israel was

the victim of such catastrophes. To this end, they employed a distinctive theology which they superimposed on the texts, and which serves as the Deuteronomistic evaluation of the history of Israel.

However, the Deuteronomistic activity was not confined to the creation of their collected history of Israel, as they also engaged in the 'publication' of at least one of the works of the major prophets, namely the book of Jeremiah. There are numerous passages in this work which may be traced back to the prophet whose name graces the book and who was active during the last years prior to the destruction of Jerusalem. These passages, however, are interspersed with purely Deuteronomistic sections, by which means the Deuteronomists were able to adapt the works of the prophet to their own ends. But what happened to the book of Jeremiah also happened to most of the other prophetic works, since they, too, contain authentic materials deriving from a particular prophet, side by side with later interpretations or expansions of such materials.

All this means that the prophetic books, too, are the results of the conscious redactional reworking of pre-existent traditional material. However, it was by no means always the Deuteronomists who were responsible for such redactional activity. There are no indications that their redactional efforts are elsewhere anywhere near as extensive as is the case in the book of Jeremiah.

These facts suggest a number of possibilities for the reader. Concern may focus on the present form of a given prophetic book, in which case the task will be to interpret it on the basis of that final form. This effort would seek to discover the aims of the redactor who 'published' the work in question. But the reader may also choose to work with the expressions which derive, or which may be supposed to derive, from the original prophet in question. The goal of such efforts would naturally be to attempt to rediscover the original message of that prophet and to interpret it within its original historical framework. Finally, the reader may be concerned with the redactional process itself which took place in the interval between the prophet's activity and the final redaction of the book. In the sections which follow we shall see that the reader is invariably confronted with the same possibilities no matter what biblical text is under consideration. On the one hand, there is a need to distinguish between the final redaction and possible earlier redactional phases; on the other to differentiate between this redaction and earlier versions of the text. Thus, that peculiar dilemma arises which enforces itself upon every serious reader of the Old Testament, namely the discovery that while the present text does indeed 'say something', that is, has a message to convey, yet there are also other messages in the text, namely those which earlier editions of the traditions in question attempted to convey.

3. *The Old Testament as a Historical Source*

3.1 *Introduction*

After the short sketch of the developmental history of the Old Testament presented above, we shall proceed in this section to examine the implications of the recognition of numerous layers of redaction and tradition for the evaluation of the Old Testament as a historical source. It should be immediately obvious in the light of what has been said above that we cannot use the book of Jeremiah as we now possess it as a source for understanding the proclamation of the historical Jeremiah at the close of the monarchical period. It is essential to distinguish between the programme of the final redaction, that is, the intentions which lay behind the publication and interpretation of Jeremiah's own words by the interpolation of redactional texts, and Jeremiah's own programme, on the assumption that it is possible to 'cleanse' the book of Jeremiah of inauthentic sections of text.

An analogous situation applies to other parts of the Old Testament, such as, for example, the book of Isaiah, the present form of which has been assembled from the proclamation of at least three different prophets. Scholars ordinarily divide the book into three parts, *Proto-Isaiah* (Isa. 1–39), which is largely derived from the original prophet, *Deutero-Isaiah* (Isa. 40–55), which derives from an anonymous prophet who preached during the Exile, and *Trito-Isaiah* (Isa. 56–66), which derives from the post-exilic period. But such considerations also apply to the Psalter, in which individual psalms were repeatedly reinterpreted already in pre-exilic times. Furthermore, as far as the historical parts of the Old Testament are concerned, it is conceivable that there may be innumerable strata layered on top of the original redactions.

These features entail that should we wish to describe the contents of a given Old Testament text, it is necessary first to distinguish between its various layers and its final redaction. Such an undertaking could produce a very sophisticated description of Israelite thought, perhaps one that stretches as far back as the pre-monarchical period before 1000 BCE and as far forward as the latest post-exilic redactions of the texts. However, the moment one attempts to reconstruct the history of Israel on the basis of these texts, the problem becomes quite different since in most cases the texts in question are significantly younger than the events which they describe. This difficulty becomes critical when one attempts to use such relatively young texts to describe the spiritual life of earlier periods, and in particular the ancient religion, since the picture present in such texts must be supposed actually to reflect the views which were current in the period in which the texts were collected and 'published'.

3.2 *Contemporary Sources*

In historical research, it is essential to distinguish between sources which are contemporary with the events they depict and sources which have arisen after the fact. The problems are many and various, depending on which part of the Old Testament we are dealing with. In this connection the associated difficulties have to do with the question of the dates to be assigned to individual texts; some scholars differ on these matters by as much as several hundred years.

This difficulty is especially acute when we study the 'writings', particularly the Wisdom Literature. Such texts are in principle timeless, since they attempt to describe general rules for the conduct of life and the direction of thought. An example is the book of Job, which is introduced by the phrase, 'Once upon a time there was a man in the land of Uz'. We are familiar with the phrase 'once upon a time' thanks to the genre of the fairytale, and the literary association of this text to this genre is additionally emphasized by the location of the protagonist of the story in the land of Uz, which is otherwise unknown. We have to do with a Timbucktoo, and with a time which is so far removed that one no longer remembers just when it was. Job himself is mentioned elsewhere in the Old Testament as one of the wise men of the past (Ezek. 14.14, 20), together with Noah, the hero of the Flood, and Daniel, who is the protagonist of the book of Daniel, which belongs to quite a different literary genre. Job was therefore a well-known figure in Israelite tradition; he derived from an ahistorical world, and thus it is appropriate that the work which bears his name is entirely divorced from indications of historical time.

3.2.1 *The Psalms*

As far as other poetic materials among the 'Writings' are concerned, not least the Psalms, it is almost certain that they once enjoyed a very precise rôle. They are accordingly to be regarded as excellent sources for the period in which they were employed; that is, they are sources which tell us about the type of worship that was cultivated in the era in question. In connection with the Psalms, however, there are two factors which significantly undermine their evidential value. One of these is, as mentioned previously, the fact that the Psalms were subjected to continuous reinterpretation after their composition; the other is that the Psalms are extremely difficult to date with any precision. The reinterpretations frequently make themselves felt in the *superscriptions* to the various Psalms, as virtually all of these are secondary in relation to the psalms which they introduce. Thus, for example, Psalm 51 begins with a superscription which introduces the psalm into a historical context with which it originally had nothing to do. Psalm 72 also bears witness to the secondary character of its superscription, since it is evident that David was not its author, as Psalm 72.1 refers to the 'royal son'. It should be noted that David was not the son of any monarch, but rather the first and founding member of a dynasty. Accordingly, the author could at best be King Solomon, even though he is not otherwise held to have written any psalms. Moreover, the psalm contains numerous pieces of information which show that it must have been composed long after the days of Solomon.

These and similar considerations suggest that it is almost impossible to date the psalms. In general, however, it may be held that those psalms which have to do with the king in Jerusalem may only be assigned to the period of the monarchy, that is, between 1000 and 587 BCE. Other psalms, such as, for example, the previously mentioned Psalm 51, could well be much later, since after the return from Babylon there was once again a temple cult capable of providing a framework for the composition of such psalms. Thus scholars generally attempt to date individual psalms by recourse to an analysis of their contents. In many cases, however, this is a dangerous undertaking since one invariably ends up in a form of circular argumentation. First, one determines what were the spiritual currents which permeated a given period. Then, one inserts the text in question in the appropriate period, on the assumption that there is agreement between the contents of the text and the dominant ideologies of the period. Unfortunately, our only knowledge of these ideologies derives from the text itself, which we have already assigned to the period in question. This closes the circle.

Finally, the use of a psalm in the attempt to reconstruct the spiritual life of a given period in the history of Israel is further complicated by the reinterpretations. In many cases, these have taken the form of dogmatically motivated expurgations of features of Israelite religion as it was during the time of the monarchy, since that religion had subsequently changed considerably. We shall return to this problem below. The result is that the psalms may not be taken at face value in any attempt to depict Israelite religion in the monarchical period; they must be carefully controlled by reference to other sources of both a written and a material nature, and both inside and outside of the Old Testament.

3.2.2 *The Prophetic Literature*
Another collection of texts, however, provides us with a better basis for reconstructing the milieu of Judah in particular towards the end of the monarchy. It also provides us with materials relevant to the period of the Exile and later. These are the texts contained in the prophetic literature, many of which ultimately derive from particular historical individuals who lived and were active at determinate times in the history of Israel. We mentioned above, however, the difficulties connected with the redaction of the book of Jeremiah and with the various sections of the book of Isaiah. On the one hand, we possess authentic pronouncements from the mouth of Jeremiah, while on the other we possess what are sometimes quite lengthy redactional passages. It should be self-evident that the latter cannot be held to represent Jeremiah's preaching; they may at best be taken to represent the interpretation accorded to his preaching by the circle who 'published' the collection. In the case of Jeremiah matters are not too complicated, since we are able to identify the circle of 'publishers', that is, the Deuteronomists. This circle is related to, though not necessarily identical with, the group who created the great Deuteronomistic History. We have other evidence as to what the main aims of the Deuteronomistic movement were, for which reason it is not surprising to find the same contents—or elements of them—in the book of Jeremiah. However, it is interesting to note that the congruence between the proclamation of Jeremiah and the Deuteronomistic programme is not total. Jeremiah's exemplars were

not the Deuteronomists, but a number of prophets who preceded him, in particular the North Israelite prophet Hosea, who was active in the eighth century BCE. Therefore, Jeremiah's message to his contemporaries is not exactly the same as that of the Deuteronomists, which was directed to the generation after Jeremiah, even though the redaction of the book of Jeremiah was so close in time to the emergence of the 'authentic' Jeremianic pronouncements that some Deuteronomists may well have known and heard the prophet themselves.

Ordinarily, however, in connection with the prophetic literature, there is a much greater temporal distance separating the phase of redaction and the original prophet whose works were assembled by the redactors. Moreover, the redaction is not usually so distinctive as is the case with the book of Jeremiah. One could mention another of the early prophets whose activity preceded the fall of the northern kingdom in 722 BCE, namely Amos. The book which bears Amos' name also contains indications of Deuteronomistic redaction; such traces, however, are limited to short insertions of material into the text, and there is no overarching Deuteronomistic framework to the book. In other cases, the tradents who ultimately 'published' the work in question are not identical with the Deuteronomists. To take Proto-Isaiah, for example, it is clear that this collection does contain some Deuteronomistic passages, especially in the concluding section (Isa. 36-39), which is largely identical with a parallel section in Second Kings (2 Kgs 18-20). Nevertheless, it seems improbable that it was the Deuteronomists who assembled the prophecies of Isaiah; yet another group must have been responsible. We do not know who this may have been, but a qualified guess suggests that it was a circle of 'prophets' who made up a sort of 'school' and who regarded Isaiah as their spiritual figurehead. In other words, scholars assume that the prophet in question formed a 'school', that is, he was surrounded by a circle of disciples; and that this circle passed on the proclamation of the prophet, perhaps to begin with in oral form, but ultimately in the form of independent, discrete, written texts. In this case the redactional activity was often confined to the joining of the individual texts, perhaps in the process reworking them a little so that they fitted better with the time of the tradent group. But in many cases, such redaction took place without making significant changes to the texts.

Thus, the prophetic writings provide us with texts which may be

dated with some precision to particular periods in the history of
Israel, and they are important witnesses to that history, since they
are contemporaneous with the events which the texts both depict and
interpret. Thus, for example, the book of Isaiah contains texts which
refer to the events of the years 734-732 BCE, when there was war
between the kingdoms of Judah on the one hand and those of Israel
and Aram, on the other (e.g. Isa. 7). It is obvious that Isaiah 7 mainly
relates Isaiah's understanding of the event in question, or at least of
one aspect of it, namely the attempt by the Judaean king to find allies
to defend him against the northern kingdom. But this fact also shows
us the limitations on the worth of the text in question as a historical
source. Apart from the fact that the text has been bracketed within a
redactional (Deuteronomistic) framework, it is also solely concerned
to reproduce Isaiah's understanding of the events. We have no idea at
all as to the reaction of the man on the street to either the events
themselves or to Isaiah's proclamation. The prophetic texts express
the interpretations of individuals of their own times.

Now, there is often a degree of agreement between the prophets as
to how they understood their own times, that is, there is a sort of
dogmatic scheme which recurs in text after text. Nevertheless, the
expressions in question remain those of individual persons and do
not reflect the views of their society. It is evident that these views and
those of the prophets were not the same, since we frequently read of
confrontations between the prophets and other members of the
society to which they addressed their proclamation. Thus, for
example, there would have been no reason for the prophet Hosea to
launch extensive criticisms of the cult of his day—in particular of the
cult of the bull calf at Bethel—if the main part of the populace did
not in fact participate in that cult. Nor would there have been any
reason for a number of prophets to offer savage criticisms of the
social conditions in their times if people were not directly profiting
from those conditions, and it is unlikely that such individuals shared
the prophets' critical opinions—although in this particular instance,
it is probable that a significant section of the populace did agree with
them. We have no information as to the 'ordinary' Israelite's
understanding of his or her existence; we possess only the interpretations of outsiders, and it would be a misunderstanding to
imagine that such views were identical with the general understanding
of things. Indeed, it is unlikely that we shall ever know what the
ordinary Israelite thought or advocated, but we cannot permit

ourselves to ignore the fact that he or she had opinions and ideas, and that these opinions and ideas were more representative of the opinions of the Israelite or Judean peoples than were those of a few prophets.

3.3 *Sources Later Than the Events They Describe*
3.3.1 *The Chronological Gap*

Most of the historical sources in the Old Testament were first collected and perhaps shaped at a time which was more or less removed from the epochs which they describe. To take the most obvious example, the biblical chronology assigns the patriarchal period to around 2000 BCE, whereas the oldest collection of traditions about that time is at least 1100 to 1500 years younger. There is no reason to discuss in these pages the various attempts which have been made to redate the patriarchal period. Rather, it would be more appropriate simply to show what consequences such a chronological gap must have for the reliability of the traditions about the patriarchs, and for corresponding epochs in the history of Israel. The question may be posed as follows: what does a narrative about the patriarchs tell us about? Does it tell us about a patriarchal era in a long-gone past, or about the understanding of a later society of its own past? The answer to this question is dependent on the precision with which one has studied the history of the society in which such traditions were collected.

Scholars have not always been attentive to this problem; rather, they have attempted to winnow out *the historical truth* from a complex of traditions, as, for example, in the case of the patriarchal materials. We shall discuss below the various methods which have been developed to aid the scholar in the search for the original tradition. Here it will suffice merely to note that at the end of the day all the various methods are employed to 'peel off' the younger accretions of a text in order to reconstruct the earliest form. To use the Pentateuch as an example, this would suggest that when we have finished our critical work, we shall be left with—ideally—the Yahwistic version of the tradition. Even assuming the success of such a procedure, however, this would not remove the previously mentioned chronological gap. Scholars have repeatedly ignored this gap and so have been content to utilize the oldest tradition, no matter how young it may actually be, as a reliable historical source. In so doing, one has managed to produce a text which merely tells us how the period between, for instance, 900 and 600 BCE understood the past (depending on the date we assign to the Yahwist).

As far as other Pentateuchal traditions are concerned, it might seem that we are better off, since the gap mentioned above decreases successively down to the time of the Settlement, which the Old Testament chronology dates to the fifteenth century BCE. Thus if we proceed forward in the Deuteronomistic History, the gap between the events described and the age of the tradition is further reduced, until we arrive at the time of the formation of the state, around 1000 BCE. Ordinary logic dictates that the Old Testament tradition as it is preserved in the books of Joshua and Judges should—from an objective point of view—become increasingly reliable as we approach historical times. Accordingly, as we proceed through the period of the monarchy, the gap is further reduced, until we arrive at a rough approximation between events and traditions about them.

3.3.2 *The Focus of Historical Interest*
Important for the evaluation of the usefulness of these traditions as sources for information about the past is the question whether we can determine that the editors who collected and/or shaped the traditions were motivated to do so by historical interests, or by other considerations. To put the matter simply: were these editors concerned to write a *history of Israel*, or did they have some other intention? If the former is the case, is their historical writing 'objective' (the traditional goal of European historical research), or was it utilized to provide a subjective explanation of conditions in the time of the editors themselves? Finally, one ought to ask whether the editors attempted to describe an event 'as it happened', or whether they made use of ideological patterns in order to depict particular historical relations.

As an example, we may take the narrative of David's rise to power (1 Sam. 16–2 Sam. 6). This account relates how the young shepherd, David, makes such a successful career at the court of Saul that he provokes the jealousy of the old king. He is accordingly obliged to flee from Saul's court. Saul subsequently pursues David, and on a number of occasions gets himself into situations in which it is possible for David to kill him. David, however, continues to believe in the possibility of reconciliation with Saul, and therefore spares his life. Ultimately, David's situation becomes so precarious that he is forced to seek asylum among Israel's ancestral enemies, the Philistines, into whose service he enters. Saul is eventually destroyed in battle with the Philistines, a battle in which, however, David does not participate. One of Saul's sons, Ishbaal, is made king of the northern kingdom (Israel), but is not up to the task, and is soon murdered by some of his subjects, who are in turn executed on David's orders when they apply to him for a reward for their deed. At the same time the real 'strongman' of the northern kingdom, Abner, dies in connection with some negotiations with David, who has in the meantime become king in Hebron. David himself is not guilty of the death of Abner; it is instead his general, Joab, who is the responsible party. After the disappearance from the scene of Abner and Ishbaal, the north Israelites make David their king as well, so that he then reigns over both Judah and Israel, and is in a position to make Jerusalem his capital.

This narrative has often been regarded as an authentic account of the events which led to David's accession to the throne. Scholars have accordingly proceeded by paraphrasing the biblical account; in so doing they have generally acquitted David of any suspicion of complicity in the deaths of Saul and his relatives. It was the will of Yahweh that David should succeed Saul. However, it is vitally necessary to insist on a more subtle historical evaluation of the tendencies contained within this complex of traditions. For one thing, it is clearly strongly pro-Davidic, as it is based on an inflexible scheme which seeks to acquit David of all guilt. For another, it is obviously a literary composition which adheres to a pre-existent narrative pattern. If one examines the individual events, one is forced to conclude that every one of them is to David's advantage, and indeed this is so often the case that it can hardly be coincidental.

If we therefore attempt to discount the pro-Davidic tendency of this work, the sequence of events may be seen in quite a different light. Instead of being an innocent but hotly-pursued victim of royal jealousy, David emerges as a cynical power politician who avoided neither treachery nor murder in the pursuit of his goal.

Thus the traditional materials about David cannot be regarded as an attempt to write *history*, as such. Rather, they represent an ideological programmatic composition which defends the assumption of power by the Davidic dynasty, and it must have had one particular group of readers in mind, who required to be convinced of David's innocence. Furthermore, this apologetic construct follows a literary pattern which was already well known and exploited in the ancient Near East during the Bronze Age. Thus, for example, in the fifteenth century the throne of the north Syrian state of Alalah was usurped by a pretender to the throne by the name of Idrimi, who had his royal scribes compose a short work defending his accession to the throne; the composition was engraved on a statue of Idrimi. According to this work, Idrimi had been expelled from his ancestral inheritance and obliged to seek refuge in the desert, where he assembled a troup of outlaws around him in order ultimately to return to Alalah—which, to be candid, was not his ancestral inheritance. This narrative has recently been analyzed on the basis of literary criteria. In this way scholars have demonstrated that the work is not a historical account of actual events, but rather a literary composition utilizing a scheme borrowed from the genre of the fairy tale. Thus, when the author of 1 Sam. 16–2 Sam. 6 used this scheme, he did so in order to present his own case better than he would have done by publishing an objective recounting of the events in question. The audience he had in mind were not familiar with precise historical narratives; rather, they were used to getting their information about historical events clad in literary garments.

If it was the case that the ancient Israelites (and their neighbours) did not use historical writing as we know it, we ought not to expect that it should be possible to rediscover the 'objective' or 'actual' historical events. The author attempted to present his narrative in such a way that it advanced his own cause. The concern to do just this is abundantly evident in the great Deuteronomistic History, which was composed under the influence of the destruction of Jerusalem in 587, and which explains that Yahweh had rejected Israel, leading to the destruction of the city. The authors of this work presented the various traditions, or indeed even selected them solely as they supported their own intentions. This is accordingly 'subjective' historical writing—we might even prefer not to term it history writing at all. Authors always attempted to accommodate their narratives to the need of their own times, and they were always prompted to do so for very concrete reasons.

3.4 *Types of Tradition*
3.4.1 *Oral and Written Tradition*
Thus it appears that one's point of departure for the study of the 'historical' traditions in the Old Testament must be the acknowledg-

ment that these traditions primarily reflect the period in which they arose, and that they tell us primarily about that period, and only secondarily about any earlier period which they may purport to describe. In fact, the only reason we use such sources at all is simply the fact that in many cases, they are the only witness to the past available.

Nevertheless, at the time when such traditions about the past were redacted and written down in their present form, the editors must have been in possession of a number of traditions of one sort or another about the past. We possess a patriarchal tradition, an Exodus tradition, narratives about Sinai, the Settlement, and so forth. It is reasonable to suppose that a number of these narratives are older than the date at which they received their final literary form. There are various ways in which an ancient tradition may conceivably have been passed on. The primary media were either *oral* or *written*. Previously, when we discussed the prophetic books we noted that individual prophetic utterances may have been preserved among circles of disciples in either oral or written form. It should be noted that certain social factors may have determined which form of preservation was employed. For example, if there are any so-called 'popular' traditions in the Old Testament, that is, narratives which were dear to the broad mass of the people, then it is likely that such materials were passed on orally. Such narratives may have had the form of short and poignant stories or anecdotes, although we cannot rule out the possibility that such lengthy narratives as, for example, epic poems, may also have existed, and that they have since been lost. If we proceed up the ladder of social prestige, however, it is probable that certain traditions were preserved in written form, since the higher strata of society were familiar with the art of writing and were able to express themselves in written form. This is naturally true of the administrative layer in the towns, that is, the royal chancellery during the period of the monarchy. This milieu must naturally also have included the centres of learning where such administrators received their education, and the upper echelons of the priesthood who officiated at the official royal sanctuaries.

As far as the oral tradition is concerned, it should be clear that none of it has been preserved, as all of the sources we possess are either written or material remains. Thus we need to consider the problem of the reliability of this means of preserving information. It has long been something of a dogma in Scandinavian research that the Old Testament oral tradition must have been extremely reliable, on the assumption that the Israelites were powerfully concerned to retell the stories they had heard precisely as they had received them. For this reason we sometimes encounter the paradoxical argument that the oral tradition is the most reliable one, in spite of the fact that it is by far the most difficult to control. We should note that modern studies of oral tradition in pre-literary societies which have used oral tradition to reproduce sometimes even very lengthy stories show that the tradents of such materials usually understand the demand for precision in quite a different way to us. For one thing, such tradents are concerned to reproduce the main features of a course of events, that is, they attempt to preserve the intentions underlying the stories; for another, they tend to understand these efforts as 'literal' reproductions.

As far as historical research is concerned, the study of folklore has been able to demonstrate a number of factors which severely limit the usefulness of oral tradition in historical work. Many things may go wrong in the course of oral tradition. For example, the chronological connection between individual events may be disturbed, reversed, or completely ignored. Similarly, historical personalities may be left out of the tradition, while others may tend to draw to themselves traditions once associated with the now forgotten figures. Finally, of course, oral tradition always has to fulfil the entertainment expectations of its audience, which entails that it invariably accepts some degree of colouration from the time in which it is told.

Obviously, this type of tradition is the only one available in a society which does not ordinarily use writing for interpersonal communications. In reality, it usually appears in societies which have not been organized as states, since there is no need in such societies to preserve information in written form. In such societies, it is easy to recollect the things which it is essential for the tribesman to know; property rights in such societies are, for example, not so formal that anything more than verbal agreements are necessary to license them. There is no official census to be performed, nor are there national reserves of grain and foodstuffs to be administered, or official taxation requiring systematic record.

In this connection, it shold be noted that Israel was a tribal society prior to the formation of the state, and also that later on the ordinary Israelite managed to be both a member of a tribal society and a citizen of a nationstate. This means, as far as our attempts at historical reconstruction are concerned, that the traditions from the pre-national period must have survived as oral traditions, with all the difficulties that this entails for our attempts, as described above. Moreover, if such traditions continued to be preserved in local societies within the state, then they were presumably preserved in oral form here, too.

On the other hand, we do not know that this was the case. Earlier scholars who maintained that the Yahwist was to be dated to the tenth century BCE were of the opinion that the tribal traditions were collected and assembled in written form already at the beginning of the period of the monarchy. Against this, if we assume that the Yahwistic work came into being towards the close of the monarchical period, this would imply that the written preservation of Yahwistic materials first took place at this late date. This might also imply that even during the period of the monarchy traditions may have been preserved among ordinary Israelites in oral form. No matter what the truth of the matter is, we cannot ignore the fact that at an early date we encounter first one, and then another nationstate formation, meaning that written documents must also have been in use. Knowledge of the art of writing was extensive in these societies, at least within the official sector, and possibly also outside of it, among such groups as wealthy Israelites, merchants, landowners, and so on. This assumption is based, among other things, on the fact that the writing system was simply constructed, consisting as it did of a regular alphabetical system in which the vowels were not written. This means that unlike Mesopotamia or Egypt, where the writing systems were extremely complex, in Israel the scribal education need not have been an insurmountable obstacle for anyone who had the means and the interest to pursue it.

It is also frequently the case that when a state is founded the society in question changes its system of administration. A need is felt for archives which may contain, in addition to the purely businesslike inventories of state coffers and warehouses also the correspondence between the central leadership and its provincial centres, as well as the correspondence with foreign state administrations. There will often also be official reports and surveys, as well as, in some cases, annals of one sort or another, that is, short records in chronological order listing the more important events from year to year. Annalistic sources are extremely valuable for the scholar, since they make it possible not only to establish a chronology, but also to relate the various events with some precision to this chronology.

It seems likely that Israel and Judah maintained such annals, since we read in the Deuteronomistic History various references to the 'Book of the Chronicles of the Kings of Judah' and the 'Book of the Chronicles of the Kings of Israel' (1 Kgs 14.29; 15.7, 31; 16.5, etc.). Quotations from such annalistic sources are possibly present in such remarks as 'In the third year of Asa king of Judah, Ba'asha the son of Ahi'jah began to reign over all Israel at Tirzah, and reigned twenty-four years' (1 Kgs 15.33), or perhaps 'In the thirty-eighth year of Asa king of Judah, Ahab the son of Omri began to reign over Israel, and Ahab the son of Omri reigned over Israel in Samaria twenty-two years' (1 Kgs 16.29). The latter notice is particularly interesting, as it seems to imply that lists were kept in Judah which synchronized events in the northern kingdom with things taking place in the southern one.

3.4.2 *The Redactional Use of the Traditions*

This sort of official list will naturally have facilitated the job of any writer who intended to depict Israelite history during the monarchy, and will have made the composition of historically correct accounts possible. Furthermore, the use of the annals reveals the identity of the historians in question, since they must have had access to the royal archives. They must accordingly have belonged to the circles of the higher administrative officials. It is a much more difficult question whether the Yahwist, who may have worked around the same time as the Deuteronomists, belonged to the same class and wrote for the same audience, or whether his origins were in a different milieu. In many respects, the basic viewpoint of the Yahwist does not seem markedly different from that of the Deuteronomist. For example, the Yahwist maintained that Israel's right to the land of Palestine derived from the fact that it was a gift from Yahweh, and, moreover, a gift which Israel had received on certain conditions imposed by Yahweh (adherence to the Covenant, worship of Yahweh as sole God, etc.); this view is not notably different from that of the Deuteronomists. On the other hand, it is difficult to determine whether the traditions which have been recorded by the Yahwist in the Pentateuch derive from the upper classes or from the local societies, or whether both groups have not made their own contributions to the final product. Many of the narratives which have been assigned to the Yahwistic sources seem on the face of them to be more 'popular' than 'official'. This impression, however, may result from the fact that we understand something different today from the notion of 'popular' media than people did in antiquity. It is also conceivable that the higher strata in Israelite society utilized the popular narrative as a vehicle when they attempted to depict the distant past or to explain current events, namely by referring to events that were supposed to have happened in the past by means of so-called *aetiological legends*.

We encounter such legends in Genesis, for example in connection with the establishment of the sanctuaries (so-called cult legends, or *hieroi logoi*, as in Bethel, Gen. 28, or Shechem, Gen. 12.6-7; cf. Gen. 33.18-20). Aetiological legends are also to be found outside of Genesis, as, for example, in the Deuteronomistic History, where the existence of a ruin in the days of the Deuteronomists is explained by the notion that Joshua had destroyed a city there during the invasion of the land (see Josh. 8, the account of the destruction of Ai). There are also other sorts of aetiological legends, such as narratives which serve to provide explanations of particular cultural relations or general human phenomena. Many such are to be found in the primeval history in Genesis. Thus, for example, the story of the Tower of Babel (Gen. 11) serves to explain the name of the city while simultaneously explaining why mankind speaks so many different languages. Similarly, the narrative about Cain and Abel (Gen. 4) tells us about the first murder and goes on to explain that it was in this fashion that murder became one of the basic facts of human life. For contemporary readers of such stories, it cannot have been important whether an aetiological story was of one or another sort. It would be unreasonable to expect such a reader to differentiate between an aetiology which explained a feature of his own culture and one which explained a historical event. The fact that we cannot expect to do this should serve to illustrate just how cautious we must be when we attempt to utilize the Old Testament as a historical source. The Old Testament arose within the context of a society which did not have the understanding of *history* which is such a commonplace in our culture. For us, history consists of past events which deserve study in their own right. For the Israelite, however, history was able to explain circumstances prevailing in his or her own time, but also to explain his or her own destiny. The intention to use history in this way is evident both in the tendencies which the individual texts reveal on analysis and in the very selection of events

about which Israelite narrators were concerned to speak. The process
of selection is in fact most easy to discuss in connection with the
Deuteronomistic History, since in a number of cases we are informed
via other sources about features which are not mentioned in the
biblical tradition (see below, Ch. 4 §1).

In many respects it is accordingly possible to speak of a
comparability between the sources relative to the history of the
monarchy and those bearing on the pre-national period. In connection
with both periods we possess a chronological frame of reference in
the Old Testament. As far as the period of the monarchy is
concerned, this chronology is useful for the reconstruction of the
historical course of events. As for the prehistoric period, however, it
is first necessary to determine whether the chronological scheme
may be used at all, or whether we should simply ignore it and
attempt to reconstruct this part of Israel's 'history' without reference
to the biblical chronology. These questions are to be answered on the
basis of traditions which contain numerous anachronisms, that is,
information which is later (or earlier) than the events of which the
tradition in question speaks. For example, the patriarchal traditions
mention that the patriarchs knew the use of the camel and that they
also sometimes negotiated with the Philistines. Both notions are
clearly anachronistic in relation to the biblical chronology, since the
chronology dates the era of the patriarchs to around 2,000 BCE, when
the camel was not in use as a beast of burden, and long before the
arrival of the Philistines in Palestine. Thus one must decide whether
the anachronisms are to be explained away as later additions or
whether all such traditions are to be dated to the period in which
such conditions in fact obtained. Moreover, it is also possible on the
basis of these and similar anachronisms to maintain that the
narratives in question were composed in a society which no longer
possessed any clear idea as to the patriarchal age, for which reason its
narrators composed their stories as narratives about a distant
fairytale past.

4. *Methods of Reading the Texts*

The study of the peculiarities of the texts in the Old Testament has
shown that it is quite impossible simply to 'go straight to them' and
employ their statements as if they were descriptive of developments
in Israel prior to the time the texts reached their final form. A

number of analytical methods are available to help the reader in the encounter with the texts. In this connection, one ought, in principle, to distinguish between two main sorts of tools: on the one hand those which help to distinguish the earlier strata in a given text, and on the other those which are appropriate either for the analysis of the final form of the text, as it now stands, or for the understanding of earlier versions of it. Generally speaking the first group of approaches are the older, and it has only been comparatively recently that the monopoly of these methods has been seriously shaken by the appearance of other approaches.

4.1 *The 'Text-historical' Methods*

Scholars generally speak of four main approaches to the study of the texts: *literary criticism, form criticism, redaction criticism,* and *tradition history,* to list them in the order in which they were introduced.

4.1.1 *Literary Criticism*

The literary critic understands the task as that of differentiating various strata in a text via an analysis of the literary elements. To this end he or she concentrates on purely formal features such as style change or heterogenous terminology in a given text. This method attempts to live up to the demands of 'objective science' in that it is— at least in theory—solely concerned with objective data provided by the text itself.

The classical point of departure for this approach is the use of the two divine names, *Yahweh* and *Elohim*, in the Pentateuch, since, as has long been noted, the use of these two names differs in parallel narratives contained in the work. For example, the creation narrative in Genesis 1 utilizes *Elohim* alone, while the second creation narrative in Genesis 2 makes use of *Yahweh* (though, admittedly, in conjunction with *Elohim*). In the Flood Narrative mentioned previously, that is, Genesis 6-9, one of the two strata present in the text employs *Yahweh*, while the other prefers *Elohim*. These are perhaps the clearest examples of such distinctions available, but they have been supported and further developed with the aid of countless corresponding observations.

The advantage of this approach is that it avoids subjective evaluations to a large extent. On the other hand, its greatest limitation is precisely that it ignores the possibility that the texts may have been composed according to different criteria than those which obtain in the modern West. Similarly, it also concentrates too much on the assumption that the texts took their origins in a literate milieu. Finally, it has become clear that this approach is only of limited value once one proceeds beyond the Pentateuch.

4.1.2 *Form Criticism*

Form criticism supplements literary criticism by enquiring as to the social background of individual texts. Scholars speak in this connection of the 'Sitz im Leben' of a given text. The first step in a form critical investigation is to determine the *form* of a given text, which in practice means its genre, after which one attempts to define the use to which texts of that particular sort were put in Israelite society.

For example, the narrative about the patriarch Jacob at Bethel (Gen. 28) may be defined as a *cult legend*, since it relates the initiation of a particular cultic site. Thus, the form critics claim that it would be reasonable to assume that before Genesis 28 was incorporated into its present setting it played a rôle at the sanctuary at Bethel in the legitimation of Bethel as a true Yahweh sanctuary.

Of course, quite a number of different genres are present in the Old Testament; the list extends from entire 'novels' (or 'novellas') like the Joseph story (Gen. 37–50) to short heroic anecdotes (collected in Judg. 1–12), parenetic passages (e.g. Josh. 23 and Judg. 2), myths (especially in the primeval history, Gen. 1–11), small units of text such as, for example, the genealogies of varying lengths (including that of Esau in Genesis 36, which is composed of a number of shorter units), or short poems appearing in the midst of prose contexts (thus, for example, Lamech's 'song of vengeance' in Gen. 4.23-24). Form criticism is, furthermore, equally useful in all parts of the Old Testament. We have already mentioned the example of the various psalmic genres, but there are more yet unmentioned. In the Wisdom literature, it is possible to distinguish between proverbs as such (collected, among other places, in Proverbs 10ff.) and admonitions (like the warnings against the 'foreign woman' in Proverbs 7). Within the corpus of the prophetic writings, it is likewise possible to distinguish a number of genres, such as threats, legal speeches, prophecies of judgment, sermons, proverbs, or songs, all of which an individual prophet may have used to express his message.

However, the use to which the prophets put the various literary genres at their disposal indicates a limit on the usefulness of form criticism. The scholar is well advised not to make too much of the 'Sitz im Leben' of a given genre, since it is clear that the prophets often used literary forms which belonged to a particular context, but they used them for their own purposes and gave them the sense they themselves intended. A famous example is the 'Song of the Vineyard' in Isaiah 5 (vv. 1-7) which the prophet no doubt borrowed from somewhere (it was probably a contemporary working song), but which he also gave a new point by allowing his version to deal with the relationship between Israel and Yahweh. In other words, a given genre may have had numerous applications within Israelite society; there is in any case no reason to suppose that any genre had only a single appropriate context.

Nevertheless, form criticism is one of the most important tools available to the Old Testament scholar, and it forms the point of departure for the application of a number of other methods. It does so by giving the texts some dimensions of depth which literary criticism alone is unable to supply. The presence of a number of different genres in, for example, the Yahwistic stratum of the Pentateuch, shows that already before their incorporation into the Yahwistic work a number of traditions existed independently. This makes possible both redaction-critical and tradition-historical approaches, both of which attempt to answer the question as to how the final product arose.

4.1.3 *Redaction Criticism*

The most important difference between redaction criticism and tradition history is that the former focuses its attention on the final redaction and on the intervening phases of redaction, while tradition history is also concerned with the pre-literary tradition, that is, it is interested in a given tradition before it was incorporated into a given context, perhaps even before it was recorded in written form.

Redaction criticism concerns itself with the various source materials and their composition. In so doing it serves as a supplement to literary and form criticism by attempting to describe the ideological motives which determined the choices by the various redactors of the individual traditions. This method is not least important in the study of the prophetic literature, since it analyses a prophetic work with the goal of evaluating the redactional activity which resulted in the accommodation of an early prophetic tradition to a redactional framework. Its connections with literary criticism, on the one hand, and with tradition history, on the other, are clear, since this method does not of itself attempt to define which materials are ancient tradition and which later materials. When the distinction between primary and secondary materials has been completed, the tradition historian is then able to provide a sort of table of contents of both quantities. He is also in a position to attempt to describe the work that went into the 'publication' of the early traditions, and to characterize the motives which guided the activity of the redactor(s).

If we turn to the Pentateuch or to the Deuteronomistic History, redaction criticism also proves to be fruitful. Today a number of scholars are of the opinion that the Deuteronomistic History contains two or three different phases of redaction. Here the redaction critical method is able to describe the different motives which led to each separate redaction; moreover, it is also able to confront these motives with those which guided the final phase of redaction. By demonstrating similarities and differences between the various phases, this method makes it possible to characterize the intellectual development of the circles responsible for the individual phases.

A text which invites the use of the tradition-historical method is Deuteronomy 12, a section of great importance in the Deuteronomistic literature as it contains the demand for the centralization of the cult. A literary critical analysis of the text shows that four almost identical sections of text are present: vv. 2-7; 8-12; 13-19; and 29-27 (vv. 1 and 28 are the introduction and conclusion, respectively). The redaction critic may relate these four sections to one another and, in a broader perspective, to the rest of Deuteronomy. He will thus be in a position to suggest a chronological sequence for the various editions of the law of centralization, and to describe the development leading from one phase to another.

In Pentateuchal scholarship, redaction criticism has been especially interested in the Yahwistic stratum. The result of this work has been that there is now considerable uncertainty as to the redactional work underlying this stratum, and as to the date that is to be assigned to it. Rolf Rendtorff has attempted to attack the thesis according to which the Yahwistic materials made up a single connected literary stratum. Rendtorff emphasizes instead the individual units of which the stratum is composed, and which he maintains existed independently prior to their inclusion within the Yahwistic work. At the same time, Rendtorff and others have attempted on the basis of their studies of the ideologies which motivated the creation of the collection to approximate the emergence of the Yahwistic stratum to the time of the Deuteronomists. In other words, they advocate moving the date of the collection down towards the middle of the first millennium BCE.

4.1.4 *Tradition History*

In principle, tradition history studies a given tradition independently of whether it is to be found in a literary or a pre-literary, that is, an 'oral' context. The questions which one asks of a text, and the answers one receives, are accordingly of a different character from those appropriate to other methods. In this connection, form-critical evaluations are particularly significant, since they suggest possible uses of the pre-literary tradition, which may also provide suggestions as to the age of the tradition in question. If, for example, it develops that all of the traditions dealing with the northern kingdom (Israel) between 925 and 722 BCE are preserved in literary strata which are younger than 722 BCE, then it is possible that these texts have a prehistory which can only be approached by the methods of tradition history.

For example, the first four books of the Pentateuch and the Deuteronomistic History contain a number of traditions about the north Israelite town of Shechem and its sanctuary. The sanctuary was founded by Abraham (Gen. 12.6-7), or, perhaps, by Jacob (Gen. 33.18-20), but the town was destroyed by Jacob's sons (Gen. 34). After the settlement in Palestine the Israelites are supposed to have celebrated a number of rituals there (Deut. 11.26-32; 27), and the settlement itself was concluded by a popular assembly in Shechem (Josh. 24). During the era of the Judges, an Israelite king, Abimelech, reigned in Shechem for a time (Judg. 9). Finally, the Davidic empire was split into two parts at a meeting between the Jerusalemite king and the Israelites in Shechem (1 Kgs 12). Subsequent to this the Old Testament is silent about the town, although the archeologists have been able to demonstrate that it continued to exist in subsequent centuries.

The traditions about Shechem were not part of the official religious tradition of the northern kingdom, as this was associated with Bethel. Thus, the survival of the Shechem traditions must be the result of the fact that the circles which were behind the production of the Tetrateuch and the Deuteronomistic History were concerned that they should survive. They must also have possessed certain information about the site. Such a tradition-historical analysis thus tells us not only something about the process by means of which the Shechem traditions were passed on, but also about the presence of different currents in the northern kingdom than the 'official' ones. It also informs us that such currents ultimately had some influence on the formation of the historical tradition after the demise of the northern kingdom in 722.

This method is equally applicable to an extensive complex of materials as to a limited corpus of them. An example of a narrow textual basis for a tradition-historical analysis is provided by the Ten Commandments. Literary critical analysis reveals that in both of the contexts in which the Commandments figure they have been fitted into a redactional framework (which in both cases is Deuteronomistic). Form critical analysis shows that the Commandments belong to a special genre among the Old Testament laws. Most Israelite cultic legislation is casuistic, that is, of the type: 'If a man kills another man, that man shall die'. By way of contrast, the Ten Commandments are apodictic demands: 'You shall not kill!' A tradition-historical analysis would suggest that whereas the casuistic type was (and had always been) associated with the usual administration of justice, the formulation of the apodictic commandments seems to presuppose a different and higher instance, a deity or a prince. Commandments of this type are most of all reminiscent of the commands issued by a sovereign king to his subjects.

A tradition-historical analysis might also be able to connect the series of commands which make up the Ten Commandments with other genres, such as the so-called 'entrance liturgies' (Pss. 15 and 24), in which a number of preconditions are imposed upon those seeking admission to the cult. Such conditions have to be met before the seekers are admitted to the sacred area. Thus one could imagine that such things as the Ten Commandments were a collection of those demands levied by the deity, that is, Yahweh, on those seeking entrance to his temple. Such an analysis would also show that the site of such demands need by no means to be the temple in Jerusalem, as it could just as easily be a question of a north Israelite sanctuary, like Shechem.

The weakness of the tradition-historical approach lies in its subjective character, particularly when it is concerned with the question of oral tradition. In this connection, the method suffers from the lack of objective controls, since we ordinarily do not possess other sources which could show that the results arrived at by the method are correct. Thus, this method has little appeal for the scholar who requires 'assured' results. It is clear that such analyses allow scholars to arrive at widely different results, and that it is almost impossible to determine just which result most closely approximates to the truth. But for the scholar who is concerned to utilize these many possibilities in the interests of arriving at a broad mosaic of tradition-historical analyses, this is the only way to achieve some understanding of the development of the Old Testament traditions.

4.2 *Literary-scientific and Sociological Methods*
In recent years, a variety of new methods have been introduced into the study of the Old Testament. Some of them have been borrowed from contemporary literary study; others derive from the field of sociology. However, the inclusion of these methods is as yet still at a provisional stage, and many Old Testament scholars remain sceptical as to their usefulness.

4.2.1 *The Literary-scientific Approach*
The literary-scientific methods are mainly applicable to a given text in its final form, meaning that they attempt to interpret it 'as it stands'. Such approaches are unconcerned with the division of the text into older and younger elements, or with the process of tradition. Thus, for example, if one regards the narratives about patriarchs as historical sources bearing on the 'age of the patriarchs' and not as examples of how during the monarchical period people told stories about the past, such approaches will be quite superfluous. If one's goal is to seek back to the 'Ur-tradition', then one will have little joy with such things as semantic analyses of individual concepts. On the other hand, such approaches are well suited to extend our understanding of ideological and cultural patterns among the circles which were behind the composition of a given tradition. Narratives about the people's past may reasonably be supposed to contain considerable information about attitudes during the period of the monarchy, or during the exilic period, when these accounts were recorded in written form. The narratives in question are in all probability

witnesses to the time when they were formulated, and only to a lesser
extent are they sources about earlier times. For this reason analytic
approaches which concentrate on the study of narratives in their
final form are extremely germane to the study of the history of Israel.
The only caution to be observed in this connection is that one must
be quite precise as to the nature of the information one seeks in a
given text. When, for example, we discover that the author of the
account of David's rise to power employed a literary scheme which
he had borrowed from the genre of the fairy tale, this implies that he
was not interested in exact or 'historical' treatment. To the contrary,
the literary form he chose was intended to play a decisive rôle in the
transmission and preservation of his message.

Other approaches entail study of the communicative patterns in a
given text to determine which literary devices were used, which rôles
were assigned to individuals in the narrative, how they relate to one
another, and, no less important, the persons with whom they are *not*
associated. Such studies can provide us with considerable information
as to how Israelites during the monarchy and later understood their
fellow human beings, as to which individuals were found interesting,
as to attitudes towards the 'stranger', and so forth. In short, such
studies should eventually make it possible for us to offer a precise
and sophisticated description of Israelite 'mentality' and to determine
the ideological basis of the Israelites' life together with others.

4.2.2 *The Sociological Approach*
Sociological approaches to the texts may be combined with literary-
scientific methods. As they have been employed so far, however,
sociological approaches have been mostly historically orientated, for
which reason they have been more or less easily accepted. The
underlying insight is that literary remains are the results of
sociological processes at work in the population. This means that
literature expresses the historical and cultural situation of the
population at the time the literature was composed. To date this
approach has mostly been associated with quasi-philosophical
'sociological' evolutionary theories which have been intended to
make it possible for us to determine a scheme illustrating how people
behave and how societies develop under particular types of influences
and conditions.

The extent to which this approach has been confined by its
research tradition is also evidenced by the way its practitioners make

use of the classical procedures of analysis. Generally speaking, the advocates of this approach have adopted the results of the classical methods; they are also, broadly considered, fairly conservative. Many such scholars have concerned themselves with the prehistory of Israel. In so doing they have dated a number of traditions back to the pre-national era, and then attempted to describe the social structure and the ideology which were then dominant. They have also attempted to describe the socio-political developments in Israelite society on the basis of the sources in question.

The difficulty confronting scholars attempting to use both of these new approaches is that the training of most Old Testament scholars does not ordinarily include either of the relevant disciplines (literary study and sociology). Instead, their training has primarily been of a philological nature (based on the notion that the text should ideally be 'correctly translated'). At present, however, this picture is rapidly changing, which means that even if the methods in question have not as yet any striking successes to their credit, it would not be amiss to predict that they will be utilized to a much greater extent in future.

5. *Other Sources*

A major obstacle to the use of the Old Testament traditions as sources for the history of Israel is the lack of other witnesses to supplement and/or correct the biblical materials. In principle, such sources would be of two types: either *written* or *material* sources. Written sources might consist of the same sorts of literature as those which are preserved in the Old Testament, or they might consist of short inscriptions which merely confirm such things as the existence of a person or institution which is mentioned in the Old Testament. By way of contrast, the material sources are 'silent'; not having been deposited in written form, they are merely remains which may be excavated from the earth, dated, and used to provide information about the periods from which they derive.

5.1 *Written Sources*
As regards the period beginning at the end of the Late Bronze Age around 1200 BCE extending down until the time of the formation of the Israelite state around 1000 BCE, Palestine offers us virtually no inscriptions. Furthermore, the countries surrounding Palestine are also lacking in such sources. There is, therefore, no written material

outside the Old Testament which can either confirm or contradict the Old Testament witness for this period. In the period of the monarchy, on the other hand, individual pieces of information from Israel's neighbours do pop up, and these may be seen in relation to events and information which is mentioned in the Old Testament, particularly from the ninth century BCE and later. The main part of such materials derive, however, from Israel's surroundings, while historical inscriptions from Palestine are still few, small, and, generally speaking, without greater significance. The more extensive Assyrian and Babylonian royal inscriptions, however, occasionally contain information bearing on the relationship between these great powers and the mini-state of Israel during the monarchical period. Unfortunately, the sort of information such inscriptions provide is mostly confined to warlike developments between the respective countries, or else they refer to the results of such confrontations (i.e. Israelite subjugation and payment of tribute).

Ordinarily, such external sources are regarded as providing more reliable information than the Old Testament does, since they are contemporaneous with the events they depict. However, this need not inevitably be the case. To mention a single example, that of the siege of Jerusalem by the Assyrian king Sennacherib in 701 BCE, we possess both a record of this in the Old Testament (2 Kgs 18-19) and Sennacherib's own version in the Assyrian annals. The biblical version records that Yahweh saved Jerusalem from the hand of the Assyrians, whereas Sennacherib himself reports that Hezekiah 'bought' him off by payments to tribute. The two records do, however, agree on at least one point, namely, that the Assyrians did not conquer Jerusalem. The obvious conclusion is that the biblical text has 'decorated' the truth, and this is probably the case. Nevertheless, it is also essential to take the peculiar character of the Assyrian inscriptions into consideration. These documents, too, are not neutral reports of past events; they are propagandistic writings intended to show the Assyrian king in as favourable a light as possible. The Assyrians, too, liked to 'decorate' the facts. Thus, the possibility that Sennacherib had to abandon his siege of Jerusalem for one reason or another, perhaps including an epidemic among his troops (cf. 2 Kgs 19.35-36), still exists. For this reason, it is necessary to consider also the attitude towards history prevalent in the societies in question. Just as the Israelites were not interested in authentic historical accounts, the Mesopotamians betrayed a similar disinterest.

Instead, people generally attempted to describe the various courses of events in whatever light and by whatever means were regarded as useful for the purpose. Nevertheless, the Mesopotamian inscriptions are of considerable value. Among other things, they have contributed importantly to the establishment of the chronology of the period of the monarchy because of the so-called *synchronisms* (time intersections) between the Israelite and Assyrian or Babylonian kings.

Written sources outside of the Old Testament are also able to inform us of other matters than political ones. As the collections of Old Testament laws (esp. the Book of the Covenant, Exod. 21.2-23.16) indicates, there are marked points of comparison with corresponding social conditions which are reflected in the legal collections mainly deriving from Mesopotamia. Religious features, not least of these being the identities of a number of deities who are mentioned by name in the Old Testament, acquire 'flesh and blood' from the religious documents from Israel's environment. The value of the various Near Eastern sources is, however, limited by reason of the distance in time separating them from the Old Testament tradition as well as by the spatial distance separating them from Palestine. Nevertheless, this literature must necessarily play an important rôle for any scholar who intends to understand the ancient Near Eastern context of Israel, that is, of that world of which little Israel was only a small part.

5.2 Material Sources
Matters are somewhat different with the *archeological* materials or sources which have enriched Old Testament scholarship in so many ways during the last century or more. They have, however, also created serious problems for that scholarship—problems which it is today quite impossible to escape. Countless sites have been rescued from oblivion by the archeologists, and on many occasions the discoveries have awakened much scholarly delight. For example, when ancient Jericho was discovered in the Jordan Valley near Arab Ariha (which has preserved its ancient name), scholars immediately assumed that the narrative of the conquest of this town (related in Josh. 6) had been confirmed as a historical account. When archeologists working in Galilee encountered the biblical Megiddo, in the process finding considerable structural remains, it was felt that we now had evidence of the structures which Solomon built (1 Kgs 9.15). In other words, the archeology of Palestine has until recently

been almost exclusively a *biblical archeology*, in which archeologists and biblical scholars have attempted hand in hand to demonstrate the 'truth' of the Bible.

Archeological evidence, however, does not consist of *objective data* (i.e. data whose meaning is immediately clear) like the data of the natural sciences. It consists instead of *subjective data* (i.e. they are the results of the interpretation of an archeologist), and their age, precisely as is the case with the literary strata of the Old Testament, is of decisive importance, but very difficult to determine. For example, subsequent examination of the buildings at Megiddo has shown that they cannot derive from the time of Solomon, as they must be at least fifty years younger. As far as Jericho is concerned, the previously mentioned excavations created more problems for the biblical tradition than they solved, since it is now clear that Jericho had lain in ruins for several centuries at the time scholars had assigned to the Israelite conquest of the city.

These two examples provide some impression of the problems associated with the use of archeological materials in conjunction with the Old Testament traditions; it would not be difficult to offer other similar examples. It is also possible to point to an extensive number of areas which might be difficult to understand for the non-specialist, but which nevertheless indicate that biblical traditions often lack any historical foundation.

In spite of all this, it would be incorrect to claim that the archeology of Palestine is without significance. In a number of cases there really is direct correspondence between the results of excavation and the Old Testament tradition. Thus, for example, the town of Samaria is supposed to have been founded by Omri (1 Kgs 16.24), and excavations have indeed shown the town to have been first founded in the ninth century BCE. Similarly, destruction layers from the period of the monarchy, which may be compared with information preserved in the Old Testament, are frequently revealed during excavations. Thus, for example, the Babylonian conquest of Jerusalem in 587 BCE left behind it thick layers of rubble which are easy for the archeologist to identify. We are also in possession of a number of material remains such as household items, house structures, and the like, which allow us to form some impression of the material culture in the country. There are also statuettes, images, and so forth of a religious nature which tell us something about the religion of the average person in antiquity. Archeology is also able to give us some idea of the differences in standard of living of the various strata in the population, just as it can provide information on the importance of the introduction of the monarchy by excavating the monumental architecture which the central authority created, and which may be compared with the wretched remains dating from the pre-national period. Archeology is furthermore able to demonstrate the presence of cultural loans, which indicate trade relationships between Palestine and her neighbours, whether these consist of directly imported materials or domestic copies of such things. Finally, archeology may be used in a historical study which does not so much aim at demonstrating the truth of the biblical tradition as at illuminating such factors as the patterns of settlement, forms of organization, and demographic dispersal of the population in various periods.

If archeology is correctly used, it is an inexhaustible source of information for understanding the history of Israel. It is also able to give us a *contemporary* impression of cultural and social conditions which at all times underlay the historical developments. What it is not able to do is to inform us about individual historical events, as long as the excavations do not produce a richer supply of written sources with historical contents and as long as it provides no certain bridge to other sources whose historical veracity is unassailable. Archeology is normally unable to give us a causal historical explanation of individual events, although it may be able to provide illustrative material for such explanations if we possess other information on the events themselves.

Chapter 3

THE PRE-MONARCHICAL PERIOD

1. *Palestine between 3000 and 1500*

When David brought most of Palestine under the control of a single
king around the year 1000 BCE he created at the same time a new
political phenomenon; however, he also continued an old and well-
known political system which had already existed in the country for
close to 2000 years. David's kingdom followed a traditional model,
since the population of Palestine had known of *kings* for a long time,
which is to say that the region had previously been organized in
states led by a central authority, namely that of the crown. David's
kingdom was also something new, however, in that all indications
suggest that this was the first time that the main part of the country
was subordinated to the authority of a single king.

   Unfortunately, as far as the first 1500 years of the Bronze Age are
concerned, that is, from about 3000 BCE to about 1500 BCE, we
possess practically no written sources capable of telling us anything
about Palestinian society. However, the existence of what must have
been at times quite sizable urban societies already in the Early
Bronze Age (c. 3000 BCE to c. 2000 BCE) does suggest that even then
there existed centrally organized political systems. Between 2300 and
2000 BCE this political and social system, which was based on the
presence of a number of urban societies, was replaced by a different
political order which entailed that for the most part the urban
societies disappeared. In this period the centralized political systems
were largely replaced by other social forms, and the population was
probably organized in tribes, as was the later Israelite society during
the Early Iron Age. The population of Palestine lived mainly from
agriculture combined with stock-breeding. There was a decline in
other activities such as manufacture and, particularly, trade, since
there was no longer anyone to trade with, because the contemporary

neighbouring cultures were in socio-cultural declines themselves, as was the case in Palestine.

In earlier times scholars attempted to relate these socio-political changes to large scale *migration of population*. Thus earlier scholars spoke of a *Canaanite* migration around 3000 BCE, followed by an *Amorite* one around 1000 years later, each 'wave' of 'migration' being named after the population groups which lived in the region in the third and second millennia BCE. Today there is a tendency to abandon this explanatory model, as the notion of large-scale migrations of population has been discredited by historical research. Historians—including Old Testament scholars—were previously inclined to employ hypothetical population migrations to explain almost any significant change in the cultural pattern of a region. Today, however, we have learned that *most social changes take place within the population that is already present in a given region*, since that population will follow the social, economic, and political developments of the society; change is only secondarily to be ascribed to the agency of external causes. Population migrations are, naturally, an exception, but in every case very good grounds must be offered for supposing them to have taken place.

Thus, when the cultural decline during the Early Bronze Age gave way to new advances, this was synonymous with a return to the social and political system which existed earlier, and in which the city-states were dominant. A number of towns which had existed in the Early Bronze Age re-emerged: others arose and flowered throughout the subsequent period, which is normally called the Middle Bronze Age (c. 1900 to 1500 BCE). As sources for this period we possess a few Egyptian texts which mention a number of Palestinian towns and cities. These are the so-called 'Execration Texts'. They are divided into two groups, with about 100 years intervening between them. Scholars have held that these texts demonstrate a development within Palestinian society corresponding to the description above, namely from a tribal system and back to a system consisting of centralized states ruled by kings. The Middle Bronze Age was the actual floruit of Palestine, at least prior to the Hellenistic and Roman periods. The wealth of this period is reflected in the archeological excavations, which show that the cities and towns of the time were large and prosperous, and that they were more numerous than at any time prior to the Hellenistic and Roman era.

The transition from the Middle Bronze Age to the Late Bronze Age was quite different from the transition from the Early Bronze Age to the Middle Bronze period. There is no sign of a medial period in which the social system changed character. Urban culture did not disappear, although it did experience a crisis which was primarily the result of political factors. At the beginning of the Late Bronze Age the Egyptians forced their way into Syro-Palestine and at this time conquered the entire region all the way to the Euphrates on the northeast. The Egyptian conquest entailed considerable destruction of Palestinian cities and towns. However, this destruction did not as a rule mean the end of these communities, although it did lead to changed political and economic conditions for their continued existence.

2. The Late Bronze Age

2.1 The Late Bronze Age Society in Palestine
2.1.1 The Sources for the Late Bronze Age

In connection with the Late Bronze Age we are well informed about a particular socio-political system, which predominated in Syro-Palestine at this time, by a significant quantity of *administrative sources* (extensive collections of both international and domestic correspondence, international treaties, economic documents, legal decisions, and so forth, all of which illustrate trade relations, price structures, exchanges of goods, systems of taxation, and so on). These sources have been made available in this century by excavations, and they permit us to depict the social structures of two West Asiatic states, namely Ugarit and Alalah; they also permit us to characterize the history of both cities fairly precisely. It is further possible for us to describe the economic and cultural forces which manifested themselves in these cities. However, both states were situated to the north of Palestine. Moreover, we do not possess such extensive sources, and certainly not ones covering the whole period, from Palestine proper, although this situation is ameliorated by the extremely important collection of letters which consists of the correspondence between the Egyptian vassal kings in Palestine and the Egyptian court at the beginning of the fourteenth century. These are the *Amarna Letters*, and they not only tell us about the connections between Pharaoh, the Egyptian king, and the local princes in Palestine and Phoenicia (Lebanon), they also tell us about the crisis which Syro-Palestine experienced at this time. In other words, the Amarna Letters make it possible for us to reconstruct some of the factors which led to the collapse of Late Bronze Age society, and which prompted the emergence of new social formations during the transition to the Iron Age. Some other Egyptian documents, mainly royal inscriptions, also provide other evidence.

2.1.2 *The Palace Administration*

All of this documentation shows that in Syro-Palestine during the Late Bronze Age there was a system of small kingdoms, usually defined as *city-states*, since they all had the common feature of having a city as centre in which the local ruler resided. There was considerable variety as to the relative size of these mini-states. In Syria they were sometimes of considerable extent, while in Palestine and Phoenicia they were commonly quite small. The reasons for these size variations will not be gone into here, but they included, among other things, the ecological conditions in the regions in question—in the case of Palestine this meant the geographically fragmented character of the area.

If we try to imagine a purely fictive Palestinian city-state and try, further, to reconstruct its structure and functions, bearing in mind that we are dealing with a fictive and not a real state, and to this end utilize data from the many known petty states of the region as well as from Alalah and Ugarit, for the sake of completeness, it would be appropriate to start at the top of the state, which means with *the king and his family*, since this combined entity was determinative for all relationships in the kingdom. The king's position was ensured by well established rules governing the succession. Moreover, he was a member of a *dynasty* and more or less 'owned' the kingdom; all others were by definition his 'slaves', meaning they were either employed by the king or were dependent on him. This status applied to the class of *public administrators*, who were simply entitled 'slaves of the king', and whose function it was to expedite his wishes. In reality, such officials enjoyed considerable influence because of their direct access to the king and their control of the apparatus of power, to which they had acceded by reason of their education. These officials were that stratum in society which could both read and write, and for this reason they were in a position to dominate the entire administration of the kingdom, with the king as their ultimate chief.

A number of social sectors were directly subordinated to the central administration, which was concentrated in the royal palace (which is why this system of government is often referred to as the *palace administration*). These sectors were concerned with crafts, trade, and defence. The artisans were employees of the palace; they did not sell their products themselves, but delivered them instead to the palace in return for a salary which at the time consisted of rations and other goods, although the worth of these commodities was valued against silver (a money economy as such first arose in later times). The products of such manufacture were employed by the palace to produce income, not least through the international system of trade. Such trade was carried out by *merchants* who were likewise employees of the palace administration. In other words, they were more representatives of the firm which the palace really was than independent traders (although there are some indications of private activities in connection with and alongside of their official duties). The group of merchants, too, received their pay directly from the palace.

2.1.3 *Military Personnel*
The military consisted of two sectors, one of which was *professional* while the other was *conscripted*. The professional soldiery were further distributed over a number of specialized weapons proficiencies, each with its own relative hierarchical placement. Some were bowmen (in fact, the Egyptian elite soldiery of the time were simply called 'bowmen'), others were ordinary garrison troops, while still others served in the palace as a royal guard. Since it was available for service at all times, it may be supposed that the guard also doubled as a police corps and so ensured political stability in the kingdom. Ranged above all the others were the corps of chariot soldiery, who were a specialized élite within the military body, and who were expert in the employment of the then-dominant horse-drawn war chariots. Many studies of these forces describe them as comprising a warrior nobility but this, however, they were not, at least not in a European sense, since they remained in any case the 'slaves of the king' and as such received their remuneration from the palace. On the other hand, some of their payments took the form of endowments of land, that is, small estates, from which they were able to provide for their own needs. Such estates were originally only loans, for which reason they continued to be regarded as possessions

of the Crown. They also reverted to the central administration when their 'owner' died or was discredited and fired. At a relatively early date, however, this situation changed, so that the smaller estates became heritable possessions and thus the system began to resemble a fief system similar to that employed in Europe during the Middle Ages (and, incidentally, making the term 'warrior nobility' not unreasonable).

The professional soldiery were never very numerous. To take the case of Ugarit as an example, in this city the palace guard numbered only a couple of hundred soldiers, and in this connection we should note that Ugarit was one of the larger states in the region. Thus in Palestine the numbers in question must have been even more restricted. It should be obvious that forces of this size would have been insufficient to wage war with neighbouring states, so that their primary task must have been to maintain internal law and order.

2.1.4 *The Peasants*

When war broke out, the main forces of the army were immediately called up. Conscription, however, cannot have been universal, since the various groups of specialists within the private sector, that is, the administrators and artisans, were too important to waste their lives on military campaigns. In short, it must have been the lower parts of society who had to ensure that such a city-state system could survive. The lower elements will have provided cannon fodder for military service and, to the extent that the palace administrators thought it necessary, they will also have served as a source of untrained labour, that is, as corvée labourers. This sector of the population was practically entirely employed in the agricultural sector, whether they resided in the cities (especially in Palestine) or were residents of the villages surrounding the cities.

Scholars have questioned whether or not there was such a thing as a free peasantry, or whether the peasants, too, were dependents of the palace. In reality, this reduces to the question of whether the peasants owned their own land, or whether the king was the official owner of all lands. There are some indications that the latter was in fact the case, since the languages of the time lacked any term for 'farmer' or 'peasant'. Instead, the term *hupshu* was frequently employed, and this term seems rather to describe a semi-free class of 'clients' analogous to the Roman 'clientes'.[1]

Thus in all likelihood it was a question of a mixed system in which the peasants disposed to some extent over their lands, meaning that they could bequeath them to others, but in which they were also copyholders or indeed simply serfs of the palace administration, with which they enjoyed the status of clients. They probably had to deliver a sizable part of their agricultural production to the palace, in return for which they received no pay—except in times of famine—and no doubt had to live off the produce which remained after taxes. What they did receive from the palace administration was an assurance of protection. The state guaranteed the peasants their lives and welfare, protected them from robbers and the depredations of hostile powers, and, additionally, parcelled out supplies to them in the event of poor harvests. But that was *all* that the state did for them.

2.1.5 *Nation-State or Territorial State?*

Last but not least, it is important to realize that in antiquity there were no national states in the Middle East, with the possible exception of Egypt. By this is meant that there was no ethnic difference between the inhabitants of the various small kingdoms; the peasants of the city-state of Megiddo in Palestine were not ethnically different from those who belonged to the city-state of Hazor. They all spoke the same language, and so could from one day to the next, if the political situation dictated it, change their allegiance from Megiddo to the king of Hazor, or vice versa. The nation state, which we today take for granted, was a development which actually arose at a much later date. This is to be emphasized, because otherwise it creates a false impression of the city-state system in the Near East of the Bronze Age. In reality, this system had only one thing in common with the *polis* of classical Greece, as represented by Athens and Sparta, namely the fact that in both systems the city was the centre of the state. However, the inhabitants did not identify themselves as 'Athenians' or 'Spartans', and in

1. The term 'client' signifies a person who belongs neither to a private individual nor to a state as a slave. On the other hand, a 'client' is not a 'freeman', since he is economically, socially, and politically dependent on some other instance to which he owes his allegiance, and which is in a position to aid him in hard times.

general they can have had no influence on the political or economic life of the state.

2.2 *Palestine and the New Kingdom in Egypt*
2.2.1 *Political Tensions within the City-State System*
In order for this socio-political system to function, equilibrium had to exist between the burdens placed by the palace administration upon the wider segments of the populace, namely the peasantry, and the few advantages, in the form of security and political stability, which the power of the state was able to guarantee. Such equilibrium had necessarily to apply across the board. Accordingly, it is more than doubtful whether the states in question ever managed to function in agreement with this ideal. Indeed, the Amarna letters leave quite a different impression as far as the small city-states of Palestine and Phoenicia are concerned. There were several reasons for this. Of the more important ones, the physico-geographical features, that is, the ecological picture, imposed certain obstacles on the city-state system. In Palestine, as we have seen, these features entailed that the region was subdivided into small enclaves. Most of these were situated in the plains in the north and along the coast, although a few were also located in the central highlands, like Shechem in the northern part and Jerusalem in the middle section. It has also been pointed out that the resources of the country were few and limited; thus, if a Palestinian city-state desired to increase its income, this had necessarily to occur at the expense of its neighbouring states. Expansion beyond the limits of Palestine itself would, on the one hand, require more resources than a single city-state would have been able to assemble, while on the other, it would also have required more political unity than was ever the case in the region in the Late Bronze Age.

Thus the 'natural' situation in Palestine was inevitably characterized by internal rivalries among the various mini-states, each of which attempted to advance its interests at the expense of its neighbours'. For this reason we may assume that hostilities between the various states were common occurrences, perhaps to such a degree that this situation may be regarded as the 'normal' picture, except in those periods in which either internal political circumstances or external political pressures kept the many petty kings in check. During the Middle Bronze Age the city of Hazor was far larger and contained a vastly greater population than other urban societies in Palestine. It is accordingly possible that at this time Hazor played the part of maintainer of law and order, which may have paved the way for the economic growth which characterized this period. Hazor's pre-eminence at this time is indicated by the fact that it is one of the very few Palestinian cities which is mentioned in the royal archives of the north Mesopotamian city of *Mari*, on the Euphrates, in the eighteenth century BCE. It is possible that a late reminiscence of Hazor's special status is preserved in the notice in the Old Testament according to which 'Hazor formerly was the head of all those kingdoms' (Josh. 11.10).

2.2.2 *Integration into the Egyptian Empire. The Amarna Age*
In the Late Bronze Age, the Palestinian mini-states were governed by an external force which was far more powerful than their combined resources would have enabled them to oppose. From the fifteenth century BCE onwards, Palestine was part of Egypt's Asiatic empire. Naturally, the Egyptians were not interested in having their provinces decimated by internal strife, for this would doubtless have influenced the income they expected to derive from the region in the form of taxes and payments of tribute. Nor was it in the Egyptian interest that the trade routes leading to Syria and Mesopotamia should be interrupted by the petty feuds of Palestinian princes. On the other hand, the Egyptians did not intervene in the internal affairs of their vassals as long as the income rolled in as expected and required. Thus in reality there was no central force in Palestine in the Late Bronze Age which guaranteed the maintenance of the political and social status quo. To the contrary, the flood of goods which were sent off to the centre of the empire from the provinces, taken together with the usual taxes which were levied by the provincial centres on their own subjects led to a considerable economic pressure on them and to lower standards of living, a feature which is demonstrable thanks to archeological evidence.

It was therefore the case in the Late Bronze Age that the petty kings had few resources at their disposal, a situation which can hardly have contributed to the maintenance of order within the region. Clearly, if the Egyptian grasp on the country weakened, the results would speedily be intolerable. The Amarna letters tell us in fact that the situation in Palestine and its environs was one of perpetual internecine strife. Also the reports which were sent from the Asiatic provinces to the Egyptian capital bear witness to the then-prevalent social unrest.

Scholars have ordinarily regarded the *Amarna period* as an unusual episode largely influenced by two aspects of the external situation. On one hand, the religious reform movement in Egypt under the aegis of the 'heretic king', Akhnaton (1379-1362 BCE) is supposed to have entailed that at this time Egypt was too preoccupied with her internal difficulties to be able to expend time and energy on troubles in the provinces. On the other hand, at this time the great Hittite empire arose in Asia Minor as a competitor to Egyptian dominance. During the course of the fourteenth century BCE the Hittites assumed control of part of the Egyptian Asiatic empire, down to a border which ran only a few kilometres north of Palestine.

2.2.3 *The End of the Bronze Age. The Sea Peoples*
Recent studies of this period have, however, demonstrated that it was by no means so exceptional as scholars have supposed. The failure of Egypt to intervene in internal Palestinian affairs seems also to have characterized other parts of the Late Bronze Age. It appears that the Egyptian authorities allowed the local petty kings to do as they pleased—as long as the tribute owed to Egypt kept coming in on time. By the same token, the rise of the Hittite empire in the fourteenth century meant that the Egyptians had to find some way of dealing with the threat from the north. They accordingly sent armies into Palestine and Syria to check the Hittites, and in point of fact they did this under both Akhnaton and his successors. Thus it would be incorrect to assert that the Egyptians allowed the Asiatic provinces to fend for themselves, or that the Egyptians did not care whether they remained Egyptian or were annexed by the Hittites. In reality, the Egyptian armies utilized Palestine as a staging-ground for their offensives and as a source of provisions. This fact cannot have helped the economic situation in Palestine, which was already acute. Thus the trends of the Late Bronze Age contributed to a development which only served to reinforce the general tendency towards conflicts among the mini-states; moreover, this development was irreversible, even though the Egyptians intensified their grasp on the region in the thirteenth century BCE as a result of their *entente* with the Hittite kingdom. The two great powers made peace with one another and divided the region, and in fact both sides kept this peace as long as the Hittite kingdom endured. This was not to last long, however, as the Hittite empire broke up only a few years after the peaceful accord

was achieved because of socio-political tensions within Asia Minor.

Towards the end of the Late Bronze Age, the ancient Near East experienced a sizable population migration, one which is well attested by both contemporary sources and by the results of archeological excavations. These were the so-called 'Sea Peoples', who presumably came from the Balkan and Illyrian-Aegaean region. Travelling in hordes by both sea and land, they ravaged throughout the eastern part of the Mediterranean territory, leaving behind them numerous towns, cities, and states in ruins. Only Egypt was able to resist the advance of the Sea People, and it did so through a series of battles in the Nile Delta at the beginning of the twelfth century BCE. Some of the Sea People groups subsequently settled down in Palestine, as, for example, the well-known *Philistines*. The Sea-People-Philistine settlement further contributed to the existing tensions in Palestine, as it intensified the already existing forces of political fragmentation. In reality, this process led to the final dissolution of the Egyptian empire in the twelfth century BCE.

2.3 Transformations in Late Bronze Age Society. The 'Habiru Problem'
2.3.1 The Habiru as Refugees and Outlaws

> When you buy a Hebrew slave, he shall serve six years, and in seventh he shall be a *hophshi*, without pay (Exod. 21.2).

Who is this 'Hebrew' slave? Why does he want to sell himself? What does he achieve by becoming a *hophshi*? This law, which introduces the 'Book of the Covenant' in Exodus, is in reality an indication of the social situation which applied to the ordinary population of Palestine towards the end of the second millennium BCE. By 'Hebrew', one is tempted to imagine that an 'Israelite' is intended, at least on the basis of the present use of the term in the Old Testament. However, this term had a much more extensive significance, in that it is identical with the sociological class designation *habiru* which was in use throughout the second millennium BCE. The term *habiru* appears in one form or another throughout the entire region spanning from Mesopotamia to the Mediterranean and from Asia Minor down to Egypt; it designated those people who had abandoned their home regions and become *refugees*.

What reason had they, though, to abandon their lands? Of course, a state could always elect to banish one or more of its inhabitants if they proved troublesome. Such individuals would, however, mainly be prominent individuals who either belonged to the ruling family, and so could conceivably threaten the reigning sovereign, or they might be administrators who had exceeded their authority. However, there is little indication in the sources that such a procedure was actually employed. No doubt there were other ways of dealing with potential troublemakers. Some, though, surely chose exile voluntarily in order to save their lives. An example of a nobleman who sought refuge beyond the borders of his kingdom is the previously mentioned Idrimi of Alalah, who in the course of his flight collected a group of *habiru* around him.

In general, we may say on the basis of the occupations which the *habiru* undertook in their exile, or which were imposed upon them, that they mainly belonged to the peasantry—with the important difference that these were peasants who had abandoned their homes and sought refuge in some part of the Near East other than their own state. Such refugees had really only two courses of action open to them: they could choose to be *refugees* in foreign lands, or they could become *freebooters*. Ordinarily, they chose the former course of action. Because of the already existing rivalry between the mini-states in the region, rulers no doubt accepted refugees from their neighbours and used them to fill in the ranks of their own military organizations, or else they were employed as ordinary unskilled labour, which of course lessened the demand for corvée labourers among one's own populace.

It appears, however, as if the mini-states of the Late Bronze Age eventually arrived at a general accord with respect to the refugee problem. Their reasons for doing so were influenced by the fact that the advantages of accepting refugees were outweighed by equally important disadvantages, that is, if one's own populace started fleeing to neighbouring states. Accordingly, the states in question made reciprocal agreements as to the repatriation of runaways, as a way of making sure that they got their own citizens back.

In the course of the Late Bronze Age, the repatriation of runaways led to a change in the character of the refugee problem as a whole, since it transformed the *habiru* into virtual *outlaws*. Because of the enforcement of provisions against them, the *habiru* had to take to the noble calling of banditry, which entailed that they had to settle in regions where the authority of the states was not able to affect them. In Palestine, it is not difficult to point to such areas: they were particularly the mountainous regions in the north and the middle of the country, where there was room for the settlement of groups of outlawed bandits. The Amarna archives are well supplied with data about the activities of such *habiru*, even though in these records the term received a somewhat new significance. *Habiru* was also used of political enemies such as, for example, nearby hostile monarchs, so that it came to signify something like 'enemies of the public order'.

2.3.2 *The Refugee Problem and Developments in the City-States*

The change in the contents of the term *habiru* gives us some indication of the dimensions the refugee problem had attained in the course of the Late Bronze Age. Thus the ground was prepared for the growth of such groups until they constituted a threat to the very existence of the mini-states. Eventually, the Egyptians themselves had to try to deal with the problem and sent forces to combat the hordes of bandits, or what looked like hordes of bandits in the eyes of the established states.

We have already mentioned some of the circumstances which might lead a Palestinian peasant to desire for himself and his family a different way of life. The balance between the imposts which he had to pay to the state and the services which he received in turn, can hardly have existed any longer. The state was unable to guarantee the security of the peasant, since it was constantly at war with neighbouring states. To the contrary, the state required ever increasing taxes in order to finance the military sector, and it also required the peasant's person in order to fill in the holes in its regiments. The result was the general impoverishment and disenchantment of the peasantry. The question of survival had always been a live issue; now, however, it had become acute. Thus, any peasant seeking to get by on the terms which existence then offered had to choose between finding a new occupation and finding somewhere else to live. Alternatively, one could attempt to change one's social situation by selling oneself and one's family as slaves to one or another nobleman. However, if one wished to retain even a minimal amount of freedom to decide the future for oneself, then moving to a new territory was the logical thing to do, and this course was generally followed.

Naturally, this development was a disaster for the city-states, and, in reality, they had no way to prevent it. Moreover, there are some indications in the Amarna letters that individual kings even took advantage of the general discontent by encouraging the populace of neighbouring kingdoms to try their luck as *habirus* in their service. Thus the solidarity between the petty monarchs concerning the refugee problem which had previously been achieved began to disintegrate in the Egyptian Asiatic provinces, since the problem took on dimensions which appeared to be threatening the very existence of the states.

The last part of the law in Exod. 21.2 suggests that a *habiru* also had a way of being re-integrated into society. He could give up his status as an outlaw, seek refuge in a state and there offer his services. After some period of service he could then reckon with being able to re-enter the peasant class as a *client* or *copyholder* (*hophshî* is the Hebrew equivalent of *hupshu*, see above) either in the service of some private noblemen or the palace administration. We do not know to what extent this loophole was exploited, but we do know that the problem continued to exist even after the close of the Amarna period. Because of the coincidence of the designation *habiru* in contemporary sources and the *Hebrew* of the Old Testament, we may conclude that the refugee problem was of central significance for the emergence of Israelite society in this and the subsequent period.

3. *Israelite Tribal Society*

3.1 *The Origin of the Tribal Society*

The name *Israel* is first mentioned in an Egyptian inscription of the thirteenth century BCE in which Pharaoh *Merenptah* boasts of having destroyed a number of Palestinian towns, after which he adds, 'Israel is desolate; its seed is no more'. Because of the way the name 'Israel' is written in the text in question—it differs noticeably from the way the other references to Palestinian localities are written—it is possible that the society in question was of a different sort than the others, which agrees with what we otherwise know about Israelite society in the pre-national period. It was not a city-state, but a tribal society.

From this one fact, however, we cannot allow ourselves to conclude that the historical Israel, twelve tribes strong as described in the Old Testament, already existed at this time. As far as we know, the name 'Israel' in the Merenptah inscription could as easily refer to a single tribe or to a group of tribes. The location of this 'Israel' seems to be implied in the inscription, since a particular line of march for the Egyptian army's passage through Palestine seems to be evident (although whether the campaign actually took place as described is another matter entirely): from Ascalon in the southwest, to Gezer in the Shephelah, to Janoam in the central highland north of Jerusalem, that is, right in that part of the country in which the tribes which later composed the historical Israel of the Northern Kingdom resided.

These facts tell us that at least parts of the later Israelite tribes and in particular the name *Israel* already existed around 1200 BCE in the highlands in the central part of the country. According to the Old Testament list of tribal territories in Joshua 13–21 the Israelite tribes lived precisely in the highlands of central Palestine and Galilee. We are accordingly led to the question as to whether there was a connection between this society and the conditions which obtained in the Late Bronze Age corresponding to the linguistic identity between the terms *habiru* and 'Hebrews'. Here we must insist that there are no indications whatsoever to suggest that the hordes of *habiru* of the Amarna Age were already at this time organized in tribes which lived in the highlands. The bands probably consisted of rootless individuals, outlaw robbers from the peasant class who were to a certain extent supplemented by their families, but in the fourteenth century BCE such groups can hardly have possessed the technical skills which would enable them to cultivate the highlands, which otherwise were beyond the effective control of both the city-states and the Egyptian empire. An Egyptian inscription from c. 1300 BCE, found in Beth-Shan, and which mentions a punitive expedition against *habiru* in the vicinity of Beth-Shan, mentions what seem to be the names of some tribes, but these very names are nowhere preserved in the Old Testament as tribal names. Thus, if we follow the line demarcated by the Amarna letters, the inscription from Beth-Shan, and the Merenptah inscription, and compare this information with the data contained in the Old Testament, which must be used with the utmost caution, we may see the outline of a picture of an alternative society which emerged in the mountainous regions of Palestine in the second half of the Late Bronze Age and the beginning of the Iron Age.

The groups which were once more or less randomly assembled bands of robbers evolved in the course of time into real tribal societies with permanent social structures and established norms which dictated the way of life of the tribes in question. To the extent that it was possible, groups of *habiru* returned to their old way of life, which is to say, to agriculture, but they did so in other areas and on other terms than would previously have been possible. Some technological advances were necessary for this process, and these actually did make their appearance in the thirteenth century BCE. For one thing, it was now possible to retain large quantities of rainwater in *cisterns* which had been lined with asphalt and so made watertight. For another, it was now possible to preserve the fertility of the mountain slopes after the natural undergrowth covering them had been removed by the introduction of the process of *terracing* the slopes to protect the topsoil. It has also often been maintained that the introduction of *iron* in tool production further contributed to the settlement process by enabling the removal of the natural growth of the highlands in the thirteenth century (for which reason scholars assign the transition to the Iron Age to around 1200 BCE). However, this is incorrect. Iron had been known long before, although it was quite useless for tool production until the smiths had learned to temper the metal sufficiently, which first occurred in the tenth century. Thus, throughout the pre-national era use was made of the usual tools, that is, made of stone or bronze, which had been used previously, and were reasonably useful even for the hard task of refashioning the highlands into arable areas, which was the ultimate presupposition for the presence of the Israelite tribes in the regions in question.

3.2 *Its Social Structure*
3.2.1 *Introductory Remarks*
This development from outlaw *habiru* to sedentary Israelite mountain peasants took place over a couple of centuries, and can be followed directly in the archeological record of conditions in the highlands. In the thirteenth-twelfth centuries BCE a number of village societies arose in both the Galilean mountains and in the central highland (as far as the territory east of Jordan is concerned we are as yet insufficiently informed), in regions which had not been previously inhabited, as far as we can tell. The reason for regarding these villages as the results of an internal Palestinian evolution is that the material culture attested in them represents what is merely a further development of the culture which had already characterized the land for centuries. Similarly, the technology necessary for cultivating the difficult regions in the highlands itself presupposes knowledge of

cereal cultivation by those who undertook the project and ultimately were successful with it.

But more important are the questions as to how a random assortment of individuals could evolve into members of an organized tribal society, and further, questions concerning the structure of this society in the pre-national period.

As far as the latter problem is concerned, we are forced to seek recourse to analogies based on much later sources, with all the risks for false comparisons and distortions such a procedure entails. On the other hand, there is some reason to trust such data, since they have to do with a type of society which did not arise in connection with the formation of the state, but which at most received a change of operative circumstances after state formation. We must regard the society described in the Old Testament as an archaic relic of a vanishing time, although it has continued to preserve certain features which ultimately derive from the second millennium BCE. This interpretation of the sources is different from the approach one has to use in connection with the accounts of individual events or of individual personalities, since the tribal society existed over a vastly longer period of time. Therefore, we may only attempt to say something quite general about a given period, while as far as the individual heroic traditions are concerned we must attempt to date these as precisely as possible.

A narrative in the first part of the book of Joshua (ch. 7) tells us about a juridical procedure in which the culprit is discovered by means of lot-casting. The contents of this story are of no interest for our present purpose; what is interesting, however, is the picture of the structure of Israelite society which emerges from this text, since the lot-casting seems to follow the various elements in the social structure as follows: first the *tribe,* then the *lineage,* and finally the *family.* Of course, this narrative is part of the Deuteronomistic book of Joshua, and even though it would be reasonable to assume that an earlier tradition underlies it, and, furthermore, even though a similar procedure is attested in connection with the election of Saul to the kingship (1 Sam. 10.17-27, which, however, also wears Deuteronomistic attire) it should be evident that we cannot without more ado simply identify this tripartition of Israelite society into families, lineages, and tribes with the actual social structure of the society four or five hundred years earlier. Israel's prehistoric period also possessed living people, for which reason this tripartition of the social structure is entirely too schematic. At best it indicates the existence of three central levels within the social system, whereas in reality many more must have been present. Similarly, the borders between the various levels will have been quite fluid. Finally, the terminology employed in our own languages is not very precise, so that the translation of Hebrew kinship terms into 'tribe', 'lineage' and 'family' may be more or less arbitrary.

3.2.2 *The Individual and Society*

An individual may conceive of his social environment as a series of concentric rings proceeding in ever widening distances from the centre, that is, from himself. The closest circle consists of his immediate contacts, his family, while the remotest one consists of those people with whom he has fewest linkages. This circular construct is understood differently by a contemporary member of a western state than by a man who lived or lives in a pre-industrial society like, for example, ancient Israel. In our culture, one of the most proximate circles consists of our colleagues at our place of employment, rather than remote members of our family whom we practically never see. In ancient Israel, however, the innermost circle consisted of the immediate family, one's wife or wives, children, and parents; but even the outermost circle also consisted of individuals with whom one acknowledged some form of kinship, such as members of one's own tribe or even of the tribal coalition. In a society like that of ancient Israel, ties which for us need not entail any implication of kinship are literally always described in kinship terms. Relationships between the individual and other individuals are dependent on the kinship connections which link them to one another. Thus persons with whom the individual has no connection are not related to him, for which reason they are assigned to the great grey mass of non-kinfolk.

In the Old Testament this relational system is expressed in terms of *genealogies*; its central importance is attested to by the fact that even the Priestly stratum of tradition in the Pentateuch devotes a great deal of space to such lists. In these genealogies, Israel is regarded as a single great kinship group, and all Israelites can trace their ancestry back to a single tribal ancestor, Jacob. Thus every Israelite was in principle able, by describing his ancestry, to demonstrate that he was an Israelite; he was also in a position to tell someone else in what relation to one another the two stood, and how they should relate to each other. It should be obvious that the ties between individuals who have daily intercourse with one another can be quite strong when they are also part of the same kinship group, irrespective of the degree of actual relatedness. These ties were intensified by the fact that in Israelite society no one could survive if he stood alone. There was no external court of appeals or a national police agency to which someone with a grievance could address himself. One's security was assured through one's relations to other people, that is, to one's 'kin'.

3.2.3 *Everyday Life: The Family*

In pre-national Israel, everyone was a member of a *family*. The main part of the populace consisted of small *nuclear families*, numbering six or seven individuals. More than 90% of the families made their living through agriculture. The only differences between them were accordingly contingent on their respective luck and skill. However, there were also some more powerful and wealthy families which were on occasion much larger than the average, *extended families* containing from ten to twenty individuals. The extended family could be even larger, if it increased its workforce by the acquisition of *slaves* or *clients*, who participated in the daily work of the family and assisted it as well in the event of conflicts with other families.

In a given local Israelite society the extended family also enjoyed some advantages which the nuclear family did not, although these advantages were to some extent counter-balanced by the expenses of maintaining the family. On the one hand, slaves were useful labourers, but on the other they were also expensive. Like other members of the family, they had to be fed even in the relatively 'dead' period when they had nothing to do in the fields. There is no indication that Israelites were able to sell their slaves on the open market; rather, the slaves were, in a manner of speaking, part of the 'family'. This is supported by the previously mentioned law on slavery, the so-called 'law of the Hebrew slave' (Exod. 21.2-11), in which it is presupposed that the slave had the right to marry and have children even while he belonged to his owner, and also by the fact that he could choose to remain a slave of his owner, who in the event apparently no longer had the right to get rid of him. It should also be observed that the Hebrew term for a slave, *'ebed*, may also be translated as a worker, so that it seems there was no difference in principle between a slave and a labourer; the term merely designates a relationship of dependence. In English Bibles the term is often rendered 'servant'. Thus the difference between the slave and the man who worked for pay was one of degree, and the slave was far from being the poorer situated of the two, because the pay—invariably disbursed in food rations—was the same; the slave, however, could be sure of getting his pay, whereas the labourer was dependent on the job situation. On the other hand, if there was sufficient work available, the latter could decide for himself whom he would work for.

The clients (*hophshî* or *hupshu*) of an extended family were also its support group in the event of conflicts within the local society. It is clear that the families which possessed the most clients were likewise in the best position in terms of mutual competition. However, the clients also expected to be rewarded for their service. The law in Exod. 21.2-11 indicates that the Hebrew slave could change his status to that of a 'client' (*hophshî*). This entailed either that he received a plot of land which he could cultivate himself and live off, or that he continued to receive rations to ensure his survival. This was true of the clients of the small city-state-kingdoms as also of those of the lesser noblemen, as far as the Hebrew law is concerned. If such rations were not disbursed, a lord could not continue to reckon with the loyalty of his clients, as they would have to attempt to find some other master who would be able to support them.

Against this, the nuclear family had no possibility of collecting a sizable group of people within its framework. Whereas at least in theory the extended family stayed together, all members continuing to live under the same roof, the nuclear family fissioned every time one of its sons left the family to form a family of his own. Of course, individual related nuclear families retained contact with one another because of their kinship ties. The advantage of the nuclear family was that it was not necessary to provide for the needs of more than a limited number of individuals. Conversely, the disadvantage was that the wealth of the family was continually being subdivided, through the establishment of new family units. Thus, as soon as a new nuclear family was formed it had to increase its earnings as quickly as possible in order to provide for the departure of the sons at maturity.

It was furthermore possible to expand the social solidarity circle by trading in the one 'commodity' one had to offer, namely *women* or, more specifically, the *unmarried daughters* of the family. By entering into marital alliances with corresponding families one created a community of interest with them. If such marital connections continued to be joined over a substantial period of time, some feeling of fellowship could arise between the individual families, and this could provide some active help in times of crisis. This possibility was of course also available to the extended family, which was able to ally itself with other extended families. In this fashion powerful kinship units and social differentiation occurred in the society, and these paved the way for a different type of social order in which the allied great families dominated the life of the society, comprising as they did a phalanx which the small families, even acting in unison, were unable to match.

3.2.4 *Ramifications of the Family: The Lineage*
In this way kinship groups or, in socio-anthropological terms, *lineages*, arose. They were composed of a number of greater or lesser families which were interrelated by marriage. The Israelite family was accordingly a member of a larger lineage. Every local Israelite society must have been composed of a greater or lesser number of lineages. Of course, such lineage-formation cannot have followed an invariable pattern; there must have been small, middle-sized, and large lineages in the society. Furthermore, there were a number of levels within each lineage. There were differences between the various ways of 'belonging', as, for example, if one derived from the nuclear group which had founded the lineage, was a son of the family which comprised its centre, or was allied to this nucleus by marriage. There were also differences depending upon whether one's family derived from an eldest son, youngest son, and so forth.

In everyday life the individual families were fully *autonomous*, meaning that they had to take care of themselves. Each family cultivated its own fields, harvested its own grapes, and sold its produce, if there was any surplus to sell. As long as everything functioned all right the larger kinship group had no rôle to play. On the other hand, when problems arose it was suddenly important to which lineage one belonged. Such difficulties as conflicts concerning the boundaries of fields could, for example, lead to confrontations between different lineages. Similarly, bad harvests could easily spell economic disaster for a family. Conflicts within the circle of the lineage were internally resolved; conflicts between non-maritally-affiliated families will either have been resolved through peaceful negotiations or through *feuds*.

It would have been impractical for the entire lineage to participate in all the details of the negotiations with a non-related lineage. Thus, even in pre-national times there must have been a tendency for individual leaders within some of the lineages to act as spokesmen for the whole kinship group. If necessary, such persons could also act as co-ordinators of the battle with other lineages, and they probably also helped to resolve conflicts between individual families within the lineage. Thus, their status within their own group was such that people were willing to accept their advice, acknowledge their decisions in connection with negotiation with representatives of other lineages, or even allow them to lead in battle. We do not know how such leaders were chosen, but in all likelihood the *pater familias* of the leading family, being the one who represented the most important of the units within the group, often served in such capacities. However, our knowledge of quite a number of corresponding societies both past and present indicates that other people could be considered for such tasks as well, and also that it was possible to distribute the various functions among a number of individuals according to their respective gifts and abilities. Thus an acknowledged orator could be chosen to speak for the group, even though he was not necessarily the most powerful or wealthiest person in it. Similarly, a well-proven warrior might be selected as leader in the event of open conflict with other lineages. However, it is characteristic of societies of this type that such leadership functions are not formally constituted; they usually arise instead in connection with the problems that have to be solved. They play no part in ordinary life, and such leaders accordingly do not have authority over the existence of individual families. Within the circle of the family the *pater familias* is the sovereign authority, with the power of life and death over its members.

3.2.5 *The Circle Widens: The Clan*

If the kinship system attains permanent significance, that is, if a lineage persists through what might be numerous generations, then its members may end in the paradoxical situation that they no longer remember the precise way in which they are interrelated. From this point on, it is usual to describe such lineages as *clans*. The clan's position in the kinship structure in such that its influence on the daily life of its members is quite limited. Most of all, it serves as a frame of reference enabling the individual to describe his relationship to a particular group of people who inhabit a particular locality or who are primarily associated with a particular place. However, the clan may sometimes be mobilized in time of war.

It would be unrealistic to expect that all of the members of a clan belonged to it in the same way at this level within a social complex like that in ancient Israel. Some were perhaps not at all related by blood to other members, but are nevertheless regarded as 'kinsmen', and have therefore been included within the genealogy of the lineage. The reason for this is the way of representing social relations within such societies. In the West of today we can socially locate an individual by calling him, for example, 'president', 'general manager', 'manager', or whatever. We have an evolved system of titulature with which to distinguish between individuals. In a society in which practically everybody does the same sort of work (like peasants) however, such a descriptive system would not be sufficiently differentiated to accord a 'place' to every member of the society. This is why kinship systems tend to be used, as they make it possible to assign a place in society to everyone by describing them as members of lineage A, B, or whatever. Of course, in our culture an individual advances from general manager of a concern to president of it, and this is signified by a change of title. In a society which is organized according to kinship, an individual might for one reason or another enjoy more contact with family B than family A, to which he belongs himself. Thus it may happen that family B sooner or later 'forgets' that the individual in question belongs to family A, and subsequently reckons him to be a member of its own polity and accordingly also assigns him a place in the genealogy. This way of describing the structure of a society as a system of kinship is thus in reality just a different way of establishing the identity of the members of a society. It is much older than our own system, which still preserves a few reminiscences of it.

Such kinship systems—including the one used in ancient Israel—are therefore fictive and do not necessarily express actual genetic or marital ties. A genealogical system like the one we find in the Old Testament depicts the composition of Israelite society at the time the system was written down—and when it accordingly became fossilized. Thus, for example, if we note that the genealogical lists in the Priestly tradition in such texts as Num. 1.1-47; 48-54; 3.14-39 and so forth seem to be stereotyped and stiff, this is because they were committed to paper in a period in which the understanding of the

Israelite tribal system no longer reflected a living reality, but only a stereotyped conception of the social structure of pre-national Israel.

3.2.6 *The Farthest Ring: The Tribe*

Above the clan in the system of social organization we find the *tribe*. But what was an Israelite tribe? In actual fact, we are forced to reply that we have no way of knowing, for there are a multitude of scientific definitions of 'tribe'; moreover, there are also a great many different sorts of tribes, so that not very much is really said by speaking of Israelite 'tribes'. The various Hebrew words for 'tribe' mean something like 'staff', and some scholars have taken this to refer to the ruler's staff of authority. However, we have no way of telling whether this is correct. Furthermore, even if it was, this would still tell us nothing about the principle of leadership, nor would it inform us about the social structure of Israelite tribal society.

Israelite tribal names in the Old Testament frequently function as geographical designations. When a man is characterized as 'of Issachar', we do not immediately know whether membership of the tribe or habitation in the territory is referred to. However, this fact does tell us that the Israelite tribes were associated with particular territories, to which they lent their names. There were historically either three or four groups of tribes: one in *Galilee* (including Naphtali, Asher, and Zebulon); two in *Central Palestine*, one in the northern mountains between Jerusalem and the plain of Jezreel (Benjamin, Ephraim, and Manasseh), and a southern one between Jerusalem and the Negeb Desert (Judah). A fourth group, located in the territory east of the Jordan (Gad, Ruben, and Machir) was perhaps more closely linked with the second group than a group in its own right. Thus, the membership of a tribe was largely identical with the membership of the lineages and clans which lived in the region with which the name of the tribe in question was associated. The inhabitants of a given territory identified themselves with the appropriate tribe because they lived in the same area and had a common interest in keeping the territory in their own hands.

Tribal association was expressed in terms of kinship. Thus in the narratives about the birth of the sons of Jacob (Gen. 29.31–30.24) we read of the origins of each of the tribal ancestors, organized in such a way as to place them hierarchically in relation to one another. This understanding of the concept of 'tribe' differs from earlier accounts, which usually presuppose that the 'ties of blood' entailed that the people in question really were related to one another. Scholars were not aware that this way of describing social location is a metaphor, a euphemism, designating what were really political and social relations. Today most sociologists and historians are surrendering the notion that actual genetic ties link together the individuals in a tribe or nation. Instead, they point out that an individual's social affiliation is always the result of a choice. Such choices are made on the basis of a vast number of factors, of which 'the ties of blood' are merely one. Others could be such things as a common history, common destiny, common economic interests, common external enemies, and so on. Affiliation to a tribe, like one's relationship to a nation, is accordingly primarily an expression of where one feels that one 'belongs'; moreover, such affiliations can change. For example, if one moves from one place to another, sooner or later one will have to decide for oneself whether one wishes to become part of the new environment, or whether one should attempt in some way to keep a distance from it. Thus, for example, an Israelite from the tribe of Ephraim who settled in the tribe of Manasseh could choose to remain an Ephraimite, and sooner or later the Manassites would reject him. He could also choose to become a Manassite, and perhaps in the course of time he (or his children) could be accepted as Manassite and be incorporated into the tribal genealogy. What was decisive for membership of the new social unit was whether it accepted the new arrival or whether he accepted it, and not whether all parties were in fact descendants of the same tribal ancestor, who either may or may not have been a historical individual.

3.2.7 *Tribal Leadership*
We do not possess much in the way of hard evidence as to the forms of leadership in the Israelite tribes. For example, we do not know whether an Israelite tribe was led by a single individual. On the one hand, we do possess some traditions—which unfortunately may only be late legends—which inform us that under certain circumstances particular individuals could be temporarily installed in a given leadership rôle, where they exercised a certain sort of authority. On the other hand, we are also occasionally informed as to the presence of a more or less *collective tribal leadership*; in this connection the terms 'elders' and 'heads' are most prominent. It is not obvious just who these individuals were, although they were presumably the same

people who in the tribal society served as spokesmen for the lineages to which they belonged. Alternatively, they may have been elected from the circle composed of such spokesmen. If this was the case, then we have no reason to suppose that there was any permanent collective leadership of the Israelite tribes. Leadership will have functioned in basically the same way as it did in the local group, that is, in the lineage and between lineages, and on the same occasions. Admittedly, we sometimes hear of individuals, such as Abimelech, who became a local king in the vicinity of Shechem (Judges 9). On this occasion, however, special circumstances obtained, so that it is possible that this was an exception; but even so, this would tell us what could happen if tribal society experienced a crisis.

3.3 Tribal Society in Times of Crisis

Israelite tribal society arose as the result of a crisis which affected the small city-states of Palestine in the Late Bronze Age, and it collapsed as the result of a crisis which occurred at the close of the second millennium BCE. This period accordingly witnessed a development from centrally organized states to tribally organized societies and back to a centrally organized state, only one of a different type than previously. In other words, society did not merely return to an archaic type, since it had in the intervening period passed through a phase which so influenced it that when it was reconstituted it did so with a new content.

3.3.1 The First Crisis: The Emergence of Tribal Society

The reasons for the collapse of the city-states in the Bronze Age have already been mentioned. The question at this time concerns how a population which had been organized in states could change its character and become a tribal society. It was mentioned previously that among the concrete results of the crises of the Late Bronze Age were the movements among the peasantry. In many cases the peasants abandoned their traditional homes and attempted to find a more tolerable way of life in the highlands of Palestine outside the reach of the centralized states. There is accordingly some question as to whether this Palestinian peasant population was not constituted in such a way that it could relatively easily be integrated into a new social order beyond the kings' effective control.

An important presupposition for this was the social structure of the Palestinian peasantry in the Late Bronze Age. Unfortunately, as far as Palestine is concerned, indeed, even as far as the northern coastal cities of Ugarit and Alalah are concerned we possess either few or practically no data about the social structure of the agrarian society. What follows is accordingly merely a suggested *model*, that is, a *hypothesis*, which is based on experience of the relationships which have obtained in traditional peasant societies and pre-industrial urban societies in the Third World in recent times. Much is based on observation of relationships in the Near East, to the extent that these societies have not yet been affected by the Westernization of their territories. If we use these materials—and the weakness of such a procedure is obvious—then we can sketch out at least a *possible* way in which the development from state-organized peasant society to tribal society and back again could have taken place.

The peasant and town societies of antiquity were characterized by a very limited division of labour, apart from the leadership stratum and the small groups of specialists. The main part of the population consisted of the 'grey' mass of peasants. As we emphasized earlier, the reason why kinship organization was so important in these societies is that there were no other ways to differentiate between their members. By analogy, we may assume that the Palestinian peasantry was organized along the same lines. Palestinian society was basically organized in terms of kinship, which made it possible for individuals to locate themselves with respect to others who were on the same level as themselves by reference to kinship relationships.

Another reason for the existence of such a kinship system was the type of government in the city-state, for there, as far as we are informed, the palace administration did not concern itself with the doings of the local societies as long as these did not effect the central authorities or the relationships between them and the local units. Thus, whatever local forms of leadership happened to be employed in the lower levels of society were uniform, whether these mini-societies were parts of an official state or not. Since the matters with which these circles of local leaders were concerned were of no interest to the power of the state, the state archives also contain no information as to local politics, but only concerning contacts between the state and the local population.

In the event that the central administrative power disappeared, either because the state in question no longer existed or because the inhabitants had absconded from the control of the authorities by moving to areas outside of the state's domain, there was no power above the level of the lineage or perhaps the clan which could then intervene in social life. When the mini-societies which lay outside of the control of the state experienced a crisis which necessitated co-ordinated action, these societies had, of necessity, to replace the authority of the state. It was first of all essential to provide for the security which the state had previously guaranteed, even though these societies had also contributed to their security either by military service or paying taxes. In a way, we could say that *'tribe' is a metaphor for this function*; that is, a tribe may arise in order to replace the centralized authority that vanishes when a state breaks down.

3.3.2 *Later Crises: Centralization Tendencies in Tribal Society*

Of course, the Israelite tribes could not become complete replacements for the absent states as long as their forms of leadership remained more or less ad hoc, that is, as long as the tendencies to organization of the tribal society only manifested themselves on certain occasions and in certain contexts. On the other hand, some changes in the structure of tribal society had to occur if the crisis in question persisted. If the Israelite tribes only functioned as such as long as they were exposed to aggression from without (for example, if a city-state attempted to take over the tribal territory, or if another tribe or parts of it attempted to enrich itself or themselves at the expense of its/their neighbours), then permanent external pressure would naturally entail a change in the significance of the tribe. The function of the tribe would attain a permanent character, which would produce the need for a more permanent type of leadership than that provided by the ad hoc leaders. The ad hoc leaders had previously been adequate to the task, but possessed neither the status nor the authority to coerce the members of the tribe as it was necessary to do under the new circumstances.

The lack or stability of the tribes was yet another reason why they had to change their nature in the event of external aggression. Admittedly, with some exceptions, the Pentateuchal tribal lists continually refer to the same twelve tribes. However, the Old Testament also hints here and there that other tribes existed besides the authorized twelve, such as, for example, Gilead in the territory east of the Jordan, and Machir, which may have lived west of the

Jordan at an early time, but which had been reduced in the Priestly census in Numbers 26 to being a part of Manasseh whose homestead was east of the Jordan (Num. 26.29). Finally, it has already been mentioned that the Egyptian inscription from Beth-Shan from around 1300 BCE refers to tribal names which are nowhere preserved in the Old Testament, not even as names, although they belonged to the same territory as some of the north Israelite tribes.

A paradoxical consequence of the lack of solidarity within an individual tribe was that several tribes could choose to band together in order to increase the number of persons who could be mobilized in the event of an external threat. Such tribal alliances were possibly not uncommon among the Israelite tribes, although—as usual—we only possess relatively young materials which tell us about this. It was noted earlier that the *Israel* which figures in the Merenptah inscription could have been a tribal alliance which could conceivably have consisted of the tribes of Ephraim, Manasseh, and perhaps Benjamin, or else of groups which later went to make up these tribes. Other coalitions may also have existed, as, for example, in the north, in connection with which the Song of Deborah (Judges 5), which describes a battle between Israelite tribes and a coalition of city-states, might be a reference to such a tribal coalition. The Song of Deborah, however, is most noteworthy because of its condemnation of those who failed to participate in the common defence. This fact provides additional evidence as to the consequences of the lack of central authority of the tribal societies. Similarly, the tribe of *Judah* in the south may have emerged out of an earlier tribal league which had taken its name from the locality in which it was based (Judah). It is impossible to date the time when these alliances were formed precisely; some of them may have arisen early in the Iron Age or in the close of the Bronze Age, while still others, as, for example, Judah, may first have come into being shortly before the formation of the state. It is to be noted, however, that it would be wrong to regard tribal leagues as permanent alliances. There is, for example, nothing which suggests that the tribal alliance mentioned in the Song of Deborah ever functioned as intended, nor that it existed for any length of time. The tribal alliances were no more stable than their individual component tribes, and often less so.

The Palestinian city-states continued to exist throughout the Iron Age, or at least some of them did so, but the archeological excavations do indicate that in the period between 1300 and 1000

BCE their material situation was far from good. Thus it was hardly
from the city-states that one could have expected any serious
pressure on the tribal societies in the mountains to be exerted, which
might have introduced disruptions of their existence and so lead to
changes in their respective structures. For this reason it is clear that
there was no significant pressure on the tribal societies before the
eleventh century BCE. This pressure was a function of a new political
reality which had come into being in Palestine on the ruins of the
previous city-state system in the coastal plains, namely the *Philistine
pentapolis*. This entity consisted of a coalition of five city-states
formed by the remnants of the earlier groups of Sea Peoples who had
arrived in the region at the beginning of the twelfth century BCE, and
who had consolidated and assumed the inheritance of the previous
local city-states. All indications suggest that the amalgamation of
these five urban communities into a league led to an expansive policy
which was in part aimed at the plains to the west and north of the
central massif and in part at the central Palestinian highlands. The
Philistine incursions represented a permanent crisis for the Israelite
tribes, and it changed the Israelite social and political system quite
drastically. These developments occurred just prior to the time of the
formation of the state, and will accordingly first be dealt with below
(see Ch. 4, § 3.1.2). In this connection it shall merely be emphasized
that in this period the Israelite tribes were confronted with two
alternatives: either to find a more permanent form of leadership, or
to disintegrate utterly. As we shall see, they chose the former
alternative, although paradoxically enough the result was in the end
the same as if they had chosen the latter, since the introduction of the
monarchy nevertheless led to the destruction of the tribal system.

4. *The Pre-national Period in Earlier Academic Discussion*

As already mentioned, the decisive problem facing anyone who
intends to make use of the Old Testament traditions in the study of
the earliest history of Israel is that of the gap separating these
traditions from the history of which they speak. A number of earlier
scholars have been aware of this problem, and they have attempted
to overcome it by dating the historical traditions of the origins of
Israel back to the pre-national period. Thus it has been claimed that
the Sitz im Leben of the historical tradition was the period of the
Judges, and more specifically the twelve-tribe league which, or so

they assumed, was a political reality prior to the introduction of the monarchy. Accordingly, any approach to earlier scholarship must take its point of departure in this conception of a permanent coalition, of which the twelve 'canonical' Israelite tribes were members.

4.1 *The Period of the Judges*
4.1.1 *Hypotheses Concerning the Amphictyony and the Traditions of Israel's Past*

In the traditions of the period of the Judges, Israel usually simply figures as 'Israel'. The entire Israelite society, all twelve tribes, were mobilized when there was need of joint action. *All of* Israel functions in a similar way in the traditions concerning the periods antedating the era of the Judges; thus, for example, it is Israel that flees from Egypt; Israel, to whom Yahweh manifests himself; Israel, which conquers the Promised Land; and this Israel, we should note, consists of the official twelve tribes.

In 1930 the German Old Testament scholar, Martin Noth, advanced his famous thesis according to which the Israelite society of the period of the Judges was organized as a *twelve-tribe amphictyony*. Noth had borrowed the term *amphictyony* from ancient Greece, and his description of the institution was to a considerable extent based on Greek analogies. The Greek amphictyony was the name given to a sacral coalition of Greek states whose common centre was the sanctuary of Apollo at Delphi. It was here the membership could meet in peace, even if the member states were otherwise at war with one another. The leadership of the amphictyony was in the hands of a college of administrators who were employed by the Delphic sanctuary. Noth assumed that Israelite society also possessed a corresponding sanctuary, for example Shiloh or Shechem, which served as the religious, but in reality also the political, centre of pre-national Israel. He further held that the membership of this group is preserved in the lists of twelve tribes in the Pentateuch.

On the one hand, the amphictyony hypothesis managed to provide a sociological model for the structure of Israelite society during the first two centuries of the Iron Age, that is, between 1200 and 1000 BCE. On the other hand, though, it also provided us with a home for the formation of the Old Testament traditions and for the religion of Israel. The twelve tribes in the traditions about the past were held to be identical with the membership of the coalition in question. Thus, the source materials dealing with the past came into being in this league in agreement with the ideology which held it together. But Noth and, particularly, some other scholars, also employed the twelve tribe hypothesis to emphasize that Israel was something special, a unique society, by reason of the specifically *Yahwistic* religious tradition which formed the background of the league. However, Noth differed significantly from his contemporaries in his understanding of the historical worth of the Old Testament source materials since he was the first to acknowledge that if these sources had been formed during the period of the Judges, then they reflected Israelite society in the period of the Judges and its ideological currents, rather than any earlier Israelite past. Therefore, as in this account, Noth attempted to depict the emergence of Israel up to the time of the foundation of the amphictyony without reference to the 'historical' content of the Old Testament sources.

Other, more conservative scholars, however, held that since the original formation of the sources was to be dated to the close of the second millennium BCE they were so old as to be reliable. They accordingly maintained that these sources could provide us with a point of departure for the study of pre-national Israel. Such scholars cheerfully ignored such things as the chronological gap between the patriarchal age and the period of the amphictyony which, like Noth, they also dated to the beginning of the twelfth century, although the more conservative among these scholars pushed the foundation even further back.

4.1.2 The Demise of the Amphictyony Hypothesis and its Consequences for the Understanding of Israelite Tradition

In recent times, the idea that the formation of the Old Testament tradition took place in the pre-national period has been shattered by studies which have destroyed the basis for the existence of any amphictyony. There is not a single concrete detail dating from the second millennium BCE which indicates that Israel was ever constituted as a permanent coalition, which could have been the basis of the conception of a united Israel. Nor is it possible to point to any single sanctuary which might have been employed as the centre of such a league and around which the formation of a tradition might have crystallized. On the contrary, careful tradition-historical readings of the sources on the period, particularly those in the book of Judges, have shown that the twelve-tribe ideology is, in the first place, Deuteronomistic, and hence late, and second, that the pre-Deuteronomistic tradition never refers to all-Israelite actions, but only to those of small units, in some cases these being a single lineage, while in others they may be a tribe or clan.

A good example of this is provided by the traditions about *Gideon* in Judges 6–8. The Midianites, a tribal people from the territory east of the Jordan, have been plundering Israel, but their depredations awaken Gideon, of the Abiezer lineage of Ophrah in Manasseh, to action. Gideon, who in some traditions is called *Jerubba'al*, starts by mobilizing the Abiezrites and then subsequently the surrounding tribes, beginning with Manasseh, and then the neighbouring northern tribes, all of which are subsequently referred to as 'all Israel'. More than 3,000 men respond to Gideon's summons, which is many more than is necessary to perform the task in question, so that two thirds of the force are sent home. In order to get down to an appropriate number of warriors, Gideon then reduces the force additionally until only 300 are left, and with these he defeats the 'tribes of the east' and once more obtains security for the region.

The entire account seems rather artificial; above all, the sections about sending unneeded manpower home seem to be unnecessary, although they do make a good story. This good story now has a part to play in the Deuteronomistic redaction, which regards Gideon as one of the great heroes who 'saved' Israel and later 'judged' her— to his death. However, a reader who takes a tradition-historical approach has little difficulty separating out an earlier version of the narrative, one in which the Manassite clan of Abiezer, under the leadership of one of its leaders, rid itself of a threat to its own territory in the form of the marauding east-Jordanian nomads. It was only later that additions to this story expanded its perspective so that at last it deals with the entire Israelite tribal society as if it had participated in the events in question. It has also proved impossible to find a common Israelite leadership rôle in the sources which bear on the pre-national period. Admittedly, the 'Judges', of whom Gideon was one, are described as pan-Israelite leaders, but it is easy to see that it is only late editions of the narratives which make them into leaders of all of Israel, while the pre-Deuteronomistic tradition describes them as local nobility. This was acknowledged by Martin Noth himself, but he thought to find in some short lists of a fragmentary character which refer to various 'Judges' (Judg. 10.1-5; 12.7-15) an old list of the actual leaders of the tribal league. However, closer investigation of these lists shows that some of the individuals in question can hardly have existed at all, for the reason that family or lineage names (gentilicia) have in these case been regarded as the names of historical persons. Such analysis also shows the only difference between the 'Judges' in the heroic narratives and those in the lists in question is that they figure in two different sorts of literary contexts.

The hypothesis of an Israelite twelve-tribe league, and indeed the notion of a permanent league in the pre-national period in general, is thus neither reconcilable with the results of recent studies of the traditions of the period of the Judges nor with our knowledge of the usual way of life in societies which resemble that of Israel at the time in question. Israelite society of this period must instead have been highly fluid with respect to socio-political relations; it was a situation in which alliances were hurriedly formed and then fell apart by themselves. The date at which such alliances developed into permanent institutions was in reality shortly before the introduction of the monarchy into Israel. Moreover, this phase persisted on into the first part of the monarchical period. There is accordingly reason to ask whether it was not first with the introduction of the monarchy that the presuppositions for the all-Israelite character of the Old Testament tradition were present. In other words, there was no Israelite league in the time of the Judges in which such a pan-Israelite tradition could have been developed. On the other hand, there may well have existed numerous local traditions, as, for example, in connection with the larger sanctuaries, which, subsequently, in the course of the monarchy, were worked into a pan-Israelite framework.

Now although there were some ancient traditions which derived from the pre-national period, there is no guarantee that these were reworked so that these local traditions came to deal with 'all of' Israel in the tenth century BCE. The reign of David merely provides us with a *terminus a quo* for the emergence of a pan-Israelite ideology, and it is entirely conceivable that such an ideology was first effective at a much later date. If this is the case, and if, for example, the present form of the traditions in question derives from late monarchical times, then it is also conceivable that we do not have any traditions which actually come from the pre-national period, even if some do attempt to describe this time. If this is the case—and it might also be true even if the traditions in question were from the time of David or Solomon—then what we possess is in reality the late Israelite reconstruction of the early history of Israel.

4.2 *From Egypt to Canaan*
4.2.1 *The Traditions of the Exodus and the Desert Wanderings*

It is generally acknowledged by scholars that the traditions about Israel's sojourn in Egypt and the *exodus* of the Israelites are legendary and epic in nature. The very notion that a single family could in the course of a few centuries develop into a whole people, a nation, consisting of hundreds of thousands of individuals, is so fantastic that it deserves no credence from a *historical* point of view. And yet these narratives are quite intelligible from the viewpoint of a society which is based on kinship, since they wonderfully express the ideological self-understanding of Israelite society, namely the view that 'we are all members of the same family'. There is accordingly no real reason even to attempt to find a historical background for the events of the Exodus. According to the biblical chronology it was supposed to have taken place in the fifteenth century BCE, that is, during the eighteenth dynasty, but, as has often been observed, the Egyptian sources make no mention of it at all. Naturally, this is not because the Egyptians wished to conceal such an event as the so-called 'miracle at the Reed Sea' (Exodus 14), but because there was no massive emigration from Egypt under the eighteenth dynasty or later in the form described in the Old Testament.

We must regard the account of Israel's *forty years in the desert* in the same way. In addition to the fact that the duration of this 'phase' is in reality merely a round number signifying a generation (and therefore in any case suspect as a historical datum), the narratives of the desert wanderings are quite striking in that it is clear that their authors had never set their feet in a desert region. It has been pointed out that if one desires to survive for a considerable period of time in deserts like the Sinai or the Negeb, a nomadic way of life would be the only possible way of doing so. However, people who are knowledgeable about the behavioural patterns of nomads report that the course followed by Israel, and the way of life she is reported to have led during the desert years, have nothing to do with a nomadic existence. If one examines the organization of the Israelite community on its way through the wastelands, it becomes clear that what is described is a cultic procession in which a sacred object, the Ark of the Covenant, leads the way, its priesthood collected in a phalanx about it. The authors of the account of the desert wanderings were therefore not attempting to describe the peregrinations of nomads, but the Israelite congregation on its way to a Temple festival, that is, to a sacred territory, which in the case of the desert wanderings was, of course, the Holy Land of Palestine.

4.2.2 *The Tradition of the Settlement*

We arrive at the same result as far as the historical basis of the tradition of the Settlement is concerned by means of an analysis of the traditions in question. According to the account in the book of Joshua, Israel conquered Palestine from north to south in a series of pre-planned campaigns, in the course of which they annihilated the indigenous population. None of this is historically demonstrable. There are no indications that either a new people or a new nation arrived on the scene, or that any genocide took place. The cultural pattern after the so-called Israelite Settlement was the same as before the settlement, although in this period Palestinian society was in the midst of developments which changed its appearance in many respects over a long span of time.

Finally, it should also be noted that even the Old Testament date for the settlement is out of the question. If Palestine was conquered by Israel around, say, 1425 BCE (a date advocated by some scholars in recent times), then we must ask just what had become of this 'Israel' in the Amarna period, only fifty years later? None of the many letters from all parts of Palestine to the Pharaoh knows of any political or national entity known as Israel. This society first appears on the stela of Merenptah about 200 years later.

Most commonly, however, scholarship has attempted to date the settlement to the close of the thirteenth century BCE, although there has been considerable uncertainty as to the form this invasion must have taken. A number of attempts have also been made to divide the Israelite conquest up into a number of phases on the basis of the subdivisions of the Israelite tribes resulting from the patriarch Jacob's marital practices, that is, they are ordered on the basis of his wives as listed in Gen. 29.31–30.24. However, there is as little reason to date this particular Israelite 'settlement' to around 1200 BCE as to any other period between 1500 and 1000 BCE. The reason for this is not contemporary written records, however, but archeological considerations.

According to Joshua 2–6, Israel conquered the city of Jericho immediately after fording the Jordan. The account of the storming of the city is well known, and it has notably little to do with a description of any sort of military undertaking. If one adds to this observation an analysis of the contents of the texts, they prove not to represent a conquest narrative, but a cultic tradition associated with the region of Jericho and in particular with the Israelite sanctuary at Gilgal, which was situated only a few kilometres from the Jordan and from Jericho. The narrative has an unconcealed aetiological intention, namely to explain why there was a sanctuary at Gilgal, why that sanctuary contained a cultic circle of stones, and why the nearby Jericho lay in ruins. As in the case of other Israelite cult legends, Gilgal is legitimated by tracing its foundation back to the 'beginning'. As far as late authors were concerned, this 'beginning' was, naturally, the patriarchal age; but as far as Gilgal was concerned it was more appropriate to associate it with the settlement phase because of its situation near one of the fords of the Jordan.

Any historian who intends to deal with the materials contained in Joshua 2-6 must be prepared to approach his subject with enormous caution. He has no reason to suppose that a narrative of this type, or those dealing with the events prior to the fall of Jericho, contains any historical information. Such caution would serve to protect the historian against unpleasant surprises in the event he should set his spade into the earth somewhere in the vicinity. Since the account of the 'fall of Jericho' is one of the classical legends which everyone knows, the region has attracted numerous archeologists of Palestine, and it has been repeatedly excavated, most recently by the late English archeologist, Dame Kathleen Kenyon. Her conclusions are unambiguous and leave no doubt that there was no historical event behind the narrative of the capture of the city, for the good reason that there was no city on the site after the middle of the sixteenth century BCE. In other words, if Joshua wanted to conquer Jericho around 1200 BCE, then he arrived 300 years too late, since the site at that time contained only an uninhabited heap of ruins. It might further be mentioned in passing that if we proceed to the subsequent narrative of the conquest and destruction of the town of Ai (Joshua 8), the discrepancy between the presumptive time of settlement and the destruction of the site is even more striking, since Ai was laid waste around 2300 BCE, that is, around 1000 years before Joshua. The narrative of the covenant between Joshua and the inhabitants of the town of Gibeon offers us a third variant of this misery (Joshua 9),

since according to the excavator of this town it, too, did not exist at
the time of the settlement, since it had not as yet been founded.

4.2.3 *The Social Location of the Tradition about the Exodus and Settlement*

If we compare the archeological evidence with the biblical account of
the conquest of the country, it seems clear that such a conquest never
took place. Thus what we possess are a number of traditions about
Israel's past, stretching from the sojourn in Egypt to the conquest of
the Holy Land, which are not historical sources about the past. The
events in question did not take place in any way that even remotely
resembles the narratives describing them. Here, more clearly than in
any other part of the Old Testament, we may see how the Israelite
society after the formation of the state attempted to reconstruct its
own past, although nothing resembling adequate sources for such an
effort was available. In all probability, no one was ever concerned
about the fact that such sources did not exist since, as has been
emphasized a number of times, it was never the intention of the
authors in question to depict Israelite prehistory as it actually was.
To the contrary, these writers were concerned to give their own time
an account which might serve as an ideological basis for their society,
or else one which corresponded to the ideological basis which their
society already possessed.

It would be appropriate to ask as to the purpose of the settlement
narratives, that is, why they were invented. For one thing, it is clear
that their intention is to legitimate Israel's claim to the lordship of
Palestine, which they explained as in part because Yahweh had given
the country to Israel, and in part because the Israelites were the
original inhabitants of the country, since those who had lived in the
region before Israel were dead. Scholars have debated about the time
when such a legitimation would have been appropriate; in this
connection the most telling observation is simply that it must have
been provided at a time when there was a need of such legitimation.
In the first half of the monarchical period there can scarcely have
been any internal or external political factor which could bring into
question the fact that Israel was a Palestinian state. First after the
destruction of the northern kingdom in 722 BCE, which was
accompanied by the deportation of the leading circles in Israelite
society, and subsequently, down towards the time of the fall of
Jerusalem in 587 BCE, when the leadership strata of Judah were

deported, we find a period when Israel's right to Palestine must have appeared, to put it mildly, rather uncertain.

Of course, this leads to the issue of why the authors in question chose a settlement narrative as their vehicle of legitimation. The answer is that the best conceivable argument for the right to possess the region was the claim that Israel had lived in Palestine since the days of Adam, that is, since the creation of the world. Nevertheless, the writers chose the concept of an Israelite *nationhood*, that is, the idea of a nation which forced its way into the territory of others and seized it. They chose to claim that the older population was wiped out, although even the Old Testament itself (not least in the so-called alternative settlement narrative in Judges 1) reveals that this was an illusion, and that the earlier population continued to live alongside the Israelites. One reason for choosing this viewpoint could, naturally, be the fact that Israel really had come from somewhere else. However, there is also the possibility that the notion of a settlement was a fiction; its literary record being 'invented' at what may have been a rather late point in the history of Israel. This is by no means as improbable as it might sound, and in fact we do know of numerous analogies from other cultures. In this connection, we may briefly mention the more or less hazy account from Danish prehistory about the fabled king Dan who came out of the blue and gave Denmark her name. Also the numerous traditions which social anthropologists have discovered in a number of traditional societies, which contain accounts of immigrations rarely based on historical events. We may also point to the well documented and quite conscious attempts to create a new prehistory for a nation (which at the time was quite well established) made by Virgil and other Roman poets in the first century BCE. They attempted to trace Roman origins back to ancient Troy in Asia Minor which, according to the Homeric epics had been destroyed by the Greeks in 'the past'. Now, there is nothing in the history of Rome, not to speak of the earlier tradition, which suggests that the Romans regarded themselves as having other than Latin origins. Nevertheless, in Virgil's *Aeneid* we find a fully finished account of the events leading from the burning of Troy to the arrival and settlement of the Trojan refugees in Latium. This settlement tradition was created in a time of cultural crisis in which the Romans suffered from serious cultural pressure from the Greeks they had subdued, but towards whom they still felt themselves to be culturally inferiour. Thus it is conceivable that

Virgil's *Aeneid* is intended to explain to the Romans, and particularly
to the Roman upper classes, for whom Virgil was writing, that the
enmity between them and the Greeks was ancient, and that Roman
culture's roots were every bit as ancient, and respectable as that of
the Greeks. The past is always reconstructed with an eye to the rôle
which the reconstruction in question is to play in its own time.

In the case of Israel, it is possible that the writers chose to speak of
a 'settlement' instead of an origin in the country in order to
emphasize the *racial purity* of the people of Israel at a time when
people were convinced that the Israelites were something quite
special and different from all others, and when they also felt
threatened by impurity because other peoples had been relocated
into their territory (historically this occurred after the fall of the
northern kingdom in 722 BCE). Thus it is entirely possible that the
emergence of the Old Testament account of Israelite prehistory was a
function of the separation of an Israelite nation or Israelite people
from other peoples. It was the result of a polarization which had
occurred between the Israelite society and groups which were not
members of it, and it was a consequence of the historical development
which bound Israel together, that is, gave the population which
acknowledged themselves to be Israelites, an identity. The choice of
the concept of a 'settlement' may be an indication of the fact that this
polarization took place in the first instance outside of Palestine. This
means that the circle which was responsible for the formation of the
historical tradition must itself have lived in exile, and accordingly
wrote for people who were in the same situation as themselves.

4.3 *The Traditions of the Patriarchs*
The Old Testament description of the 'history' of Israel from the
sojourn in Egypt to the period of the Judges is to be regarded as a
reconstruction made by a much later Israelite society of its own past,
and not as a collection of historical reports. The same applies to the
Old Testament account of the earliest history of Israel, the so-called
patriarchal era. Admittedly, appreciable numbers of Old Testament
scholars have been of the opinion (and some still are) that there once
was such a period. This position was above all based on the general
cultural relations described in the narratives in question, and which
scholars thought to recognize in the Near Eastern sources (both
material and written) from the second millennium BCE. An example
would be the curious familial customs of the patriarchs, which some

thought reflected practices also known from ancient *Nuzi*, in the fifteenth century BCE. It is also possible to refer to the references to Abraham's family in the northern reaches of Mesopotamia, since their names actually reproduce a number of town and city names which also figure in documents from as early as the nineteenth-eighteenth centuries BCE, such as Abraham's brother *Haran*, whose name is identical with that of the important trade and caravan crossroads town, *Harranu*, in northern Mesopotamia. Arguments of this sort have led many scholars to attempt to regard the patriarchal narratives as historical accounts.

However, already the two examples mentioned indicate that there are problems confronting anyone attempting such a historical reconstruction. In the first place, there is no clear chronological horizon for the Near Eastern parallels which have been adduced to the patriarchal narratives. In other words, some of the features mentioned in these narratives may be compared with conditions in the Middle Bronze Age, while others only find parallels in the Late Bronze Age. Only a modern reader of the Bible who reasons along the lines that 'it all took place so long ago that half a millennium doesn't mean anything' will be able to ignore the consequences of such discrepancies. In the second place, the parallels between the names of *persons* who are mentioned in the patriarchal narratives and those of *towns and cities* require a rationalizing analysis of the biblical texts for their cogency, since towns do not happen to be identical with people. By this is meant that a serious analysis of the narratives in question cannot proceed by transforming town names into historical personalities. Instead, it is essential to ask how in the course of the tradition these names became the names of individuals. And this in turn means that we must abandon the attempt to reconstruct a patriarchal age on the basis of this sort of information. Instead, one ought to try to explain the present appearance of the traditions and trace it backwards, if this is at all possible.

A third point is that scholars have often felt that when we have found the oldest parallel in Israel's environment to one or another feature mentioned in the Old Testament then we have also established just when the biblical tradition was influenced by this particular cultural feature. Two recent American scholars, however, Thomas L. Thompson and John Van Seters, have pointed out that this assumption rests on a confusion between a *terminus a quo* and a *terminus ad quem*. For example, parallels have been found to the name 'Abraham' as early as the Middle Bronze Age, and it has then been claimed that such parallels *prove* that Abraham lived at the date in question. This is obviously illegitimate, since these parallels to the name 'Abraham' are also to be discovered at any point throughout the next 1500 years. Therefore, since the hero of the narratives is called 'Abraham', they could have been written at any point between 1800 and 300 BCE. Thompson, who has in particular concentrated on the parallels to the patriarchs, also goes so far as to maintain that the patriarchal narratives have no chronological horizon, since all of the relevant parallels may be dated over a period of 1000 years or more. Thus he holds that these accounts are in principle impossible to date, and he goes on to conclude that we ought not even to try to do so. This perhaps somewhat harsh conclusion has been slightly modified by Van Seters' study of the Abraham tradition, as Van Seters thinks it possible to date it to the time of the Babylonian Exile, for which reason he regards it as the result of a conscious literary attempt, in a manner of speaking, to 'invent' the figure of Abraham.

5. *Concluding Remarks*

These considerations bring us to the conclusion of this chapter, since the opposed positions of Van Seters and Thompson, respectively, give us some idea of the restraints forced on the modern scholar in his attempt to study the history of Israel. On the one hand, it proves to be impossible on the basis of the texts themselves to point to any particular date as the time of origin of the so-called historical tradition of the Old Testament, while on the other hand there is not much to suggest that this tradition dates from before the latter part of the monarchy, that is from the seventh century BCE. However, there are isolated indications that this is not completely tenable, as there are, for example, some references to the patriarch Jacob in sources which are older than the seventh to sixth centuries BCE, among other places in the writings of the north Israelite prophet, Hosea.

In Hosea 12 we encounter a proclamation of judgment which the prophet, who was active around 730 BCE, delivered against the northern kingdom a few years before its destruction. This proclamation refers several times to the 'patriarch' of the northern kingdom, Jacob; his activities are cited as examples of the crimes which the northern kingdom had committed during the monarchical period. For example, Jacob is said to have cheated his brother already in the womb (Hos. 12.4-5), and that he fled to Aram where he slaved for the sake of a woman (Hos. 12.13). It is not difficult to find the relevant passages in Genesis (although there the attitude towards Jacob is quite different); thus 25.19-28 tells us about the births of Jacob and Esau, while Genesis 28ff. contain stories about Jacob's flight to Laban, whom he served for seven years to obtain Rachel in marriage. By reason of these references in Hosea, which are surely to be regarded as authentic pronouncements of the prophet (there is no reasonable ground to suppose otherwise), we may surmise that certain parts of the patriarchal tradition were in circulation in the eighth century BCE. It is probable that certain parts of it may be even older, but there are no *contemporary* sources which confirm this supposition. The acknowledgment of this fact leads us to a second conclusion, namely that if we move back in time and attempt to find other sources for the tradition of Israel's earliest history up to the time of the introduction of the monarchy, it is impossible to demonstrate that this tradition was known before the middle of the eighth century at the earliest. It is furthermore impossible to say just how much of it was known at this time, because there are only a very few references to it or mentions of it in the old historical sources which can with certainty be dated to the last couple of centuries of the period of the monarchy. Thus if we wish to go further back, we are relegated to attempting tradition-historical studies, with all the uncertainties which are associated with this method. In the event, however, our loss is not great, because it compels us to undertake a more fruitful way of reading the biblical texts than is offered by attempting to reduce the texts rationalistically in order to force them to yield a 'historical' nucleus. The main emphasis on the future study of the historical tradition of the Old Testament is accordingly the analysis of the period of the monarchy, since it was in this period that traditions about Israel's past came into being. The acknowledgment of this fact forces the reader to ask why the historical reconstructions in question took the particular forms they did; it also forces the reader to be concerned more for the concrete aspects of the contents of the texts, and to ask what significance they can have had in the period in which the Old Testament understanding of Israel's earliest history was formulated.

Chapter 4

THE PERIOD OF THE MONARCHY

1. *The Deuteronomistic History*

One does not have to read much of the Old Testament description of the fortunes of Israel under the rule of her various kings before one realizes that we seem to be extremely well informed about the events in question and about the sequence in which they occurred. We have already previously mentioned a number of factors which made it possible for, first, the united monarchy, and, later, the divided kingdoms, to leave behind them traditions which might have been employed by a historian to reconstruct the past (cf. above Ch. 2, §§ 3.4.1 and 3.4.2). Such a historian, if he had access to the royal archives, might have had at his command administrative documents of all sorts, as well as international correspondence, treaties, and the like. Most important of all, however, were the royal annals, since these probably contained information about the most significant events, the lengths of reigns, and perhaps even synchronistic dates correlating the kings of Judah with their counterparts in Israel.

However, there are no indications at all that any account was ever composed of the era of the monarchy prior to the appearance of the Deuteronomistic History. Admittedly, this history contains traditions about the time of David which might be regarded as sizable collected historical works. These are such works as the previously mentioned account of the history of David's rise to power (1 Samuel 16– 2 Samuel 5) and the so-called Succession Narrative (2 Samuel 7–20; 1 Kings 1–2) which inform us about the struggles for power which occurred within David's family and which were concerned with the question of who was to succeed the old king. However, reference has already been made to the ahistorical character of the first body of stories, but it should be noted that the Succession Narrative, too, is to be regarded as a tendentious programmatic tract which was either

intended to legitimate Solomon's accession to the throne or to accuse
him of having unjustly seized power (scholars disagree on this issue).
Accordingly, the Succession Narrative is also to be used with care in
any historical reconstruction. We are apt to be disappointed when we
attempt to test the feeling immediately exuded by the work that its
author possessed an intimate knowledge of the events at David's
court. The work could indeed be better regarded as a sort of *novella*,
that is, a piece of creative writing, since ordinarily it is only the
authors of fictional works who happen to know precisely what their
dramatis personae are thinking and feeling. Thus, when we encounter
this sort of information in the Succession Narrative in connection
with its main characters, there is reason to suspect that its author is
claiming to know more than it was possible for even an eye-witness
to know.

In the Deuteronomistic History we find a number of narratives
and narrative cycles which deal with various prophets and with their
relations to the monarchy, and which we can dismiss without further
consideration as primary sources. They are instead to be regarded as
legends and sagas from the period of the monarchy. In fact, in the
books of Samuel and Kings the authors alternate between narrative
genres in such a way that we more than suspect that the authors did
not much care whether the materials they used as sources for their
work were of one sort or another.

A good example of the mixture of several genres is the account of
the introduction of the monarchy, 1 Samuel 8-12. This section not
only contains numerous different types of stories; they are also at
least partially contradictory with respect to events and the attitudes
towards the monarchy which they display. This complex of
traditions is introduced by the Israelite demand for a king who will
be able to help them, a king like those of the other peoples (ch. 8).
Samuel, to whom the Israelites address themselves, represents the
old order and is opposed to their wishes; thus he describes all the
misfortunes the adoption of such a king will entail, a catalogue of the
'law of the king' which in reality is a parody of the expectations the
Israelites had towards a just king. In the following narrative,
1 Sam. 9.1-10.16, we read the story of the young Saul, who is sent to
find his father's runaway asses, and who has a number of
extraordinary experiences in the process. Among other things he
meets a prophet who later turns out to be Samuel. Samuel annoints
Saul to be king of Israel, after which Saul returns home. In the

following version of Saul's election, 1 Sam. 10.17-27, the locale shifts to the sanctuary at Mizpah, where Samuel assembles the Israelite tribes and Saul is chosen as king by lot-casting. Then Saul goes home yet again, but only to be acclaimed king for the third time in the sanctuary of Gilgal as the result of his success in leading a rescue operation to save some kinsmen in the territory east of the Jordan (ch. 11). The entire narrative of Saul's election is ultimately concluded by a general rejection of the institution of monarchy by Samuel in ch. 12. Samuel ends by saying that now that Israel has got herself a king, one must hope that all will go well, but his concluding remark does not augur well for the future: 'But if you (Israel) still do wickedly, you shall be swept away, both you and your king' (1 Sam. 12.25, RSV).

Now, there is no good reason to suppose that the historical Saul had to submit himself to all three election procedures before he could seat himself on the throne, but we do nevertheless possess three different versions of his election, each associated with a different locality. It is accordingly tempting to suppose that we have to do with local variant traditions which were at some time worked together, although narrative continuity suffered in the process. A historian might see it as his task to compare the three versions and then to decide which of them is historically most correct. The first narrative (1 Sam. 9.1–10.16) is clearly a fairytale or at least adheres to the structure of the fairytale. Characteristically, to begin with there is no mention of Samuel, nor of any particular locality where Saul encounters the prophet; rather, we find the neutral idea that 'there once was a town where dwelled a holy man', which is characteristic of the fairytale. Only later are we told that the holy man is Samuel, so that the town in question must be Ramah, Samuel's home town. Thus, most scholars would regard this account as a legend possessing little historical value, if any. The second narrative, that of the lot-casting (1 Sam. 10.17-27), does not appeal to scholars either, as lot-casting would seem to be an odd way to choose someone for so important an office. Most researchers seem to prefer the third account, and it is often held to be a historical report of the election of Saul (ch. 11). Of course, this is quite conceivable; on the other hand, we must not ignore the fact that the narrative in question is quite similar to the heroic legends that we find in the book of Judges. In principle, there need be no more historical background underlying ch. 11 than is behind any of the stories of the various Judges. The story could well be a legend which is constructed according to a well-established pattern, a fairytale, which ends when the hero obtains the entire kingdom.

In working these three accounts together, the Deuteronomists have not, as modern historians surely would do, attempted to distinguish between the various versions, let along attempted to decide which of them was most 'correct' from a historical point of view. They simply present all three versions one after another, and link them together with rather improvised 'bridges'. They could not avoid the fact that at least two of the accounts, and perhaps all three of them, are favourable to the monarchy, but they changed this impression by framing these stories with their own evaluation of the monarchy, which they inserted into Samuel's mouth.

This is yet another indication that in the Old Testament we do not find a history of Israel of a type which is any way reminiscent of a modern scientific reconstruction of the past. All varieties of traditions are cited in the 'historical' literature of the Old Testament without the editors' attempting to assess their respective value. Such an attempt would in any case have been foreign to the world of the redactors; it is a modern criterion which is introduced from without, that is, from our insistence on the historical character of the Deuteronomistic History. Accordingly, we see all of the events of the Israelite monarchy through the glasses of the Deuteronomists. In the later parts of the work, these views may be supplemented with the witness of those prophets who have left behind them testimony as to the history of Israel during the period of the monarchy. To put the matter another way, we possess only very delicate materials for the purpose of reconstructing the life of Israel during the monarchy. In a manner of speaking, we must recreate this history on the basis of the available sources, and on the basis of the extra-biblical source materials mentioned previously, which may be able to help us control the information in the Old Testament.

2. *The Political History of the Monarchy*

2.1 *The Relationship between Event and History*
As far as the details of the political history of Israel between 1000 and 600 BCE are concerned, one could almost follow the advice of the Old Testament itself and say, 'whatever else there is to read about in the history of Israel, you may look it up yourself in the books of the

Kings!' By this is meant that a detailed study of the individual events in this part of the history of Israel can hardly be very profitable, since in by far the majority of cases it must be undertaken on the premises of the Deuteronomists. A historical datum is, in and of itself, of no importance. Therefore, the significance of our determining whether Joash of Israel defeated Amaziah of Judah or the reverse (cf. 2 Kgs 14.8-14) is not that our curiosity is satisfied, but that this event characterizes the political relations that obtained in the region during a particular period (i.e. the beginning of the eighth century BCE). It is likewise unimportant whether the Judaean king who succumbed to the Babylonian attack in 587 BCE was called Zedekiah or not. The significance of a name consists in the fact that it makes an event *personal* for us, since we experience the individual event as personified by the named historical figure whom we regard as the centre of the event. This eases our attempts to structure our knowledge about the past, since we ourselves experience a need to know precisely when something happened in order to accommodate to our system of historical knowledge. This is a major difference between us and the peoples of the ages here discussed, since they had no such need; for them, instead, the *typological* interpretation of a course of events was far more important. People in antiquity no doubt felt, to a much greater degree than we do, that is is possible to learn from history, and this concept was so much more important to them than it is to us since they regarded the history in question as an expression of the will of the deity, and of his evaluation of the society, or people.

Both views, that of antiquity and our own, are ways of seeking causal explanations, but the similarities end at this point. We attempt to obtain a grasp of the various factors which underlie a particular event, and to fit the event itself into a wider framework. In our conceptual framework the factors may be economic, social, ideological, or purely political (i.e. the struggle for power). People in antiquity sought causal explanations which in a way went deeper than ours, since the events were invariably regarded as a message from the deity to those men who worshipped the deity, and the message had also to do with the relationship between that deity and other deities. When, in an inscription which dates from the middle of the nineth century BCE, we find that king Mesha of Moab writes that Chemosh (the god of Moab) was angry with his land and therefore delivered it into the hands of the Israelites, this message corresponds to similar expressions in the Old Testament. Thus, for example, Psalm 80 contains a prayer to the God of Israel, who has delivered Israel to the mercy of her enemies, instead to abandon his anger against Israel and save her. For corresponding reasons the Assyrian kings wrote long reports to their divine lord, Asshur, in which they accounted for the conduct of their reigns, since they regarded themselves as accountable to Asshur. Such reports were not intended for the subjects in general, for they were placed in places which were inaccessible to the public; instead, they were directed to the gods alone, since the prosperity of the country was contingent on the goodwill of the gods. In other words, in antiquity the history of humanity was regarded as a game which was played out by the gods, in which people were more or less like chess pieces, with the reservation that they were independent pieces who had the potential to oppose the will of their lord and thus incur his displeasure. In such a case it was up to the divine lord as to whether he was of a mind to clear the board and start a new game with new pieces, or whether he would just re-arrange his pieces in order to start again.

2.2 *The Historical Picture*
2.2.1 *The United Monarchy*
Around 1000 BCE there was, according to the Old Testament historical account, no doubt whatsoever that the board had been cleared and a new game was about to start in which old and new pieces were involved. Yahweh, who had ruled Israel up to that point, had been rejected by his subjects in favour of an important new piece which had arrived on the scene, the *king*. The subsequent national history is therefore written from the point of view that this new piece was of decisive significance for the further fortunes of Israel. The first attempt, however, soon proved to be based on a misunderstanding; the new piece turned out to be recalcitrant in every way, and it had to be exchanged for another. Saul had to give way to a king who was, or so we read, more dear to Yahweh than his predecessor.

To translate this, it seems that the tribal society of the pre-national period produced a sole ruler, that is, a *chieftain*, or perhaps already to begin with, a king. A central administrative apparatus soon crystallized around this figure, and this brought about considerable structural changes in Israelite society. Events took a new course with the accession of David. The monarchy had been introduced at a juncture when the Israelite tribal society was already exposed to considerable external pressure, and this necessitated the abandonment of the previous 'government' and created the preconditions for the emergence of a permanent type of ruler figure. Saul's entire career was dominated by the fact that his duty was to attempt to restabilize Israel, and he seems to have failed, since the crisis was apparently even more acute at the time of his death than it had been at the beginning of his reign. However, it is possible that at this time the crisis was almost over, for as soon as a new king was well in the saddle Israel returned to the offensive. The first campaign was aimed at defeating the threat to Israel's political independence, and subsequently she began to attack her neighbours. This development might at first sight seem paradoxical, in that Israel progressed from being a threatened tribal society to an empire in the course of a single lifetime. Moreover, this empire extended, according to the Old Testament, from the Euphrates in the north to the 'Brook of Egypt' (the *wadi el-'Arish* in northern Sinai) in the south. At the same time, centralization of the exercise of power accompanied the reigns of David and Solomon, his son and successor, and this centralization transformed Israel from a tribal society to a state in the true sense of the word. The profound structural changes will be dealt with below; here we shall concentrate on the external course of events.

The external course of events continued on its apparently paradoxical pathway, because the Davidic empire dissolved just as quickly as it had arisen; moreover, not only did the dissolution lead to the independence of the provinces, but to the partition of the very nucleus of Israelite territory itself. In other words, after fifty years at most during which Israel had been one, if not *the*, leading power of the first half of the tenth century, it was reduced over the next ten to twenty years to the more modest status of one of the many small states in the region. However, Israel did not abandon this position of eminence without striking a few blows, and in fact we shall have to progress down to the middle of the ninth century before the long-term consequences of the collapse of the empire become fully clear.

2.2.2 *The Divided Monarchy*
Around 925 BCE the Davidic empire was replaced by two lesser states, *Israel* (the northern kingdom) and *Judah* (the southern kingdom). Once again a paradox occurs, in that the natural heir to Davidic authority was Judah, where the house of David continued

to rule until the bitter end, interrupted only by the singular and brief occasion when a queen of north Israelite origins ruled for a space (1 Kings 11). The grasp of the family of David on their society was so sure that even on those occasions on which the legitimate king was killed in connection with one or another palace revolution no attempt was made to replace him with a representative of a different noble line. Instead, a son of the murdered king was invariably chosen, even if this meant that the days of the regicides were soon told (cf. 2 Kgs 12.20-21; 14.5 [Joash]; 14.19-21 [Amaziah]). On the other hand, it is quite clear that it was the northern kingdom which was the real heir to the great empire of David and Solomon. It was this kingdom which took upon itself the hopes and the will to carry on the traditions of greatness, which apparently were completely lacking in the south. These efforts were most marked under the rule of the Omrides, who for a time enabled Israel (the northern kingdom) to achieve the position of what may have been the most important single state in western Asia. Judah, by comparison, played a modest rôle and, as has often been noted and as even the Old Testament itself more than hints, in this period Judah was only a vassal of northern Israel. However, the northern kingdom made no serious effort to reintegrate Judah into a common kingdom with herself at the head. Omri and Ahab, the most important of the northern kings, had apparently no intention of recreating the *Davidic* kingdom. In a sense one could say that while Judah became the heir of the *ideology* of the Davidic empire, Israel took over the *political inheritance* of the first two kings of the Davidic dynasty.

This relationship between the two former parts of the Davidic empire, the independent or quasi-independent kingdoms of Israel and Judah, continued to exist throughout the following period ending with the fall of the northern kingdom in 722 BCE. During this time, the northern kingdom was involved in the whirlpool of international political events, while Judah was largely able to keep herself uninvolved. By contrast, the northern kingdom was forced to take up the battle against the other kingdoms that emerged at the beginning of the first millennium BCE, namely the Aramaeans and, eventually, the Assyrians. Thus the northern kingdom became a player in a political power-game which far exceeded its own resources, and with the mercilessness of a natural law this finally led to the destruction of the kingdom.

The actual historical course of events was, naturally, by no means so simple as the above description might suggest. In fact the fortunes of Israel alternated between periods of relative prosperity and international significance and periods of weakness, during which the demise of the kingdom seemed inevitable. These shifting fortunes, however, were functions of forces which were vaster than Israel herself, and over which Israel could exercise only very little control. During the reigns of Omri and his successors it was possible for Israel to pacify the Aramaean kingdom by means of treaties of a primarily defensive character; there was a broad alliance of the mini-states in the western part of the Near East against the quickly burgeoning Neo-Assyrian Empire. For a while this alliance succeeded in checking the advances of the Assyrians, but towards the middle of the ninth century the entente collapsed because of general strife between Israel and Aram, the results of revolutions in both states which led to the emergence of new royal houses in both Damascus and Samaria. In Israel the dynasty of Omri was annihilated by the usurper Jehu, whose descendants reigned for most of the following century.

In the subsequent period the fate of Israel seemed on several occasions to have been sealed, but on each occasion she succeeded in saving herself at the last moment. The real reason for this, however, was not any dramatic measures of her own, but the activities of the Neo-Assyrian Empire. In the beginning of the eighth century BCE the Assyrians concluded their advance towards the west by destroying the Aramaean kingdoms, and it seemed inevitable that a similar fate would be visited upon Israel in a short space of time. Instead, however, Israel survived and even experienced a brief period of prosperity which extended until the middle of the eighth century BCE. Once again the reason for this was factors which were beyond Israelite influence, no matter how the Israelites may have understood the events in question. After having destroyed Damascus, Assyria was torn by internal difficulties which brought her advances towards the west to a halt, although the respite was, in the event, to prove brief. New Assyrian rulers soon once again began to direct their attention to the west and to form new armies, which quickly subjugated the whole of the Near East down to the borders of Egypt. The fate of Israel in this period between 750 and 722 BCE is characteristic of the fortunes of virtually all the small states in the region at this time. In the first instance, Israel was forced to submit to Assyrian authority, pay tribute, and acknowledge her status as an

Assyrian vassal. Shortly afterwards, Israel attempted to revolt against her master and tried to forge alliances against the Assyrians; punishment for such audacity fell like lightning from a clear sky. The kingdom of Israel was dissolved in two instances. First, the Assyrians removed all the provinces outside of the central highland from Samarian control, meaning the Samarian possessions in Galilee, the plains, and in the territory east of the Jordan. These were made into Assyrian provinces under the immediate rule of Assyrian governors. Since the king in Samaria had not yet understood the lesson he was being taught, he was removed, his capital was conquered, and his kingdom was transformed into an Assyrian province called *Samarina*. Leading elements of the population were deported to Mesopotamia and disappeared utterly from the arena of history. In their place foreign populations were imported and forcibly settled from other parts of the empire (2 Kgs 17.3-6, 24), and Israel no longer existed as a state.

2.2.3 *Judah Alone*

While all of these events were transpiring, Judah played an ambivalent rôle. The king in Jerusalem certainly did not feel in a position to take active part in the political events. Thus he submitted himself without more ado to the Assyrian yoke and paid tribute on the first occasion that presented itself. If the evidence of the Old Testament is to be believed, in doing so the Judaean king contributed to the dissolution of the northern kingdom, since the king in Jerusalem directly appealed to the Assyrians for help when he himself had been forced into a war with Israel and Aram (the so-called 'Syro-Ephraimite War', spanning from 734-732 BCE; cf. 2 Kgs 16.7). The Assyrian king intervened in the conflict with alacrity, because among other things it was apparently the goal of Israel and Aram to force Judah into a coalition against the Assyrians. After the fall of Samaria and the accession of a new king on the throne in Jerusalem, Judah nevertheless chose to enter into the political fray, but it must be admitted that the timing of the king in question, Hezekiah, was completely off. Judah was every bit as unable, as she had been previously, to carry off such a feat of political derring-do. To be brief, Hezekiah attempted to revolt against the Assyrians in 701 BCE, and the immediate consequences of his action were unambiguous. Before the year was out, Jerusalem, the capital city, was besieged by an Assyrian army while the surrounding Judaean fortresses were eliminated one by one. The only anomaly in the whole procedure was that Jerusalem itself did not fall, as the Assyrian king allowed himself to be paid off. This resulted in, or at any rate intensified, the myth of the inviolability of Jerusalem (perhaps also because the central authorities more or less concealed the real reason for the departure of the Assyrians), a myth which was to have catastrophic consequences in the subsequent period. On the other hand, the Assyrians left the Judaean king in no doubt whatsoever as to their seriousness:

> As to Hezekiah, the Jew, he did not submit to my yoke, I laid siege to 46 of his strong cities, walled forts, and to the countless small villages in their vicinity, and conquered them . . . I drove out (of them) 200,150 people . . . Himself I made a prisoner in Jerusalem, his royal residence, like a bird in a cage . . . His towns, which I had plundered, I took away from his country . . . Thus I reduced his country, but I still increased the tribute and the *katrû* (due) to me (ANET 288).

Such was the 'greeting' of the Assyrian great king, Sennacherib, to his rebellious vassal.

For the following seventy to eighty years, Judah remained the faithful vassal of Assyria. We are not told much about events in this period of time, but everything suggests that the Jerusalemite kings continued to pay their tribute year by year. There are also some indications that Judah was even treated as a faithful vassal and so was rewarded with the return of some of her lost districts, so that the kingdom was able to enjoy the general political stability that characterized this period. The peace, however, was not to last. After 630 BCE the Assyrian empire collapsed in less than twenty years as the result of the attacks of a coalition consisting of the Median empire (in Iran), the Lydian empire (in Asia Minor), and last, but not least, the Neo-Babylonian empire. These developments entailed that practically from one day to the next the king in Jerusalem found himself liberated from Assyrian servitude and left to his own devices. This king, who at this time was the young Josiah, attempted to exploit the possibilities offered by the disintegration of the Assyrian empire to the previous vassals, who now were given a chance to engage themselves in international politics.

There can be no doubt that these developments ultimately meant that Judah was doomed, since Josiah appears to have seriously overestimated the might of his country and launched it on a foreign-political adventure, perhaps with the optimistic goal of recreating the Davidic empire. In any event, Josiah died rather pitifully when he attempted to hinder the progress of an Egyptian expedition on its way to succour the remnants of the Assyrian empire in the last throws of their struggle for existence (609 BCE). Thus Judah had become involved in the struggle to take up the Assyrian inheritance, a battle in which the main agents were the Egyptians on one side and the Babylonians on the other, and which ended with Babylonian victory. Egypt was again expelled from Syro-Palestine, and the other Near Eastern states were once again relegated to their virtually customary vassal status. In the course of these political complications, the Jerusalemite kings committed their most lethal errors and attempted for the last time to enter Judah into international politics, with the result that their kingdom was laid waste, Jerusalem was plundered, and the kingship brought to an end for ever. Parts of the population of Judah were deported to Mesopotamia, and the monarchy was replaced by the rule of Babylonian governors (587 BCE).

3. *Israelite Society during the Monarchy*

3.1 *From Tribal Society to State*
3.1.1 *The 'Reserve Ideology'*
In this section we shall attempt to examine more closely some of the underlying circumstances of the period in which the Israelite tribal society was transformed into a regular state. In the previous chapter some ways were suggested for the progress for the inhabitants of Palestine from tribal system back to state, or, more properly, for that part of the population of the country who lived in the hill country of central Palestine, in Galilee, and in the territory east of the Jordan. It was mentioned that external factors may have provoked a development of the tribal society which led to a different form of organization than had previously been employed. It was also emphasized that within the fundamental social structure there was a common denominator linking the kinship system of the tribal society and in the centralized state, which facilitated the transition from one form of organization to another.

As far as the last-mentioned factor is concerned, American social anthropologists have pointed out that in traditional societies, that is, societies in which industrialization has not yet transformed socio-cultural relations to any significant extent, there is inevitably some form of *reserve ideology*. By this is meant a form of ideological connection which serves to link people together into a community, but which first becomes operative when other forms of organization are no longer dominant. The *feeling of kinship* serves as such a reserve ideology. For example, peasants who are organized by kinship ties have no need of a higher level of social integration than that of the family or, on certain occasions, of wider ramifications of the lineage. Thus, if the state disappears, the kinship system is able to replace the central administrative forces and their rôles as protectors of society. This manifests itself as an intensification of the previously existing kinship ties, which leads to the emergence of larger kinship groups. It is even possible for kinship units to reappear which have not manifested themselves for numerous generations. In this connection, one could say that the lineage and the tribe are kinship forces which replace the state.

3.1.2 *Tribal Society under Pressure: The Philistine Threat*
Around 1000 BCE, Palestinian society was transformed into a centralized state in which the members of the tribes were citizens. One reason for this change may have been the pressure from external political forces which the tribal society itself was unable to deal with. Of course, it is also possible to imagine this development towards a centralized form of government as the product of internal con-tradictions which had arisen within the tribal society. This would perhaps have been brought about by pressure on the available resources caused by such things as a population surplus which overstrained the ability of the tribal territories to feed their respective population. However, as far as the last possibility is concerned, the Old Testament is silent, and we are hardly able to demonstrate this sort of development by means of archeological excavations, at least at present. And yet, such a situation would not be at all unthinkable, since the tribal territories in question were both of limited extent and of limited fertility. Thus, the possibility cannot be simply dismissed that towards the close of the second millennium BCE Israelite tribal society had begun to encounter internal problems as a result of the limited availability of resources, and it is not inconceivable that such difficulties would have been quite acute in the event of serious crop shortages. However, as mentioned above, we have no way of knowing whether this was the case.

By way of contrast, however, we do possess considerable information about an external political and military pressure on the tribal societies in the mountainous regions of Palestine at around 1000 BCE. In the territory west of the Jordan, the Philistine coalition based on the coastal plains was responsible for this pressure, or so the Old Testament maintains. As far as the corresponding development in the region east of the Jordan is concerned, we are informed that a number of tribal societies, consisting of the Israelites, the Ammonites, and the Moabites, were all competing for control of this territory. The development in Palestine proper is, of course, the most important, and it is also the easiest to follow. We have previously mentioned the arrival of the Philistines and their formation of a coalition. It has been archeologically possible to follow Philistine expansion because of the peculiar style of Philistine pottery. On the other hand, all indications suggest that around the turn of the millennium the assimilation of the Philistines into local culture was in other ways so advanced that the Philistines had forgotten their own ancient, non-semitic language. They appear instead to have employed a semitic dialect which more or less corresponded to the one in use in the rest of Palestine, and which we have received in its late form as biblical Hebrew.

With respect to the complete assimilation of the Philistines into the semitic population, a process which entailed the disappearance of most of the peculiarly 'Philistine' features of their culture, it would be reasonable to suppose that the Philistines as such merely comprised the élite strata of the Philistine city-states. They were a ruling class who based their claims to authority on the solidarity within the leadership group, which thus more or less functioned the way the previous palace organizations had done. In this process, at least to begin with, there must have been concrete ethnic differences between the élite and the ordinary population of Palestinian origin. Generally speaking, they were the inheritors of the city-states which had thus far existed in the same regions. Among other things, this is indicated by the fact that names of several of the Philistine city-states figure in the sources from Late Bronze Age Palestine, the only difference being that the Philistine élite had replaced the earlier Palestinian ruling strata. Considered individually, the Philistine towns did not constitute any more significant threat to the tribal societies up in the mountains than the earlier Palestinian mini-states had done. What was peculiar to the Philistine states, however, was that the Philistine upper classes in the five city-states apparently acknowledged bands of solidarity which manifested themselves in the alliance of the five states. This was a political coalition under collective leadership; taken together, these features changed the political balance to the advantage of the Philistines, and it made it possible for them to bring the plains in the coastal regions under their control in the course of the eleventh century BCE.

Of course, the tribal societies in the mountains, which the mini-states had never regarded as legitimate political formations, must have been regarded with deep suspicion by the respective palace administrations in the various city-states in the country, in part because they were created by refugees from the populations of the city-states themselves, and in part because they constituted a social system which might be able to serve as an alternative to their own. The presence of these refugee societies meant that there was always the possibility that dissatisfied peasants and refugees from the cities might seek asylum among the tribes. In this connection it is interesting that according to the Old Testament witness about the wars with the Philistines at the beginning of the monarchy the Philistines referred to the Israelites as *hebrews* or *habiru* (1 Sam. 4.6, 9; 13.3). Whether or not this is a historical reminiscence, the same connotations are found here as in connection with the *habiru* in the Amarna letters. Thus the indicated response to the challenge presented by the tribal societies was that the coastal societies assumed control of the tribal territories in the central part of the country. The coalition of the Philistine city-states made it possible to attempt the occupation of the hill country. The books of Samuel preserve a number of traditions about the Philistine entry into the hill country (1 Sam. 4; 13–14); in every case, there is no question but that we have to do with legendary traditions, but their implication is nevertheless clear. When Saul emerged as the leader of the Israelite tribes, there were Philistine governors at various points in the hill country north of Jerusalem. It must accordingly have looked at this point as if it was only a matter of time before the Israelite tribes had to succumb.

3.1.3 The Tribal Society Responds: The Introduction of the Monarchy
States and tribal societies have historically frequently collided with one another; for this reason we are well informed as to the results of such collisions. Either the tribal society in question disintegrates as

the result of a political pressure to which it has no effective answer, or it changes its character by centralizing its exercise of power. Confronted with the Philistine threat the Israelite tribes had of necessity to face one of two alternatives: they could submit, or they could intensify their internal solidarity. Had they followed the first course, they would have been integrated into the Philistine states, and within a few years they would have lost both their tribal organization and their specific identity. In the other case, they would possibly be able to resist the political and military threat from without. There is in any event no doubt about which course the Israelites chose. As a result, they chose a king whose task it was to liberate the tribal society from the external threats.

Scholars have discussed both the form and the consequences of the first attempt at monarchy by the Israelite tribes. No agreement has been reached as to the number of tribes which later belonged to the Davidic empire which supported the first effort at monarchy. However, it appears that the tribes in the southern part of the country did not recognize the new king, who was chosen by the tribes dwelling to the north of Jerusalem. Therefore Saul's kingdom probably included the tribes of Benjamin, Ephraim, and Manasseh in central Palestine, plus two or more of the Galilean tribes. His authority will not have extended south of Jerusalem, for which there may have been a number of reasons. The most important was perhaps the fact that there was a territory which was still controlled by the city-states and which separated the northern and southern states. The largest and best-known of these city-states was, of course, Jerusalem, and taken together, these states inhibited communications between the tribes on either side of them. It was first with the advent of Saul that this line was broken, and it was ultimately eliminated by David, who integrated the city-states in question into his empire.

Another explanation as to why the northern tribes more readily accepted a king than their southern counterparts, at least to begin with, was that there may already have existed a tradition among the tribes of central Palestine which moved in the direction of a centralized form of government. We have previously referred to the tradition in Judges 9 about the brief rule of Abimelech in Shechem, which had been the seat of a prince from ancient times. Although it would be methodologically incorrect to identify this tradition with a historical source, as it is obviously more of a saga than a historical account, the localization of such a narrative in the central Palestine tribal territory might nevertheless suggest that at least the tribe of Manasseh may have known a more authoritarian leadership figure than was provided by the groups of 'elders'. There is accordingly some question as to whether this tradition derived from the pre-national period, and that it might therefore indicate the nature of the motives underlying the choice of Saul as king. However, we cannot answer this question definitively, since we are likewise unable to deny the possibility that Judges 9 arose much later, that is, during the period of the monarchy, in which case it must represent the later criticism of the monarchy, as it manifested itself in Israel (cf. the so-called 'fable of Jotham' in Judg. 9.8-15). It may have been projected into the past for reasons of 'security'.

3.1.4 *The Monarchy of Saul*

The political integration achieved under Saul was not sufficient to enable Israel completely to repel the pressure of the coastal states. Even under its first king, the tribal society continued increasingly to be encapsulated within the domain of the states. There were many reasons for this, of which some deserve mention. The informal sort of leadership which had also previously been exercised had even then been insufficient to get its way in all cases. A leader who was elected by a tribe or a coalition of tribes could not compel his fellow tribesmen to take action; he could only appeal to their feelings of fellowship. If such feelings were insufficiently strong, the members of the tribes either did not meet up, or, if they did so, only those came who saw some advantage in their participation. The leader was furthermore chosen with respect to the particular task he was expected to solve, and when the crisis had passed by, he lost his leadership rôle again either voluntarily or involuntarily, because there was no longer any use for him and people wanted to return to their homes. In a situation in which the authority of the leader depended only on his personal abilities and not on an external administrative apparatus, he had no possibility of undertaking sanctions against possible dissidents.

Saul represented something new because the tribes saw themselves as confronted by a permanent threat. The tribes who were threatened could no longer manage their affairs with only a short-term leader, after whose services were ended they could return home. It was necessary for them to maintain continuously some central organ, that is, a permanent administrative apparatus which would always be present and which could assemble the tribes in precarious situations. This entailed that the leader, as previously, had to be elected, only this leader was regarded as indispensable—he had to be protected. For this reason Israelite society produced a permanent leadership group consisting of a king (although others might perhaps prefer to term him a *chieftain*), one or more administrative officials to serve at his pleasure, and finally a small standing military force of housecarls, that is, of individuals who were responsible to Saul personally and loyal to him, who served as his personal guard. In the days of Saul this apparatus cannot have grown so strong that it could not as easily have disappeared again. By the same token, it is far from certain that it was always able to command the obedience of the tribes. However, the longer there was need of its services, the more extensive such an apparatus must have grown, until the point was reached where it was indispensable, and no one any longer saw any alternative to it.

The emergence of this administrative apparatus also entailed the development of a group of specialists in which were concentrated the society's resources of manpower for purposes of war, and such an apparatus had to be paid for with regular deliveries of rations. This group of leaders and the helpers of leaders had to be fed by the rest of society, and from this situation the leap from being employees of the society to being employers of the society was not great. The decisive question was merely when the control of the leadership group over the exercise of military authority became so permanent that it would be able to carry out sanctions against disobedient members of the society. Even the rudimentary apparatus available to Saul was able to develop further, since there was continuous use for it, and in this way it became possible for the organization to get so firm a grip on the administration of power in the society that it was no longer possible to get rid of it.

The decisive expression of the fact that this development already occurred in Saul's lifetime is the fact that Saul's son, Ishba'al, was chosen king after him. Already Saul became the founder of a *dynasty*, by means of which the administration of power in the country was monopolized by a single family.

The life of the ordinary tribesman can hardly have changed significantly during the career of Saul. There was ordinarily no need in his daily life to seek the support of the central authority, which consisted of Saul and his circle. Conversely, when the central authorities called on his services in the event of war, the ordinary Israelite had no difficulty in acknowledging that it was also in his own interest. The difference between this and previous situations, however, was that with the advent of centralized power the Israelite perhaps also recognized that if he did not obey such a summons it might have negative consequences for himself. There were now forces beyond his control within his own society, and these could turn against him if he refused his services.

In economic terms the establishment of the central leadership can hardly have played any great rôle at this time. The administrative apparatus was not large, nor was the standing army; there were only a limited number of expenses, and there were many to share the burden. Thus, at the introduction of the monarchy the individual Israelite cannot have realized that a process had been initiated which was destined to change the presuppositions of his life fundamentally in only a single generation.

3.2 *The Davidic Empire*
3.2.1 *Tribe Versus State*
As we have seen, already in the days of Saul the new institution of the monarchy had achieved a position which made it indispensable. This may be seen in the reaction that set in after the fall of the Benjaminite dynasty. David's precise part in the fall of this dynasty is, in this connection, unimportant, although the question itself is fascinating. For our purposes, what is interesting is the evidence of the new socio-political reality that had arisen which was provided by the fact that the 'elders of Israel' *presented themselves to David*, who at the time in question had already won for himself the position of king in the southern part of the hill country (2 Sam. 5.3). The 'elders' in question were probably the previously mentioned leaders of the various lineages. On this occasion, it was they who elected the king on behalf of the rest of the society, and it was presumably also they who, a generation or two later, rejected the Davidic monarchy in favour of a genuinely northern Israelite royal house.

The preceding lines already adumbrate one of the conflicts which must have characterized the early days of the monarchy. The monarchy had to compete with the old tribal system, since the *laissez-faire* attitude of the tribal society to authority was un-acceptable in the eyes of the centralized state. The Jerusalemite kings extended their positions of power from above; they gradually divided the country into administrative districts which were ruled by governors, that is, royal office-holders; they imposed taxes, summoned ordinary folk to corvée labour (forced), and they organized a professional army. Nevertheless, the Davidic monarchs sat no firmer on the throne of the northern part of the country than that they could be expelled from it from, so to speak, one day to the next.

All of this suggests that the transition from tribal society to state was not a process which took place once and for all; rather, it was a gradual process which contained in it the possibilities of relapses, that is, attempts to return to conditions which had previously obtained in the country. This also warns us not to assume that the introduction of the monarchy was synonymous with the dissolution of tribal society. The conflicts in question inform us, to the contrary, that the tribal society not only still existed but that, in addition to being an important social factor, it also played a political rôle of some importance, at least at the beginning of the monarchical period. By the same token, *tribal solidarity* may be regarded as the probable origin of *nationalistic feelings*. For this reason the Israelite monarchy was to a certain degree different from the many previous petty monarchies in the country.

The ordinary Israelite continued primarily to belong to his tribe, and it was to him only of secondary importance that he also was a member of an Israelite state. His relationship to the leadership of the state, that is, to the king and the central administration, was a factor in his existence which played a far smaller part in things than did his relations to his lineage and his fellow tribesmen. If latent conflicts broke out, the lines along which the society would have cleaved would probably have followed the actual relationships among the tribes. This assumption is clearly borne out by the battlecry, 'To your tents, O Israel!' which occurs on two occasions in the traditions about the Davidic age, first in connection with a north Israelite rebellion against David (2 Sam. 20.1), and later in connection with the partition of the empire (1 Kgs 12.16). It is always clearly indicated that the dividing lines between the two subsequent petty states of Israel and Judah followed tribal boundaries. In fact, it is specifically mentioned as an exception that the tribe of Benjamin was broken up in the course of the division of the kingdom. As far as Benjamin was concerned, however, the special circumstances applied that it was situated right alongside the centre of the Davidic empire, Jerusalem, so that it was probably encapsulated to a greater degree than any of the other northern tribes within the Davidic state. It may even totally have lost its ability to make decisions as to its future as a tribe or territory.

3.2.2 *The Consolidation of the State*

If the monarchy was to survive in the long run, it was imperative for it to destroy the political significance which the tribal society still retained. This could take place either by arbitration or by compulsion. In the time of David and Solomon it was of fateful importance that the latter choice seems to have been made, at any rate with respect to the tribes in the northern part of the country. Perhaps already David, but certainly Solomon, attempted an administrative subdivision of the country which in a number of cases cut across the tribal territories (1 Kgs 4). The goal of this was presumably to reduce the political influence of the tribes in question by replacing the local form of leadership with that of a centralized administration. These kings then subsequently used their administrative apparatuses to squeeze the populations for both revenues and labour. It is hard to determine how much of this took place during the reign of David, but it is in any event clear that under Solomon the undermining of the tribal society had taken on a definite shape, and that its intention was evident: Israel was to be transformed into a state like those which had previously existed in the country, although the dimensions of this new state were decisively different. The king was to be the only authority in the country, and the population were to be reduced to the status of his slaves. In Jerusalem a central apparatus was constructed which some scholars have regarded as similar to that which had been employed in Egypt during the New Kingdom. This system may have survived in a simplified form in some of the small Palestinian city-states in which the administrative tradition from the days of Egyptian hegemony had been preserved. The basis of the power of the state was enhanced by the fact that the number of members of the tribes who were conscripted for military service steadily diminished while at the same time the military came to be based on specialist units, chariot troops in particular. Such units were garrisoned round about the country in royal fortresses which as a rule were situated in places which had previously been local city-states (1 Kgs 9.15-25). In this process, too, the inheritance from the city-state system of the Late Bronze Age was quite striking. Admittedly, this standing army of professional soldiers was intended to defend that empire which David had created, and which Solomon quickly put at risk; but the situation of these mobile attacking forces *within* the borders of Palestine tells us that they were also intended to maintain law and order in the centre of the kingdom.

The monarchy had yet another way to ensure its position, since, in addition to the means of compulsion and the creation of a centralized administration, it was also possible to attempt to exploit the possibilities which were inherent in the use of the resources of the empire. These resources were channelled to the centre of the empire, that is, Jerusalem and the royal palace, and it was here that they were used to create a picture of the Israelite king as the *lord of the world*. To this should be added the fact that some attempts were apparently made to enhance the figure of the king in the religious awareness of the populace through the establishment of a splendid royal temple cultus in Jerusalem. Such efforts required much in the way of purely external manifestations, which in antiquity was invariably synonymous with construction projects. Accordingly, we note that king Solomon, during whose rule this particular policy became the dominating force in Israelite society, also launched an extraordinarily expensive series of construction projects in his capital, projects which consisted in part of the erection of a massive palace complex, decorated with all the then existing tricks of the builder's trade, and in part of a temple which was directly connected to the palace (and rather smaller), in which the royal cultus was centralized (1 Kgs 6-7). A cruder, but nevertheless effective, way of conducting these propagandistic efforts lay in the establishment of the fortresses or, more properly, *barracks*, which were built at strategic sites throughout the kingdom. The content of this sort of propaganda differed from the first type, although the message was unambiguous: it was a warning to the populace to maintain order, so that the military apparatus would not be aimed at *it*.

However, there is some question as to whether such policies were viable in the long run, that is, as to whether the population in general were prepared to suffer in silence the yoke that had been imposed on them. There was the further question as to just what conditions the people were prepared to accept from the monarchy, if not the complete exploitation of their society. In this connection the further development of the kingdom played a significant part, since all of Solomon's attempts to strengthen his 'image' were quite expensive. In order to carry out the construction projects in Jerusalem the services of specialists from all over were required. Very expensive building materials for these projects had to be ordered from the Phoenicians, and it was necessary to obtain gold from distant countries to pay for both specialists and materials, and for the elaborate decoration of the buildings. In the beginning of Solomon's reign this system seems to have functioned well, since income and expenses were more or less equal. It was possible to exploit the distant provinces of the kingdom in Syria and the region east of the Jordan; there was also trade with foreign powers both by land and by sea through the trade expeditions which went out from Eilat and the Red Sea. However, these times were not destined to continue.

3.2.3 *Towards the Collapse of the Davidic State*
In the second half of the reign of Solomon the empire began to disintegrate, since the distant provinces successfully revolted. We possess very little information which might help us to penetrate to the causes of these events. Nevertheless, it is possible to point to some general lines indicative of a particular tendency. Paradoxically, these lines suggest that Israel lost her dominant position in practically the same way the Philistines lost control of the Israelite tribes. The empire had been created by the young Israelite state under the leadership of David, who succeeded in co-ordinating the forces which were latent in that society. Thus the Israelite development into a centralized state led to a co-ordinated effort (in the same way as the earlier Philistine alliance had been able to focus Philistine resources against Israel). The Israelites were simply in a position to put many more soldiers in the field than any of the neighbouring societies were able to do during this period. Moreover, the government in Jerusalem possessed the authority which was necessary to ensure that it would be obeyed by its subjects.

Throughout the Late Bronze Age and the Early Iron Age the neighbouring regions in Syria and the region east of the Jordan (the later states of Aram, Ammon, Moab, and Edom) had been at the same developmental level as Palestine. However, the subsequent political integration of these regions took place later than it did in Israel, perhaps because these regions were not exposed to external pressures equivalent to those exerted by the Philistines on Israel during the eleventh century BCE. Philistine pressure led to the centralization of the forces of the society, and in a corresponding way Israel (and perhaps the Assyrian empire in the east, which emerged in the tenth century BCE after a lengthy period of weakness) caused the political integration of the territories which Israel regarded as her provinces. In actual fact, these regions covered vastly more space and had much larger populations than Palestine was able to muster, and for this reason the political organization of Syria had to lead to the collapse of the Israelite empire sooner or later. Just as the creation of the Israelite state had meant the end of the Philistine dream of controlling Palestine, the political organization of Syria, which the kings in Jerusalem had neither the manpower nor the economic resources to oppose successfully, meant that the fate of the Israelite empire was sealed. Of course, things were not made easier for the king in Jerusalem by the tendency of his southern neighbour (Egypt) to 'speculate' in the rebellious tendencies of the Israelite provinces. Rebellious leaders like Hadad the Edomite, Resin the Aramaean, and Jeroboam the Ephraimite could always count on being well received in Egypt (1 Kgs 11.14-40). All three subsequently returned and became kings of their respective parts of the former Israelite empire.

The loss of the empire had severe consequences for Palestine. Following the motto that 'what is outwardly lost must be inwardly won' (a Danish maxim which accompanied Danish attempts at restoration after the loss of the Danish-Prussian War in 1864) Solomon had to replace the incomes from his departed provinces with incomes which he squeezed out of the local populace. As a result, considerable pressure was exerted on the patience of the people, who were also compelled to perform unpaid corvée labour to finish the royal construction projects. The people had further to bear the weight of taxes intended to finance Solomon's military system and the wars which he must have waged in his vain attempt to keep the empire intact. As we have seen, Palestine itself is quite poor in natural resources, and for this reason Solomon probably had to supplement his tax income by taking loans abroad, and he even had to mortgage some villages in Galilee to a Phoenician creditor (the king of Tyre; cf. 1 Kgs 9.10-14).

This account is based on the heterogeneous tradition about Solomon in the Old Testament. Unlike the reign of David, there is practically no connected pre-Deuteronomistic account of the reign of Solomon. On the other hand, a wide variety of sources have been utilized and worked together by a much later redactor who often frequently added his own commentary. Some information might derive from the national archives in Jerusalem, such as the list of Solomon's 'ministers' in 1 Kgs 4.1-6, or the description of the subdivision of provinces in Palestine in 1 Kgs 4.7-19. Other sources may have been such things as royal construction inscriptions, which would account for details of the construction of the palace complex and the temple (1 Kgs 6–7). On the other hand, these descriptions could equally well have been made from a much later account by a single individual who had either seen the buildings himself or had some memoir of them available (e.g. during the exile). Other sources are completely legendary, like the present narrative of the visit of the Queen of Sheba to Solomon (1 Kgs 10.1-13); we happen to know that the south Arabian kingdom of *Saba* had not yet come into being in Solomon's day. The confusion of the source materials tells us a number of things. In the first place it shows that the Deuteronomistic redactor(s) made use of materials he (they) had not created; rather, they were simply adopted for use from whatever source. In the second place, this also tells us that no attempt was made to evaluate the historicity of the source materials themselves. Thus, the Deuteronomists constructed the Solomon story in accordance with a well-established scheme: on the one hand, Solomon was evaluated positively, because he built the temple, while on the other he was condemned, because he lost control of David's empire. For this reason, the Solomon narrative gradually changes from a broadly positive account to a predominantly negative one (cf. 1 Kgs 11). However, if a historian wishes to undertake a historical evaluation of this period, he or she must make some attempt to penetrate this framework. As far as the following periods are concerned, I shall not attempt to evaluate the sources in a corresponding way, but the reader is hereby cautioned that in every case the situation of the sources is similar to what we have seen to be the case in the narratives about Solomon.

3.3 *The Period of the Divided Monarchy*
3.3.1 *The Partition of the Empire*
With the death of Solomon around 925 BCE the opposition between the king in Jerusalem and his northern subjects burst into flame. The son and successor of Solomon, *Rehoboam*, was forced to journey to Shechem to parley with the leading circles of the northern kingdom, who were presumably the same groups of elders, tribal and lineage leaders who had previously been influential during the coronation of

his grandfather. Even the account of these discussions which is preserved in the Deuteronomistic History (1 Kgs 12) leaves us in no doubt as to the reasons for north Israelite discontent. The Israelite representatives demanded relaxation of the burden of taxation and of corvée requirements, and the king was unwilling to give way on either issue. If the Deuteronomistic account is to be believed, the king appears to have over-estimated his own importance, with the result that he provoked the decisive break himself, and when he sent his overseer of the corvée service to the region, the latter was lynched by representatives of the northern kingdom and the king himself had to flee to save his life.

This account of the break between north and south leaves behind it a number of unanswered questions. The first of these is, where were Solomon's soldiers when this happened? Another is, how did the southern kingdom react? We have no precise information with which to answer these and similar questions, so the following account is necessarily hypothetical. With reference to the first question, it is likely that since the military consisted largely of professional troops their loyalty went by definition to the employer who paid the highest salary. Thus, if the finances of the kingdom were in a chaotic state at this time, as has been suggested above, then this must have expressed itself in terms of diminished standards all across the board, that is, in reductions which affected both the soldiers' equipment and their pay. If to this consideration we add the fact that Solomon's last years were characterized by defeat and stagnation, this fact might provide an explanation for the apparent fact that it was impossible for Rehoboam to seek help from the garrisons in, for example, Megiddo or Hazor, against the rebellious northern tribes. To the contrary, in the subsequent period we discover that when the Jerusalemite king attempted to win lost districts back he was repulsed with ease. Although the first decades following the partition of the empire were not peaceful, Judah had no success against the north. On the other hand, when we look at the *Omride dynasty* in the northern kingdom during the first half of the ninth century BCE, that is, half a century after the break, we learn that their military forces were based on troops of war chariots. Thus it is extremely inviting to assume that the northern garrisons entered the service of the new rulers in the northern part of the country without more ado.

As far as the second question is concerned, the Judaeans remained loyal to their king in Jerusalem. There were no doubt a number of reasons for this, of which the most important was surely the fact that David and his successors themselves belonged to Judaean circles. David was a Judaean, and in reality the bands of solidarity which linked the Judaeans to their king were completely different from the association which related the Davidic dynasty to the northern tribes, since the Judaean relationship was based on convictions of kinship. This means that the Judaeans regarded the king as the representative of their tribe, even though in terms of power he differed significantly from the earlier sort of leader. He was in any case obeyed, since he was able to back up his wishes with force; at the same time however, the Judaeans followed him because he was of the tribal kin.

The converse of this solidarity may have been that the burdens which had previously been levied on the population of the north were not correspondingly imposed on the Judaeans. Thus, some scholars maintain that Judah was kept out of the subdivision into districts which was undertaken by Solomon, which also means that the Judaeans will scarcely have been oppressed by the system of taxation which was based upon it. They were probably also exempt from the corvée labour obligation which so plagued the population of the northern districts. Accordingly the king in Jerusalem was regarded by the Judaean populace as their 'big brother', to whom loyalty was owed, but who also returned the favour by means of dispensations from the obligations which applied to other parts of the kingdom. The people of Judaea were accordingly entitled to regard themselves as the real centre of the empire. By the same token, however, this means that they regarded the northern part of Palestine as a province which could be exploited in the same way as the territories east of the Jordan, as long as they remained within the control of the king. For this reason, the Judaeans continued to regard the dissolution of the empire as treason, that is, as a revolt against themselves and their king; for the same reason the conception of the Davidic empire continued to be adhered to in Judah.

3.3.2 *The Differences between Israel and Judah*
If we look at the history of Israel and Judah as the histories of two independent kingdoms which existed alongside of one another for the next two hundred years, we cannot avoid noticing some significant differences between them both with respect to external and internal affairs. One of the reasons for this is to be sought in the possibilities

available to the respective kingdoms to play an active rôle in the international showplace. Israel's assets consisted in her control of the richest and largest parts of Palestine. Israel also possessed by far the largest population base, and, or so it appears, she had also assumed the power apparatus of the Davidic-Solomonic empire, namely its professional military. Judah's assets, by way of contrast, consisted solely in the greater homogeneity of the kingdom than was the case in the north. In reality, the kingdom of Judah consisted of only a single tribal territory plus a capital city with its attendant lands. Although this city had not previously been a part of Judaean tribal territory and its inhabitants were therefore not members of the tribe of Judah, this occasioned no ideological difficulties for the Judaeans. For one thing, the original inhabitants of the city, the *Jebusites*, were only few in number; for another, they were governed by the Judaean who happened to be king in Jerusalem. In contrast to this, Israel consisted of a number of tribes which, admittedly, even before the introduction of the monarchy had been able on occasion to co-ordinate their forces; but they had also been able to go their own way when they desired and to make independent decisions accordingly. Most of the sizable urban societies belonged to this kingdom, with the exception of the Philistine cities which managed to maintain an independent or quasi-independent existence in the southern part of the coastal region. These urban communities, too, possessed their own tradition which had been determined by the many centuries during which these communities had been independent, whether or not they remained autonomous states after David's assumption of power. They were either reduced to the status of Philistine vassals, or eventually became part of Israelite tribal territory. This means that in Israel the demographic composition of the population was extremely heterogeneous, which entailed that there were many possibilities for conflict between the various components of the population.

3.3.3 *The Monarchies of Israel and Judah*
There are many indications that these were the basic conditions under which the northern kingdom was to attempt to survive in the period following the partition of the empire. Moreover, in this effort the military proved to be a decisive factor. It is characteristic that no dynastic tradition ever evolved in the north comparable to the one which, in spite of all manner of misfortunes, nevertheless kept the

heirs of David on the throne in Jerusalem. In Israel, the whole of the short history of the kingdom witnessed a series of ruling families in which one family replaced the next, only to be subsequently expunged by revolution. Therefore, the German scholar Albrecht Alt held that there was some question of an ancient *democratic* tradition which had been adopted from the previous tribal societies in which, or so he held, the leaders were elected in democratic fashion. According to Alt, just as the accession of Solomon's son Rehoboam had to be approved by representatives of the northern tribes, the northern kings had also to have their election confirmed by representatives of the old tribal system. The theory is incorrect, even though it apparently explains a structural difference between the two kingdoms. In the first place, Alt's suggestion represents a misunderstanding of the procedures by which leaders are appointed in tribal societies, since such procedures are both informal and far less 'democratic' in our sense of the word than Alt supposed. In the second place, it is imperative that we look more closely at the question of just who managed to get themselves elected kings in the northern kingdom and also at the question of who elected them. In most cases, it appears, the candidates were generals, and the corps of electors consisted of their soldiery.

This tendency is most clear in connection with the accession of *Omri* (1 Kgs 16), c. 878 BCE. The legitimate king had been deposed and murdered by the chief of the palace guard in his city of residence, and the officer in question promptly seated himself on the throne. The army, which at the time in question was engaged in a border conflict with the Philistines, reacted to the events in the capital by appointing their own commander king instead, and Omri had little trouble eliminating the usurper in the royal palace. There is some question, however, as to the nature of Omri's position in society, that is, in addition to the fact that he was a general. His relationship to a particular Israelite tribe or to a given family is not mentioned. This fact corresponds to reports in other parts of the ancient Orient, when the throne had been assumed by usurpers of unknown origins, or by those whose origins were illegitimate: they were 'sons of nobodies'. Scholars have also attempted to show on the basis of Omri's name that he was not an Israelite, and since his name could well have been Arabic (identical with Omar) he may have been a professional mercenary soldier who, like David, had a successful career at the royal court and ended by being supreme commander of both the professional chariot troops and the ordinary militia. Of course, we do not know whether this surmise is correct, but some support for it may be provided by the fact that Omri's election did not go unopposed. A rival king by the name of Tibni, the son of Ginath, appeared on the scene, and the fact that his patronymic is mentioned may imply that Tibni was a member of a family which at the time in question was well known. Thus scholars have often regarded Tibni as an authentic Israelite rival candidate to Omri, the foreigner, for the throne of Israel.

Thus for a large part of her history Israel was governed by a number of successful generals; hers was a *military* government whose main base of support was the professional army, and perhaps to a lesser extent the ordinary conscripted soldiery. When it proved feasible to do so, the officers in question were succeeded in the royal office by their sons, which showed that in ideological terms the Israelite monarchy was not understood differently than it was in Judah. Rather, Israel, too, shows a dynastic tendency, and one of the Israelite dynasties, namely that which derived from a general of the chariotry called *Jehu*, lasted for almost a century.

3.3.4 *Local Societies and the State*

A completely different question concerns the reasons why Israel continued to exist as a centralized state after the partition of the empire. One might have thought that the country's experiences with the Davidic kings would have been sufficient in themselves; moreover, there are no indications that the ordinary populace received better conditions under Israelite government than they had previously done under a Judaean one. Nevertheless, the rebellion against Rehoboam resulted in the election of a local revolutionary leader in the struggle against Solomon, namely Jeroboam, the son of Nebat (note the patronymic!) as king of the northern part of what had been the Davidic empire. The correct explanation for this is most probably that there was no good alternative to the centralized system. If the society of the north intended to retain its independence of the rule of Jerusalem, then the political cohesiveness of the kingdom had to equal that of Judah. We should also recall that the introduction of the monarchy, which at this time lay eighty years in the past, must have entailed a number of both greater and lesser structural changes in Israelite society. The first of these was the creation of a class of administrators who were active on both the central and the local planes, and who were paid by the state. Of course, such a system also signifies that a system had also been erected by which it was possible to collect the taxes which supported such a class. Another significant factor is the continued existence of the class of professional soldiers. Naturally, as far as the lower ranks were concerned, it was possible to dismiss the soldiery; but as far as the élite chariotry was concerned, it is likely that as had been the case in the Late Bronze Age these forces approached the status of a warrior nobility. They were in the king's service and were remunerated directly by him in the form of rations; but they were also indirectly paid by a latifundium-like arrangement, meaning that they received endowments of land, complete with tenants, in fief. Moreover, the monarchy must also have changed the economic presuppositions of other groups in Israelite society through the creation or strengthening of the class of artisans, who either sold their products directly or else received payment for them from the central administration.

In short, even the smallest village in the Israelite kingdom had for more than a generation been part of a national economy consisting of taxation, markets, and more or less enforced military or labour service. The latter features had caused the crisis which came to fruition on the death of Solomon, but these practices had nevertheless established themselves so that they must also have played a part in the social system under the dynasty of Omri, as we may deduce from the numerous sizable remains of monumental construction projects which date from this period.

3.3.5 *Rich and Poor: The Collapse of Tribal Solidarity*
Yet another matter about which we have no information from the early part of the history of the northern kingdom, but only from the latter part, is the relationship between rich and poor in the country. In the latter days of the history of the northern kingdom under the last kings of the Jehu dynasty in the eighth century BCE, the social criticisms of two prophets seems to suggest that the land-owning peasantry were in poor fettle because of debt accumulation. The problem is well known throughout the ancient Orient, both past and present. Cultivation of land is inevitably dependent on the vagaries of climate. Within a given period of time, such as a decade, it is almost certain that there will be at least one or two (and in periods of real drought three or four) years in which the amount of precipitation

is insufficient, with disastrous harvests in consequence. For the land-owning peasant this has usually entailed that he has had to eat what grain has remained to him after nature and the state have both had their share. Thus, seed has to be purchased either from royal stores or from those of wealthy men who have been able to store up a surplus.

It is to be recalled that in antiquity there was no such thing as liquid capital, but only payment in kind. In ancient Israel this meant that in the event of poor harvests the peasant had to borrow his seed for planting from those who were better situated than himself, and he had to pay his debt back, plus interest, in the form of portions of his grain production. Accordingly, if the harvest failed for two years running the peasant was in serious trouble, for he would then be unable to pay off his creditors. In many cases he was no doubt forced to sell his lands to his creditors, in which case he may sometimes have remained on the land under contract to his creditors as a copyholder. In the Bronze Age this process was a familiar one, and it was one of the more important reasons for the previously mentioned refugee problem which arose in the second millennium BCE. In the first millennium BCE in the Israel of the monarchical period a similar process seems to have developed, although at that time the possibility of flight was no longer present, because the territory which had previously given refuge to the runaways was now the central territory of the state. Although the social criticisms in the Old Testament do not permit us to say anything at all about the extent of this difficulty which turned land-owning peasants into copyholders, there is no reason to believe that it was a peripheral problem. Analogies from the twentieth century CE show that such a social process may be completed within only one or two generations. Thus a free peasantry may totally cease to exist within the space of fifty years.

Of course, it is impossible to say with certainty how conditions in Israel really were in the last part of the tenth century BCE, although there are some indications that the process which leads to the impoverishment of the common person was already underway then. Earlier, that is to say, already prior to the introduction of the monarchy, such tendencies might have been halted by the internal kinship solidarity forces of the society, but such solidarity was no doubt weakened during the subsequent period. This is one important indication that the tribal system was slowly but surely losing its importance for the common person at this time. As a political organism, the tribe had no rôle to play within the state apart from such exceptional events as in the confrontation with Rehoboam in Shechem or during the earlier uprising against David. The state had assumed into itself all the normal functions of the tribe. Of course, kinship groups still existed and in fact continued to do so; but outside the local society they had no importance, since they were not a factor capable of opposing the centralized state. Eventually, even their local importance became reduced as local administrators were introduced in connection with the development of the national administration.

The actual relative power status of the state versus the peasant is expressed with clarity by the narrative of Naboth's vineyard (1 Kgs 21). Naboth's problem is that his vineyard is situated in the vicinity of one of the royal residential cities in the north, Jezreel, and that the king, Ahab, desires to include it among his own possessions. Naboth refuses to accede to the royal request for the reason that the land in question is the property of his lineage; he cannot sell it, no matter what the king should happen to offer for it. The king, or rather, his queen, the notorious Jezebel, knows how to deal with such matters. She had Naboth arraigned on a false charge which leads to his condemnation and execution, allowing the state to confiscate the vineyard.

This narrative is part of the cycle of legends which is associated with the prophet Elijah, and as such it cannot be used as a direct historical source relevant to events in the days of Ahab, that is, in the first half of the ninth century BCE. However, it remains in any case a good indication of the change in power relationships between the state and the traditional social structure to the advantage of the state. It is also evidence of the arbitrariness which no doubt attended the royal administration; this was a factor for which the ordinary Israelite had no remedy. He could only accept it, however unwillingly.

We are told very little about social conditions in Judah before the eighth century BCE, at which time criticisms of the social situation are made by several prophets. These criticisms more than imply that a corresponding evolution had also taken place in Judah, in spite of the fact that the point of departure was somewhat different than it was in the north. In other words, one might have expected more tribal solidarity to obtain in Judah which was, after all, a one-tribe kingdom. But, to the contrary, we are told by the criticisms launched by *Micah of Moresheth*, one of the lesser provincial towns of Judah, against the wealth of Jerusalem, that the local peasantry was to a considerable extent in the clutches of the élite class of the nation, the rich merchants and lofty administrators who resided in the capital.

Yet another facet of the socio-economic developments in Judah, and one concerning which we are somewhat better informed, if from a slightly later date, is the emergence of royal estates. Such royal estates were distributed throughout the country, but of course they were necessarily situated where the earlier local societies had once owned the land in question, and which they had replaced. Obviously, we have no way of knowing whether in each case such confiscations were at the expense of people like Naboth. However, Naboth's main argument, that he was unable to transfer ownership of property belonging to his kin, tells us about a fundamental conflict which must have taken place between the state and the peasantry as to the ownership of the land. Naboth's remark suggests that even if the land in question was his own, it also belonged to his kinfolk, so that he was obliged to let it remain in the hands of his kinfolk. This was a substantive obligation, as we learn from a narrative in the book of Jeremiah (ch. 32) in which Jeremiah serves as the 'redeemer' of ancestral property in his hometown of Anatoth, a few kilometres to the north of Jerusalem. The field in question was about to pass from the ownership of the family, for which reason there was a moral obligation on the relatives of the owner of the land in question to pay back the sum for indebtedness of the field. The state could not tolerate property relations based on kinship ties, and the emergence of royal estates in Judah demonstrates how the state was forced to co-exist in a latent conflict with the traditional socio-economic system.

This latent conflict is further implied by the speech which the Deuteronomistic redactor put in Samuel's mouth in connection with the election of the first king (1 Sam. 8.11-17). Here we are told that the king has the 'right' to conscript the general population for military service, for fieldwork, and for other functions within the purview of the state's housekeeping. He could also confiscate 'fields, vineyards, and olive orchards' and give them to his administrators in fief. He was also able to tax the produce of the private sector to pay the public sector; in short, *the populace were the slaves of the king*. Although some scholars have held that this description applies to the city-states of the Bronze Age, it is far more likely that in this passage the *Deuteronomists* are describing the experiences of the populations of Judah and Israel under their respective monarchies. In other words, the practices mentioned were those which were normally the case in Israelite society, as long as it remained a nation state.

3.3.6 *The Citizen and the State*

None of the many revolutions which took place in the northern kingdom in particular ever changed the relationship between the state and its citizens. The nation-state system had become a permanent feature in both Judah and Israel, and internal forces within the two societies were no longer able to change this fact. On the other hand, the tensions between the interests of the two states and those of their inhabitants must have been a destabilizing factor. The destruction of the land-owning peasantry, which had once comprised by far the major part of the populations in question, resulted in the creation of two social classes, the haves and the have-nots. This development must have been synonymous with a weakening of the internal feelings of solidarity in the country which linked the populace to one another. In Israel, this solidarity will, in any case, have had a hard time of it, because of the heterogeneity of the populace. Judah, of course, was more predisposed towards internal cohesion, if the necessary socio-political presuppositions were present or were to arise. However, there is absolutely no suggestion that the central authorities in either the north or the south had any intentions in this direction. In fact, we can point to a contrary instance during a drought in which the state dealt in a fashion counter to the interests of the populace at large by ensuring its right to the exploitation of the available pasturage for its horses and asses. It need hardly be pointed out that these are two rather unproductive aspects of the national economy; moreover, on this occasion the state also reserved the available water resources for itself (1 Kgs 18.2-6).

There are accordingly no indications that the ordinary Israelite identified himself with his state as the members of the later European nation-states were to do. Rather, Israel, and perhaps to a lesser degree Judah as well, developed in the course of their history into states which were not significantly different from the city-states which had existed in the region during the Bronze Age. In other words, the basis of the state was the territory it controlled, and its economic basis consisted of the taxes and imposts which it was possible to squeeze out of the local population. Just who this population was, and what traditional rights it may have had to its lands, was of no interest to the state.

The foreign powers which occupied the country, that is, in the first instance, the Assyrians, followed by the Babylonians, were quite aware of these structural properties of the territories they had conquered. There was, therefore, an easy way available to them to tackle the problems caused by the continual revolts against their authority. The population at large was essentially uninterested in the question of who happened to rule at any given time, as such changes did not change the circumstances of their existence. It was not the peasantry who led such rebellions, but the élite, that is, the ruling class and its representatives. If the élite stratum were to be removed and replaced with a loyal élite of foreign origin who would rule the country, the tendencies towards unrest would be likewise excised. As far as the Assyrians are concerned, this policy seems to have succeeded, as we find no indications of any feelings of national identity in the former Israel in the period after the fall of Samaria in 722 BCE, and certainly none in the post-exilic period. The deportees also disappeared from the historical arena, not because they were liquidated, but because their attachment to their country of origin consisted in an ideological identification with the Israelite state, whereas their connections with the land itself were mainly economic in character. The members of this stratum had lost their economic basis because of the deportations, but they encountered new possibilities to establish themselves economically in the territories where they were resettled, and no doubt on terms which were similar to those with which they were already familiar. Under such new conditions their allegiance was not directed towards a king in Samaria, but towards the Assyrian state, on which they had become dependent.

The Babylonian exile experience was different from the Assyrian deportation in that the group which the Babylonians deported did not abandon their identity and instead continued to associate this identity with their old life in Palestine. Thus, this group was later in a position to return to its former home carrying a quite evolved programme for the society which it intended to found there. In the years between 722 and 587 BCE a process had thus come into being in Judah which was ultimately to lead to the emergence of the *Jewish* society of the post-exilic period.

4. *History as Intellectual Experience: The Development of a National Identity*

4.1 *Introduction*

The background for the preservation of the Israelite-Jewish society through the crucial years of the Babylonian exile is to be sought in the history of Israel and Judah during the period of the monarchy, or else in the pre-national period. In saying this, political history is not intended, since in this respect, as we have seen, Israel and Judah did not differ significantly from other west Asiatic states which met the same sad fate and which, however, disappeared from the forum of history without leaving noteworthy traces behind them. Rather, we have to do with intellectual history, which is to say, that way the Israelite and Judaean peoples experienced their history; that is, the interpretation which they put on that history and the conclusions which they drew from it. This section will accordingly concern itself with what, for want of a better expression might perhaps be called the 'spiritual culture' of the two countries during the monarchical period. In this connection the material culture is largely irrelevant, and, in passing, it might be mentioned that the few genuinely Israelite and Judaean material remains which the archeologists have unearthed, such as the ivory decorations from the royal palace in Samaria, are either of foreign origin or were produced by foreign artisans. The decoration of the temple and palace complex in Jerusalem was similarly left to the care of foreign agents (cf. 1 Kgs 7. 13-40).

An examination of the intellectual currents which led to the emergence of a Jewish sense of national identity is necessarily connected with the question of religion. It would not be appropriate here to attempt an analysis of the history of the Israelite-Jewish religion, although a brief attempt to do this will be offered in the last chapter of this work. However, in this section it will be necessary to utilize some of the results arising from such a study. One should above all else be aware of the fact that the emergence of the monotheistic type of religion to which the Old Testament bears witness was a result of conscious reflection based on the Israelite experiences of the monarchical period. The point of departure of Israelite religion seems to have been polytheistic, like all the other types of religion which are attested in the west Semitic ambit. Somehow, and against the background of particular conditions, the emergence of a peculiar *Israelite-Jewish religion* went hand in hand

with the emergence of the *Israelite-Jewish people*. As mentioned
previously, we shall return to this issue in the concluding section on
the history of Israelite-Jewish religion. Here, some attempt to
describe these features in terms of the sociology of religions will be
useful, as it might help us to understand the circles within the region
which were responsible for these religious developments.

The concrete formulation of the new or revised contents of
Israelite religion is associated in our sources with the prophetic
movement in ancient Israel and Judah. In other words, this type of
religion tries to trace its origins back to the middle and latter part of
the eighth century BCE, that is, to the first of the writing prophets,
Amos and Hosea in the north, and Isaiah and Micah in the south.
However, it seems as if the proclamation by these figures of Yahweh
as the sole God of Israel and their rejection, or at least serious
criticism, of both official and unofficial religious practices in their
times was not without more ado either accepted or understood by
their contemporaries. Nor, for that matter, would their criticisms
have been at all relevant, if the populace had not in fact cultivated
religious interests other than those advocated by the prophets in
question. Neither the leadership strata nor the general public in
either of the two countries shared the basic religious views of the
early writing prophets. This type of religion was, rather, the
exclusive property of some *reformers*, which is probably the best
description of these early writing prophets, since their message was
at once both new and ancient.

Naturally, these observations raise the question as to the presuppositions of these writing prophets. To what extent can they be
considered the inheritors of earlier tradition? The Deuteronomistic
History is rich in legends about prophets and in speeches which have
been inserted into the mouths of prophets; these span the period
from the introduction of the monarchy to its final dissolution.
Unfortunately, we have no way of knowing whether or not, or to
what extent, the Deuteronomists actually had ancient prophetic
traditions at their disposal. Thus, in spite of the fact that the
Deuteronomistic prophetic traditions reveal a number of common
features, we cannot regard them as historical sources. Such features
may well have been the result of the redactional activity itself, which
either utilized an earlier tradition or even created this tradition
('fictionalized').

4.2 Ideological Tendencies in the Northern Kingdom
4.2.1 The Religious Struggle of the Ninth Century BCE
The central prophetic traditions in the Deuteronomistic History are
undoubtedly the narratives dealing with Elijah and Elisha (1 Kgs 17–
2 Kgs 13). We have already characterized these stories as largely
legendary; close analysis of them shows that in considerable part
they consist of miracle stories about holy men. Taken together they
make up one of perhaps two narrative cycles which the Deuteronomistic redactors worked into a historical framework, although this
provides no guarantee of historical accuracy. If, however, we follow
the approximate Deuteronomistic chronology, then the two prophets
Elijah and Elisha represented a consciously *Yahwistic* reaction to the
Omride dynasty. In a corresponding way, tradition-historical analysis
of the Elisha legends shows a connection between this prophet and
the subsequent dynasty, namely that of *Jehu*. Thus we see that it was
supposed to have been Elisha who anointed Jehu king (2 Kgs 9), and
the same prophet seems also to have played a rôle as court prophet at
Jehu's court in Samaria, although the tradition emphasizes that he
was sometimes difficult to deal with.

With all the necessary reservations because of the late reworking
of these traditions, it is nevertheless possible to use this cycle of
stories as evidence that there was popular resistance to the royal
power in the north as early as the first half of the ninth century BCE.
We hear nothing about corresponding movements in the south. This
resistance ultimately led to the expulsion from power of the Omrides
and their total destruction as a result of the revolution which brought
the general Jehu, son of Nimshi, son of Jehoshaphat (2 Kgs 9.2) to
power. Already back when Omri assumed power there had been
opposition to his ascension, opposition which was perhaps rooted
in circles that could not accept that a 'son of a nobody' could rule
over them (see above). Prior to the reign of Omri, there had been two
short-lived dynasties in the northern kingdom, that of Jeroboam
(more precisely, 'the Ephraimite Jeroboam, the son of Nebat, from
Seredah... whose mother's name was Zeruah'; 1 Kgs 11.26), and
that of Ba'asha ('the son of Ahijah, of the house of Issachar'; 1 Kgs
15.27). We should note that in both instances the familial and tribal
affiliations of both figures are carefully listed, implying that they
belonged to what were apparently old and influential Israelite
families. The name of Tibni's father (Ginath) is likewise listed; thus
it is possible to regard Tibni's supporting party as consisting of the

same families of powerful nobles which had also supported the families of Jeroboam and Ba'asha, and among whose number these royal families really belonged—at least as far as their placement in the social hierarchy is concerned.

The kings of the Omride dynasty occupied the throne thanks to their position as soldier kings, and they appear to have enjoyed little support from the Israelite noble families because of their illegitimate origins. Thus, if the Omride dynasty was to establish its power, it had to do so by building marital contacts to its potential opponents. They chose, however, a different policy, since they apparently failed to recognize just how precarious their position was. This policy consisted in the attempt to strengthen their position by entering into international marital agreements, which ultimately allowed the *femme fatale* of the Omride dynasty, namely *Jezebel*, the daughter of the king of Tyre, to make her appearance in Israel. A constant feature of the Elijah and Elisha narratives is that although Ahab appears not to have been popular in his own time (or at least in the view of later times), his unpopularity is insignificant with respect to the distinctive hatred towards his wife which fairly seeps from the texts dealing with this period. The traditions in the Deuteronomistic History concentrate on the religio-political situation in the Omride period, although the socio-political problems are not fully ignored (consider the Naboth narrative). The sources indicate that in this period the internal religious contradictions were prominent, and that they were exacerbated after the accession of Jehu to the throne, when a bloody purge of certain religious phenomena took place. Among those who participated in the slaughter of the priests of Ba'al was a figure who represents a movement about which we possess some much later information (Jeremiah 35), and which, at least in Jeremiah's day, had developed into an ascetic Yahwistic sect, the so-called *Rechabites*. The ancestral father of this group was Jonadab, the son of Rechab, who is supposed to have assisted Jehu in his purge of the official cult in the time of Ahab (2 Kgs 10.15-17).

There is some question as to whether the offical religion under the Omrides did not manifest a particular development which provoked a reaction among those parts of the populace (the important old Israelite families) who were already not favourably disposed towards the dynasty. In this connection it has been pointed out that Jezebel came from Tyre, and that the official god of Tyre was a peculiar manifestation of the west semitic deity, Ba'al, who in Tyre was regarded as the lord and creator of the world under the name *Ba'al Shamayim*, the 'Ba'al of Heaven'. It would not be unreasonable to suppose that this deity was introduced into Palestine in connection with Ahab's Tyrian marriage, and for this reason came to threaten the position of Yahweh, the national deity. No doubt one of the reasons for this development was the use of the *bull calf* as a symbol of Yahweh in the northern kingdom (see below), since it was possible to reinterpret this iconographic depiction of Yahweh as a picture of Ba'al (and this may in fact have occurred). Thus, an opposition to the ruling house whose original roots were probably social, being, as they were, grounded in the non-existent pedigree of Omri, that is, in his foreign origins, received its ideological contents in the form of religious opposition to the Omride dynasty.

Of course, we must ignore the fact that the accounts of these events are strongly tendentious in an anti-Omride vein. In fact, there are other not unimportant indications to the effect that Ahab himself attempted to reinforce his position by emphasizing the Israelite national god, Yahweh. Among other things are the names of the two sons who succeeded him, *Ahaziah* and *Joram*, as well as that of his daughter *Athaliah*, who for a transitional period was the reigning queen in Judah. It is to be observed that *Yahweh* is the *theophoric* element in all three names. However, Ahab's demonstration of respect for Yahweh, implicit in the names of his children, did not interest the authors who were behind the traditions in the books of the Kings which deal with the Omride dynasty. Rather, they directed their entire attention to the foreign religious element, the Tyrian Ba'al. If we take their account at face value (and on this point it is probably quite reliable), Ba'al's rôle in Samaria was at an end from the moment Omri's dynasty fell. Just as the dynasty itself was eliminated, the Israelites also brutally liquidated both the priesthood of this deity and the circles in Samaria who had bound their fate to the house of Omri and to Ba'al. We shall never know just who these people were, but it would probably not be wholly wrong to assume that there was a considerable Tyrian presence in the capital which may even have comprised an administrative élite, just as Tyrian or at least Phoenician artisans were active in the town in connection with the decoration of the palace. For these reasons it is justifiable to regard Jehu's revolution as a genuine Israelite reaction to a foreign dominance of both religious and political character. Of course, there is some question as to whether this contra-revolution had permanent consequences, and as to the circles for which it was important.

4.2.2 'Official' and 'Unofficial' Religion in the Northern Kingdom

There are no sources which can with certainty be said to apply to the religious development spanning the years between Jehu and the two north Israelite writing prophets, Amos (who, however, was of Judaean origin) and Hosea, that is, the period between c. 845 to c. 750 BCE. Moreover, as far as the situation in the middle of the eighth century BCE is concerned, we have to draw our conclusions on the basis of the descriptions offered by these two prophets, who are anything but neutral sources. We mentioned above that the figures in question may be regarded as representatives of a new religious attitude; they were opponents of the official cult of the northern kingdom on the one hand and of private piety on the other. The official religion was associated with the great sanctuaries, and above all with the royal sanctuary in Bethel, where Yahweh had been worshipped under the external aspect of Ba'al's bull calf at least since the days of Jeroboam Ben Nebat, but possibly also earlier (cf. Ch. 6 §4.1.2). This fact more than implies that the religious struggle against the Omride dynasty was not caused by the enmity between Yahwistic religion and the local worship of Ba'al, but rather by the collision between the local religion and the worship of the foreign deity, which had attempted to replace the local religion. Jehu's revolution entailed no changes for the unofficial local worship in the kingdom, but the Tyrian influence on the official religion was excised. On the other hand, the cult in Bethel continued to exist as long as the kingdom did.

Similarly, if we are to believe these two severe critics of the unofficial religion, unofficial piety followed the traditional lines which characterized the worship of Ba'al in the region in general. In other words, neither the state nor its populace in the middle of the ninth century BCE regarded the break with the foreign religion as an expression of any general opposition between Yahwistic and Canaanite religion. Rather, they saw it as it was, namely as a conflict between local gods and a foreign deity. If the prophets of the eighth century BCE represented a reaction against the worship of their contemporaries, then the background was a different one than that which had obtained in the days of the Omrides. It is necessary to find a different Sitz im Leben for the religious attitude which regarded Yahweh as the sole god of Israel, and which found itself in sharp conflict with all other worship within Israelite society.

The question is, where are we to seek this undercurrent within

Israelite society which led to the emergence of a criticism of the official religion of the country? As far as the structure of Israelite society during the Jehu dynasty is concerned, we may presume that there was both political and ideological agreement between the Jehu dynasty and that part of society which had supported its attack on the Omrides after the liquidation of the foreign elements during the revolution of 845 BCE. Thus it was traditional Israelite society which formed Jehu's support group and which enjoyed the fruits of the developments brought about by his dynasty, even though the tribal system as such had ceased to play any rôle in daily Israelite life. This party probably consisted of wealthy land-owners from the various local societies; these made up the élite from among whom the leaders of the kingdom were chosen. It was this social group which profited from the socio-economic developments created by the Jehu dynasty; but it was also this group who later had to be deported by the Assyrians and who disappeared in Mesopotamia. Thus it is not among ordinary Israelites that we must seek the counter-ideology on which the later Yahwistic reform movement based its efforts. The religion of the people in general was still characterized by the traditional fertility cult which we have been accustomed to call 'Canaanite'. However, the prophets, who were the spokesmen of the reform movement, had the broad mass of the populace as their target group; it was to them, and to the leadership strata, that their criticisms of the predominant religious practices were directed. They were the group who were to be reformed.

4.2.3 *Bethel and Shechem*
It is accordingly necessary to find some other instance in Israelite society in which the religious tradition which led to the reform movement(s) had its origins, and in this connection it would be natural to look to the various sanctuaries in the country. In other words, we must attempt to point to a sanctuary which was the hotbed of a religious tradition which claimed to be old, but which on the other hand was not identical with the official religious attitude of the élite of the society. On the basis of these presuppositions, Bethel is out of the question, as is evidenced by the criticisms of Bethel and its cult which were voiced by Amos and Hosea (Amos 5.5; cf. 7.10-17; Hos. 4.15; 8.5f.; 13.2). It is very likely that the priesthood of Bethel regarded themselves as the heirs of the religious tradition which formed the background for Jehu's revolution, but the

Yahwistic religion as practised at this site can hardly have agreed with the Old Testament understanding of legitimate Yahweh worship.

There were, however, other sanctuaries in the country which could be considered in this connection such as, for example, Gilgal, near the River Jordan. Indeed, Gilgal plays such an important rôle in the Deuteronomistic account of the Settlement that readers might be led to believe that it is here that we must seek the point of departure of 'mono-Yahwism', as some scholars prefer to term Israelite religion. However, Gilgal was also one of the sanctuaries against which Amos and Hosea directed their criticisms, as they did in the case of Bethel (Amos 4.4; Hos. 4.15; 9.15; 12.12), for which reason Gilgal is hardly a prominent candidate. We are left with Shechem as the hotbed of this religious tradition, which during the period of the monarchy in the north created an unofficial counterweight to the official religion. We have discussed the Shechem traditions previously, and in this connection it was pointed out that the Deuteronomistic History contains mainly positive references in the traditions about this site. The Abimelech narrative in Judges 9, however, is not unduly positive towards this town, and this section relates that the deity worshipped in Shechem was known by the name of *Ba'al Berith*, the 'Ba'al of the covenant', or *El Berith*, the 'El of the covenant'. Thus it is impossible to deny that there may be some connection between this divine designation and the Old Testament covenantal theology, which is otherwise associated with Shechem (see below). No matter how ancient or young this covenant tradition may happen to be, and in spite of the Canaanite divine names, El and Ba'al, the Deuteronomistic History is so predominantly positive towards this locality that it is not improbable that the Deuteronomistic movement regarded Shechem as its traditional home.

Shechem played a rôle in the northern kingdom at the beginning of the period of the monarchy which might be of interest in this connection. In the days of Rehoboam, Shechem was still of such importance that it was the natural place for the encounter between the Jerusalemite king and the representatives of the northern populace. When Jeroboam assumed the throne in the north, he naturally chose Shechem as his capital, although he soon abandoned the site in favour of the territory east of the Jordan, and settled ultimately on Tirza, about ten to fifteen kilometres north east of Shechem. Jeroboam's reason for changing his place of residence may have been an Egyptian razzia which was carried out by Pharaoh Shishak a few years after the death of Solomon, and which affected large parts of the territory west of the Jordan. Shishak's brief excursion into Palestine explains the first removal to the east, but it does not explain Jeroboam's subsequent abandonment of Shechem. Apparently there had arisen some tensions between Shechem and the new king which are reflected in the latter's choice of new national sanctuaries, of which the most important was located at Bethel. We have scarcely any idea what happened to the sanctuary at Shechem, although it can be demonstrated archeologically that the religious tradition of the town was interrupted at this point in time. During the monarchical period, at the site in Shechem where there once had been a temple which may have been dedicated to Ba'al Berith there was instead an official grain storehouse.

It is possible that in Shechem people did not accept the degradation of their ancient sanctuary, and that they remained in constant opposition to the new national sanctuary of Bethel. This opposition is tangible in the Deuteronomistic History, in which the description of the period of the divided monarchy is more or less framed by two traditions about Bethel. One of these deals with the curses launched by a Judaean prophet against the cult-site (1 Kgs 13), while the other deals with king Josiah's later fulfilment of this prophecy (2 Kgs 23.15-20). There are therefore good reasons for regarding Shechem as a centre for the emergence of an antimonarchical tradition in the northern kingdom, a tradition which in part criticized the monarchy as an institution and in part criticized the official practice of religion in the country. Of course, as to the rôle played by Shechem (and there may have been other sanctuaries which suffered the same fate, and in which the same resentment of the official Israel existed) during the monarchical era before the fall of the northern kingdom we can only guess. However, there is nothing which suggests that the town ever had more than regional significance in this period. As long as the sanctuary in Bethel continued to exist, the people of Israel do not seem to have turned to Shechem as the legitimate ancient sanctuary of central and northern Palestine. It is possible that Shechem first seriously became the official centre of north Israelite tradition after the fall of the northern kingdom, when the traditions which had been associated with the site received a new homeland in the southern kingdom in the time subsequent to 722 BCE.

4.3 *Intellectual Developments in Judah after 722: Deuteronomism*
4.3.1 *Refugees from the North*

The intellectual development in Judah after the fall of the northern kingdom is inseparable from the appearance of Deuteronomism. It is accordingly imperative for anyone who deals with this period to investigate the identity of the Deuteronomists, their place of origin, their message and antecedent tradition, and, finally their influence on the Judaean religious experience towards the end of the monarchy and, particularly, later. Any such investigation must also take account of the fact that other traditions were also active in the Deuteronomists' own times; these were movements which either ran parallel to Deuteronomism or were opposed to it. Finally, one ought not to ignore the fact that in the period from 722 to 630 BCE Judah was a vassal kingdom of the Assyrian empire. Cultural loans from the vast Mesopotamian sphere were not insignificant in this period, and they probably express themselves more frequently in the Old Testament than is commonly assumed. Nor should one overlook the possibility that the Deuteronomists themselves were influenced by Mesopotamian thought.

But above all else there is the question of an influence on the spiritual climate in Judah whose roots were in the sometimes northern kingdom, and which must have been imported by refugees from the north. Admittedly, we do not actually know that there was such a stream of refugees in the period after 722 BCE, but in consideration of the fate of the northern kingdom in that year and in the decades preceding it, it would be reasonable to suppose that there was a considerable influx of refugees from the north. The north origin of important aspects of the Judaean cultural picture as well as the northern contribution to the development of a specifically Judaean national ideology in this period are incontestable, particularly in view of the sizable number of genuinely northern (i.e. Israelite) traditions which were absorbed by the Judaean tradition in the time subsequent to 722 BCE. Considerable parts of this Israelite traditional material have left their imprint on the history of the religion; this applies to such materials as the Sinai tradition, the Exodus tradition, the Jacob narratives, and so forth, of which there are no traces in the Old Testament sources of Judaean origin in the period prior to the fall of Samaria. Thus, for example, not one of these traditions is so much as mentioned by the Judaean prophets, Isaiah and Micah— that is, as far as the genuine pronouncements of these two figures are concerned. On the other hand, there were references to the Exodus and the Settlement in particular, but also to the patriarch Jacob, in the works of the prophet Hosea. Against this, the main part of such references in the works of Amos derive from the Deuteronomistic redaction. As far as the Judaeans were concerned their early history began with David and with the Davidic empire, whereas in Israel we find a tradition about the past which at least superficially goes much further back.

There have been many theories as to the identity of the Deuteronomists; in reality, scholars are only agreed on the conclusion that they must have originated in the earlier northern kingdom. However, there is reason to examine the nature of the traditions which they passed on as well as their essential message. As far as the first factor is concerned, there is a notable predominance of traditions dealing with northern sanctuaries, above all Shechem. As for the second feature, the proclamation of Yahweh as the sole god of Israel is central. It would therefore be appropriate to seek the roots of Deuteronomism in a religious tradition which derived from the northern kingdom, although this could not have been the national cult as expressed and practised in Bethel. Rather, its background is to be sought in an unofficial tradition which existed alongside of the official one, but at such ancient sanctuaries as the one at Shechem. When we consider the general religious attitude of the population at large, as characterized by its prophetic critics, namely Amos and Hosea, there is no reason to suppose that Deuteronomism derived from any 'populistic' movement in the earlier Israel. Rather, its origins were most likely to have been situated among a *religious élite* which had been relegated to the outer darkness by official Israel, and which no longer played any significant rôle as far as the general religious consciousness was concerned. In short, it would be reasonable to suppose that the Deuteronomists were the successors of refugees from the north who once had their roots at sanctuaries like the one in Shechem. These individuals had most likely comprised the priesthood of these sanctuaries, and their political significance had been nullified by the central administration and its official cult. For this very reason they no doubt escaped deportation, since these figures did not belong to the leading circles of the northern kingdom in 722 BCE.

The first result of the activities of the refugees in their new homeland is perhaps to be detected in the cult reform which

Hezekiah carried out towards the close of the eighth century BCE (2 Kgs 18.1-8). Of course, we have only a vague idea of the precise programme of this reform, since only the Deuteronomistic description of it has been preserved, and we have no way of knowing to what extent this description has been 'coloured'. However, one ought to note the removal of *Nehushtan*, a cult object in the form of a bronze serpent which tradition assigns to the agency of Moses (cf. Num. 21.4-9). In consideration of the elevated status which is otherwise assigned to the figure of Moses in Old Testament tradition, both in the Tetrateuch and in Deuteronomy, this part of the cult reform must reflect a fact which the Deuteronomists found impossible to deny. Thus, the destruction of the bronze serpent informs us that, at this time the figure of Moses had not yet achieved the exalted status which it subsequently received in the traditions about Israel's past. And this fact also suggests that at this time the Deuteronomistic understanding of Moses had not yet decisively influenced the religious attitude in Judah; nor had it as yet found its final form.

4.3.2 *The 'Pax Assyriaca'*

The arrival of the refugees from the north did not entail an instantaneous change of the religious life in Judah. Both the official religion and the more popular variety continued to be practised in the following centuries to such an extent that the Deuteronomistic efforts at reform had their work cut out for them. Above all in the long reign of Manasseh, concerning which practically nothing is preserved in the Deuteronomistic History except an exceptionally negative evaluation of the king himself (2 Kgs 21.1-18), Deuteronomistic influence must have been slight indeed. This lengthy period of 'wandering in the desert' by the refugees and their successors is eloquent in its silence about a time which in most other respects seems to have witnessed considerable Judaean success, not least because Manasseh's loyalty to his Assyrian masters ensured peace for half a century. In this age when Judah was able to enjoy the blessings of the *pax assyriaca*, trade prospered, and the Assyrian cultural tradition had uncontested opportunity to express itself. We can only guess as to the extent of cultural loans made by the Judaeans in this period, in spite of the long series of traditions, particularly those in the 'primeval history' (Gen. 1-11), whose Mesopotamian origin seems evident. Nevertheless, we are forced to guess about these matters, since we have no assured criteria to enable us to distinguish between influences which may have been felt in the seventh century BCE, and those which may have expressed themselves in the sixth century BCE (the period of the Exile).

Even the Deuteronomists themselves do not seem to have escaped a degree of influence from Mesopotamian tradition. The question of the extent of Assyrian influence on the Deuteronomists has never been thoroughly explored, but it is possible to point to a number of areas in which we may infer such influence. Above all, the characteristic Deuteronomistic expression of the relationship between Yahweh and Israel, is that of a relationship regulated by a *covenant*. The formulation of this relationship in the book of Deuteronomy displays considerable resemblances to the political treaties in use at the time, particularly those which were administered by the Assyrians. Admittedly, some scholars have argued that the background of the Old Testament covenant traditions is to be sought in the Hittite vassal treaties which had linked Hittite kings with monarchs in northern Syria already back in the Late Bronze Age. However, there are many reasons for regarding the culture-historical background of the sort of covenants we encounter in the Old Testament as stemming from the treaties of the first millennium BCE, the Assyrian ones in particular. Although we cannot prove it, it is not impossible that this type of treaty was quite well known in Judah during the period when the land was an Assyrian vassal state. Such vassal relationships were ordinarily regulated by a treaty of the above-mentioned sort, a copy of which would have been preserved in Jerusalem and read publicly from time to time. The Deuteronomists appear to have been familiar with the scheme employed in such treaties, and they used *parts* of this scheme when they formulated their own special covenantal theology.

Another example of the way in which Assyrian tradition may have influenced Deuteronomistic thought has to do with the understanding of the monarchy. According to the Deuteronomistic view, the king is *the servant of Yahweh*, even though they themselves deliver countless examples to show that the kings were by no means faithful servants. The king was therefore held to be a *man* to whom Yahweh had entrusted a particular office, for which reason he was directly responsible to Yahweh for his conduct in office. Naturally, this is not a monarchical ideology which the Deuteronomists invented all by themselves, since its roots, as well as the notion that the king was the 'servant' of the deity, can be traced back to the Late Bronze Age. The

Palestinian petty kings had been 'the servants of Pharaoh', and, according to Egyptian ideology, the Pharaoh was divine.

However, a different royal ideology is expressed in such texts as Psalms 2 and 110, in which the Davidic king is regarded as god or godlike. Such conceptions could conceivably be reminiscences of the imperial period under Solomon, in which the Judaean king described himself in this way as Pharaoh's heir. It is to be noted that this ideology was wholly foreign to the Assyrians. The Assyrians regarded the king as the *vicegerent of the deity*, and they took this conception entirely literally. As the vicegerent of the god Asshur, the Assyrian king was responsible for his conduct in office to Asshur, and he was accordingly obliged to report his righteous administration to the deity. Thus it is conceivable that the resuscitation and powerful re-emphasis on the 'human' understanding of the king were features which had been encouraged by the Assyrian royal ideology, which was presumably well known in Judah during the seventh century BCE.

On the other hand, there is no reason to expect that the Assyrians directly influenced the religion of the vassal kingdom of Judah, since the Assyrians had no desire whatsoever to export their own religion to their subject peoples. As in the later Persian empire, the Assyrian attitude towards the religions of their vassals was quite liberal, and they had no inclination to get mixed up in local religious affairs. This is not because the Assyrians did not regard their civilization as superior to those of others, but precisely because they regarded themselves as 'masters', while their subjects were seen as slaves who, as such, had no right to participate in the cult of Asshur, the main Assyrian god. Therefore, in this period Mesopotamian influence will have been indirect, but it was nevertheless inevitable, because the superior Mesopotamian culture could not have avoided influencing cultural relationships in the provinces of the Assyrian empire.

4.3.3 *The Reform of Josiah*

Like other intellectual movements in its time, the Deuteronomistic movement was, as we have seen, in a position to absorb those elements of the foreign tradition which it found suitable for its own message about Yahweh as the sole god of Israel without any marked sense that this view had been imposed from some foreign source. Of course, the spiritual and intellectual climate of the day was also influenced by other currents. The entire period as such was a time of general crisis or of rethinking throughout the ancient Orient. It would almost be appropriate to say that the general attitude was one of *scepticism* towards the contemporary terms of existence, as a result of which people were inclined to seek their roots in the past. History, considered as a message about the past and the right relationship to the divine became the life-raft to which many people clung, because they felt their own identities to be threatened. This sort of 'historicizing' attitude was directly expressed in the Assyrian empire, not least under its last great king, Asshurbanipal, who collected within his royal residence a massive library. This was no accidental collection of 'popular' materials, but a conscious attempt to conserve the ancient tradition by incorporating the religious traditions of the whole of Mesopotamia in the library.

A corresponding tendency was also present at this time in Egypt, which had had its time of greatness in the second millennium BCE, and which played only a pitiful rôle in the international events of the first half of the first millennium BCE. In the beginning of the seventh century BCE the Egyptians even suffered the indignity of seeing their country, which they had long thought to be inviolable, invaded by the Assyrians. Even though this was only to prove of short duration (670-663 BCE), this invasion provoked Egyptian self-reflexion in such a way that an attempt was made to find the national identity in the past time of greatness. Thus, the *national* self-understanding was constructed with the aid of an ideology, the main contents of which consisted of the idealization of all that was Egyptian, and the simultaneous abomination of all that was known to be foreign. In terms of practical policies, this effort led Egypt briefly to re-enter the arena of international events again, in a vain attempt to recreate the ancient Egyptian Asian empire when the Assyrian empire collapsed in the years between 630 and 612 BCE.

Nor was the Judaean leadership stratum untouched by this 'new orientation' towards the past. When the Assyrian yoke practically removed itself from Judah's neck, Josiah, the king in Jerusalem, inaugurated a policy which apparently aimed at recreating the Davidic empire. We possess, in the first instance, only the Deutero-nomistic accounts of these events and their presuppositions, for which reason we cannot be sure whether the significance the Deuteronomists assign to their fundamental theological programme in this period actually corresponded to reality. But if this programme really did influence things, then it was because it provided the ideological background for Josiah's efforts at restoration. In part, it provided the legitimation for the king's attempt to win control over the territory of the earlier northern kingdom. But by the same token, this programme also motivated the break with the local sanctuaries, in particular the sanctuary in Bethel, and thus made possible the centralization of the cult to Jerusalem which was carried out around 623 BCE, and which was central to the Deuteronomistic self-consciousness. According to the Deuteronomistic account, Josiah's reform further aimed at the destruction of all local cults round about the countryside. These measures applied not only to the so-called Canaanite gods, Ba'al, Asherah, and so forth, but also the local sanctuaries which were dedicated to Yahweh. In practice this meant that the national religion would from that point on be concentrated around the king in Jerusalem, that is, the new David, and in this way the reform served to reinforce the king's *image* as an aid to the effectuation of his political programme.

The extent to which Josiah's reform was directly inspired by the Deuteronomists or by the discovery of an ancient lawbook in the Temple is a debatable issue. However, it does appear from the reform measures which were in fact carried out that Josiah's programme agreed at least to some degree with the Deuteronomists' main goal, which was that the Jerusalem temple should come to monopolize the worship in the country. Although this cannot be demonstrated, it is conceivable that lurking behind the demand for centralization was the ancient opposition between the unofficial cult and the official cult as practised in the earlier northern kingdom. Thus, it is likely that Jerusalem's claim to be considered *the sanctuary* par excellence reflects the ancient enmity between Shechem and the royal sanctuary which Jeroboam had instituted in Bethel. To put the matter slightly differently, one could say that if the Deuteronomistic movement determined the contents of the Jerusalem cult, already at the close of the seventh century BCE, then the centralization of the cult and the actual worship that took place in the country had to take place on Deuteronomistic premises. In a way, one could say that the unofficial tradition had finally been elevated to the status of the official tradition.

Although this is the impression one gets from reading the Deuteronomistic interpretation of the events which transpired during the reign of Josiah, it is still possible to ask whether this account corresponds to the actual conditions; and, it is also possible to raise doubts as to the factual extent of the reforms in question. In other words, did the reform and the Deuteronomistic participation in it survive the death of Josiah in 609 BCE, or did the death of this heir to the throne of David simultaneously entail the demise of the hopes which had been pinned upon him, so that the Deuteronomistic programme subsequently became discredited? Much suggests that the latter was the case, since the time subsequent to the reign of Josiah is described as a period which witnessed new apostasies from the right form of worship, and which serves as the final confirmation of the judgment which had been placed in the mouth of Samuel in connection with the enthronement of the first king of Israel, namely that this coronation was synonymous with the rejection of Yahweh as Israel's God and king.

4.3.4 *The Failure of Deuteronomism*
A possible reason why the efforts of the Deuteronomists in pre-exilic times only achieved a limited degree of political success is that their origins were foreign. They were never a majority in Judah, but only a very restricted minority. Nor did they extend their programme to include the broad mass of the population out in the countryside, but confined it instead to the centre of the kingdom, that is, to the capital and the royal palace complex, including the temple. As has been suggested, the Deuteronomists are most likely to be sought among the administrative élite of the kingdom and among the priesthood of the royal temple during the reign of Josiah, rather than out among ordinary people. In this connection, Moshe Weinfeld, an Israeli scholar, has attempted to disprove the notion that the Deuteronomists could have been priests of ancient Israelite origins (i.e. Levites). Weinfeld suggests instead that they are to be seen among the administrative strata in Jerusalem, since they were familiar with the pan-Oriental Wisdom, a tradition which was employed in the ancient Orient in connection with teaching in the scribal schools, or universities, if you will. Weinfeld's theory is at least partially wrong: he has overlooked the fact that the priesthood in the royal sanctuary and the administrators in the palace complex lived side by side with one another; they most likely had the same basic education in the scribal schools and will no doubt have shared the same national ideology. Thus, there was no contradiction between the priesthood and the administrative strata; in all likelihood, both groups combined their efforts on behalf of the programme of cult centralization. The

notion that the administrators could have had intentions different from those of the priesthood is mainly a modern conception. The placement here suggested for the Deuteronomistic movement would help to explain its poor success after Josiah's sudden and unexpected death, since in the eyes of the ordinary person—and those of its opponents—the movement must have seemed bankrupt after the events at Megiddo in 609 BCE, which brutally awakened Judah from her dreams of greatness.

We must also consider the fact that there were other movements in seventh century Judah which competed with Deuteronomism for influence on the Judaean consciousness, and these tendencies probably had more elbow-room after Josiah's demise. One such Jerusalemite or Judaean tradition was the *Zion ideology*, which had considerable popular appeal. It was therefore opposed by the prophet Jeremiah, among others, who lived through and commented on the events spanning the time from Josiah to the destruction of Jerusalem in 587 BCE. It was no doubt reinforced by the fact that Sennacherib was unable to conquer Jerusalem in 701 BCE, for which reason Jerusalem was regarded as Yahweh's own city—a thought held in common with Deuteronomism—but it was also regarded as a city which by definition could not fall. The political reality, of course, turned out to be quite different. The notion of the inviolability of Jerusalem and its companion conception of the continued rôle of the Davidic dynasty were both decisively shattered in the first decades of the sixth century BCE. The state of Judah ceased to exist as such, the temple and its capital were laid in ruins, and the dynasty was terminated. All of these factors contributed to the fact that the Deuteronomistic view of history as based on the right relationship to Yahweh was ultimately vindicated by posterity, since the Deuteronomists had proved to be right. They had maintained that the state would be destroyed, and their prophecy was fulfilled. However, the most important contribution of the movement was that it had also created the ideology which was to form the background for the emergence of a Judaean-Israelite (Jewish) identity after the exile.

Chapter 5

THE EXILE AND THE POST-EXILIC PERIOD

1. *The Sources*

The sources which bear on the period in which Judah and the Judaeans, or, alternatively, the 'Jews'[1] were subjected to first, Babylonian, and, second, Persian rule, are problematic.

These problems may be compared with those which accrue to the sources which deal with the pre-national period. However, there are considerable differences between the sources for the period of the monarchy and those which deal with the exilic and post-exilic times. A large part of the exilic and post-exilic epoch remains mysterious. There are no sources which might provide us with a continual narrative of the history of this time, in contrast to the collected Deuteronomistic presentation of the era of the monarchy. There is some scattered information about the period from 587 BCE, when Nebuchadnezzar destroyed Jerusalem, to 539 BCE, when Cyrus conquered Babylon. We are also told how the Jews received permission to return to Palestine in 538 BCE, and how Alexander the Great subdued the Levantine coast in 331 BCE. Some of the information pertaining to these matters has additionally been preserved in the form of official documents which are quoted either entire or in part in various Old Testament writings, but especially in the books of Ezra and Nehemiah. Most, but far from all scholars, are agreed on the authenticity of these documents. It is to be emphasized, however, that such data have to do with individual events; they shed

---

1. The term 'Jews' is employed from this point onwards instead of the previously employed term, 'Judaeans'. This signifies merely that the people in question were members of a society which had begun to develop those characteristics which are ordinarily associated with the designation 'Jew', both in relation to the character of the religion and practical life in society.

some light on isolated episodes in this era, or else they concentrate their entire attention on a very small segment of the life of the society as a whole, mainly the matter of the re-establishment of the temple cult in Jerusalem.

However, we also possess other materials from the exilic or post-exilic periods, plus some whose background, at least, is in this age. Thus, for example, some of the prophetic books contain information about the situation in Mesopotamia. These include the book of Ezekiel, which is ascribed to a prophet who had gone into exile already a decade before the final fall of Jerusalem in 587 BCE, and who was in a position to describe subsequent events from his exilic situation, as well as the collection ascribed to Deutero-Isaiah (chs. 40–55). These chapters have been ascribed to the authorship of an anonymous prophet whose proclamation has been incorporated into the present book of Isaiah, although in reality this figure was active in the decades prior to the conquest of Babylon by the Persian king Cyrus and the dissolution of the Neo-Babylonian Empire. The book of Jeremiah, however, contains information relevant to the events which occurred in Palestine shortly after the destruction of Jerusalem.

There are two prophetic figures whose works date from the post-exilic period, and they concern an especially critical phase around 520 BCE: Haggai and Zechariah (chs. 1–6). Some information about the post-exilic period is also to be obtained from the short book of the prophet Malachi, and in the collection called Trito-Isaiah, which has been ascribed to the anonymous prophet or circle of prophets who were responsible for the remainder of the book of Isaiah (chs. 55–66). Finally, there is Lamentations, which the tradition assigns to the prophet Jeremiah, but which he is unlikely to have written; it contains some information about the state of affairs in Judaea during the time just after the fall of the monarchy.

We also possess some materials outside the Old Testament which illustrate the history of the Jews in the sixth to the fourth centuries BCE. These documents do not bear on the history of the Jews in Palestine, but rather on the history of the so-called *Diaspora* (literally the 'dispersion', which is the technical expression for extra-Palestinian Jewry). Thus, a number of documents have been preserved, written by a small Jewish society in Upper Egypt which had its own temple of Yahweh on the Island of *Elephantine* in the fifth century BCE. Furthermore, Babylonian sources dating from these centuries occasionally mention Jews, and we also possess the archive of a

Jewish trading company in Mesopotamia, which tells us something about a local Jewish society in the Diaspora.

It is accordingly an extremely precarious task to attempt to depict the history of Jewish society in the period which resulted in the fact that, in Hellenistic and Roman times, the Jews appeared as a national and religious unity; a period which, however, also saw the fractioning-off of Palestinian Jewry into groups centred on Jerusalem and those which were concentrated on other parts of the country. The most important of these groups were the Samaritans, who congregated around ancient Shechem, and who have survived, though pitifully few in number, until our times. However, we are not even able to date the breach between this society and Jerusalem with any certainty, even though it is usually assumed that the schism between the Samaritans and official Jewry had taken place by the beginning of the Hellenistic period.

2. The Babylonian Exile

2.1 Judaea after 587

2.1.1 The Deportations and their Extent

The first questions which arise in connection with the dissolution of the state of Judah are, how many people were ultimately deported? How large a percentage of the Judaean population were directly involved? Which *groups* among the population were forced into exile?

There seem to have been at least three deportations: one which took place in 597 BCE, and which was probably the most extensive, as it encompassed around 5000 individuals; another in 587 BCE; and there may have been yet another which took place around five years after the fall of the city, that is, in 582 BCE. The collected number of individual exiles cannot have numbered more than 10,000. As far as the population percentage is concerned, the answer to this is naturally dependent on one's estimation of the size of the Judaean population around 600 BCE, but it is also contingent on the size one chooses to ascribe to this 'Judah'. If we estimate the whole population of Judah to have numbered between 50,000 and 100,000, and at the same time bear in mind that the real figure could as easily have been the former as the latter, then the deportations will have affected between 10% and 20% of the population.

Not all parts of this society will have been equally affected. The sources all agree that a remnant was left behind—a remnant that may have included as much as 90% of the population!—but this remnant consisted of the poorest and most wretched segment of the people. On the other hand, after the events of 587 BCE the Babylonians were nevertheless in a position to employ a Judaean administrator of good birth, Gedaliah by name, to look after their interests in the region, perhaps because he belonged to a pro-Babylonian faction in the Judaean court. It is accordingly possible that at least some of the Judaean leadership stratum received permission to remain in the country after 587 BCE because they were not regarded as constituting a threat to Babylonian overlordship, and perhaps also because it was felt that they could be employed to administer the country on behalf of the Babylonians. However, as the book of Jeremiah indicates, Gedaliah was murdered after only a few months (Jer. 41.1-3), and the general conditions which seem to have prevailed in Palestine during this early phase of the exilic period were anarchistic. The third deportation in 582 BCE is perhaps to be seen in the light of this fact. It is conceivable that the pro-Babylonian party within the Palestinian élite had been weighed and found too light, for which reason they were removed as well.

The difficulties in determining the identity of those who were compelled to go into exile have to do with the way the Babylonians conducted deportations and with the policies in general which they employed in conjunction with their newly conquered territories. The general Babylonian policy included the removal of the leadership strata, a policy whose roots may be traced back to the last half of the second millennium BCE. However, their observation of this principle was by no means as rigorous as that of the Assyrians had been in the preceding centuries. There are, for example, no signs at all that suggest that the forcible deported segments of society were replaced with individuals who had been likewise removed from other parts of the Neo-Babylonian empire. Correspondingly, those Judaeans who were carried away to Mesopotamia were not relocated to the periphery of the empire, but to its very nucleus, although not to the capital. As a result, the province of Judea suffered a significant decline in population on the one hand, but on the other, no foreign population was introduced which might have changed the ethnic composition of the populace or introduced cultural developments in Palestine in the period after 587 BCE.

2.1.2 *Those Left Behind*

Therefore, when we consider the conditions which obtained in Palestine after the destruction of Jerusalem, we must conclude that the homogeneous character of the population was either unchanged or perhaps even strengthened as a result of the disasters which had affected the capital and the élite more than any other part of the population, even though it is imperative that we not forget that the inhabitants of the Judaean province also ran the risk of being dragged off by the conquerors. As far as the books of Jeremiah and Lamentations are concerned, this was an extremely confused period, not least because the Babylonians appear to have left an administrative vacuum behind them in the country, that is, if we leave out of account the unsuccessful attempt at local government under Gedaliah.

One of the results of these chaotic conditions was an increase in the number of refugees seeking asylum in, above all, Egypt. Jeremiah himself became an involuntary participant in this stream of refugees after the murder of Gedaliah. Another result of the crisis was the reduction of the territorial possessions of Judah, not only because the Babylonians consciously reassigned some areas to the neighbouring provinces, and to Ashdod in particular, but also because of Edomite incursions on Judaean territory. These incursions ran north of the old Judaean town of Hebron and only stopped around thirty kilometres short of Jerusalem.

It is conceivable that the Babylonians attempted to ameliorate the harsh situation of the peasants after the ravages in the land by redistributing the ownership of land. This is very briefly referred to in Jer. 39.10 and is somewhat differently described in 2 Kgs 25.12. In reality what probably happened was that the possessions which had previously belonged to the deported part of the population were subdivided into lots and given to the remaining inhabitants for cultivation. There may have been several reasons for this step. For example, the Babylonians may have intended to ensure for themselves the loyalty of the local populace. Another consideration is the fact that cultivable land was always scarce in Palestine, so that it was simply too valuable to let it lie fallow. But it is also possible that the basic intention of the Babylonian reform had to do with the annulment of debt- and property-relations which were based on the accrual of debt. Peasants were frequently forced to hand over their lands to their creditors in order to pay off their debts. This custom had flourished in Babylon more than a thousand years earlier, back in the Old Babylonian period, and since in many respects the Neo-Babylonian empire represented a return to the customs and usages of the past, it is possible that the Babylonian undertaking had a socio-ideological background. And if this was in fact the case, then there might have been more than just a religious justification for returning to Palestine after the Persian conquest of Babylon, since such a return might in the event have entailed *restoration* in the form of the repossession of lands which the élite had lost in the time after 587 BCE.

Another important question, but unfortunately one which we scarcely have sufficient information to answer, had to do with the possibility of a *retribalization* of the local populace during the exilic period. Such intensification of the political rôle of the families and lineages would be a probable consequence of the lack of central administrative control over Palestinian society. Perhaps the numerous 'tribal lists' as well as the censuses which are to be found within the Priestly tradition, plus the post-exilic interest in determining who was or was not a Jew, may be taken as indications that a movement towards the re-formation of tribes was underway. However, it is far from certain that this was actually the case, because the lists in question are so stereotyped that it is difficult to say whether they reflect a living social organism. Nor should we underestimate the significance of the fact that there was an imperial provincial government in Palestine in the sixth century BCE.

But however matters may have stood, two central instances were lacking at this time which in the pre-national period had been powerful centripetal forces in Judaean society, namely the monarchy and the temple cult in Jerusalem. After the death of Josiah, the monarchy and the Davidic dynasty were played out, and it is hardly likely that any immediate hopes were attached to the notion of the resurrection of royal rule. It is first during the latter part of the exilic period that we can detect any signs of renewed interest in the heirs of David, and, it is to be noted, this occurred in Mesopotamia rather than in Palestine. The temple cult lay similarly in ruins and even though there are a few indications that some weak attempts were made to resuscitate it these efforts were doomed to failure since the most important ingredient in the cult was lacking, namely the temple. Moreover, the priesthood which had the technical knowledge and skills essential to the administration of the cult in Jerusalem happened to be in exile. In this connection, it would naturally be interesting to know if any information exists as to the presence of cult sites outside of Jerusalem during this period. Such information is not to be sought in the more sizable towns, since these had suffered the same fate as Jerusalem. This leaves the villages as the only car dates, and so far the archeologists have failed to find any complexes of the type in question from the exilic period; they have either managed to overlook them, or else such sites simply did not exist at this time. If the latter was the case, although we cannot be certain of this, in view of the status of contemporary archeological study of the villages, it would provide an interesting confirmation of the extent of penetration of the demand for centralization in the period after the fall of Jerusalem. But, as suggested above, we must be reticent on this issue, as the information is still lacking which would finally be able to clarify the question.

2.2 *Life in Exile*

We are not very well informed as to the conditions which obtained among the deportees in their first years of exile. Most of our information derives from archives from the succeeding centuries. However, if we compare these materials with the information which is preserved in the Old Testament, it is nevertheless possible to present a brief and sketchy picture of the conditions to which the exiles were subjected.

Zedekiah, the last king in Jerusalem, was cruelly punished by the Babylonians. His sons were executed, and he himself was dragged off to Babylon. The Babylonians no doubt regarded him as an unfaithful vassal who had conspired against the very lord who had originally installed him in office, thus breaking the covenant that existed between them. This, however, was not synonymous with the destruction of the Davidides, since on the occasion of the first deportation in 597 BCE the king at that time, Jehoiachin, had been taken off to Babylon together with his family, and we are informed that he still resided there in 562 BCE, when Nebuchadnezzar died. We even possess Babylonian sources which mention the dispensing of rations to this Judaean royal family, which was apparently maintained in a sort of 'golden cage', and which seems to have enjoyed more freedom after the demise of Nebuchadnezzar. Indeed, descendants of Jehoiachin assumed leading positions within the exilic community and later on in Judah after the return from exile.

It was impossible for the deported élite to maintain their social position in exile. As mentioned previously, they were in large part the leadership class, but, in the eyes of the Babylonians they could be put to little use within the complicated administrative system then in use in Mesopotamia. For one thing, the Judaeans were not educated so as to be able to undertake important administrative jobs (for which knowledge of cuneiform and of Sumerian, the 'Latin' of the day, was essential); for another, there would always be doubts as to the loyalty of the group. It appears that to begin with the leadership stratum were reduced to the status of peasants who farmed plots of land which had been assigned to them by the Babylonian state. However, later sources reveal that some elements of the Jewish society in Mesopotamia eventually established themselves in other areas, such as trade and banking.

In addition to the various élites, the Babylonians brought considerable numbers of specialists to Babylon. These included above all artisans, whose services were always in demand and who also represented the single labour commodity which the Babylonians could most effectively exploit immediately. On the reassignment of this body of manpower within Babylonian society our sources are silent, but the lists of deportees in the Old Testament, which explicitly emphasize this social group, strongly imply that the Babylonians intended to gain control of it for their own purposes (cf. 2 Kgs 24.14, 16).

Both the Babylonian sources and the information in the book of Ezekiel agree that the Jews were settled in various places in Mesopotamia. Ezekiel is said to have been a member of a local Jewish settlement called Tel Aviv, the location of which is unfortunately unknown. Also, the archives of the Jewish trading family, the *Murashus*, which date from the fifth century BCE, reveal the presence of a Jewish colony in the ancient Babylonian city of Nippur. The Babylonian materials also permit us some insight into the occupations in which these Jews were engaged, and they generally confirm the impression that although the Jews did not belong to the élite of the society, they were otherwise distributed throughout the social spectrum. It is to be noted, however, that there are only a very few references to Jews who were slaves. In spite of the fact that this information dates from after the end of the exile, it nevertheless serves to demonstrate that the Jews in Babylon were not regarded as slaves. In spite of the fact that they had been deported from their homeland they were apparently not regarded as prisoners of war (who would ordinarily have been utilized as slave labour). They were instead the clients of the Babylonian state, and the state employed them to form a *colony*; they were peasants on lands assigned to them by the state.

As regards the religious practices which were observed by the Jewish exiles, at this point it suffices to underline the fact that there are no signs of the administration of a cult in the proper sense, and no indications whatsoever of any kind of temple cult. Considerable assimilation took place between Jews and Babylonians, as is indicated by the proper names which have been preserved. A large part of these are Babylonian names, even within the Judaean royal family. However, this by no means suggests that the Jews accepted Babylonian forms of worship. At the same time, however, we must admit that there is no evidence that this did *not* take place, since such a departure from the picture of the isolated Yahweh-worshipping Jewish society would clearly have been regarded as inadmissable. This must be taken into account, since some of the Babylonain personal names assumed by Jews are names in which such major Babylonian gods as *Marduk* and *Nabu* figure, and this might be taken to suggest that some sort of acknowledgment of the gods in question did, after all, take place. All indications are that the Jews did not establish any temple worship during the exile, and that the traditions about the past and about the correct form of worship were both honoured and observed in congregations which probably assembled in private homes. Regular *synagogal worship* as such, however had, not as yet evolved.

2.3 *Cultural Developments During the Exile*
2.3.1 *The Social Location of the Great Historical Works*
If the assertion of many Old Testament scholars in recent years is correct that the main part of the historical literature in the Old Testament was created during the exile, then we are in the paradoxical situation that we do not possess much information as to what actually transpired in this period, whereas we have more information as to spiritual cultural developments. However, it should at the outset be emphasized that the study of these materials is in many cases dependent upon a somewhat uncertain scholarly procedure, to the extent that we cannot with certainty 'prove' just which of the historical sources are to be dated to the sixth century

BCE. Thus, for example, we date the Yahwistic source to this epoch because we think we find in the Yahwistic materials answers to questions which arose at this time. We then proceed to describe the cultural situation in the period in question on the basis of the very same source. If, therefore, this was the only reason to date even the primary Pentateuchal sources late, it would be quite impermissable to construct any hypotheses on the basis of them. Therefore, it would be wiser to argue a late date for the Yahwistic materials on the basis of the kinship of those materials with the Deuteronomistic ones. We can in any event be sure that the Deuteronomists were active during the exilic period, and that it was at this time that at least the main part of the Deuteronomistic History came into being.

Unfortunately, it is extremely difficult to demonstrate with any degree of assurance precisely where the Deuteronomistic movement experienced its full flowering, that is, whether this took place among the exilic Jews or among the remnant that had stayed behind in Palestine. As far as the Jews who lived in exile were concerned, only those in Babylon are to be considered, among other things because of the interest evinced by the Deuteronomistic History in the fate of Jehoiachin. However, a Palestinian homeland for this literature is also conceivable, though in the event one would also have to reckon with continuous communications between the deportees and the Jews who lived in Palestine. Logically, one would expect that precisely that part of the Judaen populace who would have been able to create this theological literature would have been among those who had had to go into exile. On the other hand, as was mentioned previously, the Babylonian deportation practice was by no means as consistent as that of the Assyrians. There is accordingly a slight possibility that the Deuteronomistic circle, or some parts of it, remained in its homeland, or that in reality it was active in both Palestine and Babylon.

2.3.2 *History as a Response to Catastrophe*
It is obvious that during the exilic period whether one was among those who had remained in Palestine or among the exiles in Babylon one's main intellectual concern would be to attempt to explain the recent catastrophe. It is characteristic of the thought of this period that the attempt to solve this problem was made through the medium of history and, moreover, not just in the history of recent events, but in the distant past as well. History was more or less understood

paradigmatically in that it provided causal explanations of current disasters, because it bore witness to the fact that the past and the present were intimately connected. It contained one and the same message for the Jews, namely a message about apostasy and rejection, but also about forgiveness and conversion. Modern attempts to analyze the Deuteronomistic literature indicate the presence in it of several layers of material, and in this connection it would hardly be wrong to maintain that the motif of rejection was probably most pronounced in the oldest section. Indeed, it would be appropriate to enquire as to whether the Deuteronomists had any expectation at all that Israel would continue to exist, since she had sinned against her God and broken her covenant—the latter being the Deuteronomists' favourite expression for characterizing the relationship between Yahweh and Israel. For these reasons reference was made to the history of Israel spanning the exodus from Egypt, the period of the judges and the era of the monarchy in order to illustrate that the rejection of Israel had not taken place without reason. The Israelites could by no means blame Yahweh, since they themselves were alone responsible. In fact, if this was the content of the Deuteronomists' message already in the days of Josiah it would additionally have been possible for them to point out that events had proved them right.

On the other hand, there is no reason to believe that this account of Israel's guilt with respect to Yahweh went unopposed at the time it appeared. There are a number of very interesting texts in which this very message is dismissed, notable, for example, in Ps. 44.17 where it is emphatically emphasized that 'we have not forgotten thee, or been false to thy covenant' (RSV)! The verse in question even plays paronomastically on the standard Deuteronomistic vocabulary. In other words, an attitude is expressed which refuses to regard the fall of the Judaean state as the result of some 'sin' which had forced Yahweh to reject his people. Furthermore, the adherents of this view even went so far as to accuse Yahweh of having broken his promises, since they were able to point to the covenant between Yahweh and the Davidic dynasty by means of which Yahweh had assured 'David' (i.e. the dynasty) that his house would endure forever (Psalm 89). This covenant now lay in ruins, so that it was possible to request Yahweh to revivify his covenant with the dynasty, that is, to recreate the state.

Still other theological currents accepted the importance of the

covenantal theology as it is expressed in the Deuteronomistic
literature. However, such thinkers preferred to emphasize the
concepts of Yahweh's election of Israel and of divine promise. The
main message here was the possession of the land of Palestine; this
was the signpost which pointed forwards to a new existence in 'the
promised land'. These themes are present in the Deuteronomistic
literature, but they receive special significance particularly in the
work of the Yahwist, and for this reason, signify some sort of
opposition to the Deuteronomistic theology of sin and punishment.

At least to begin with it was the Deuteronomists' view which was
most influential, as can be seen from the significance this view has
had for the general Old Testament understanding of history as well
as for posterity. On the other hand, as the time of the exile neared its
end and the possibility of returning to Palestine became even more
prominent the various views became confluent. On the one hand, it
was emphasized that Israel had been forced to go into exile because
of her sins, while on the other, it was maintained that the Israelites
were nevertheless the chosen people. It was accordingly possible to
look forward to a liberation which would make an exodus possible for
Israel, so that she could return to her inheritance. This, it was held,
had been the promise to the patriarchs, who themselves had been
compelled to leave the land of Canaan, that is, to go into exile,
although they still retained the promise that their descendants would
one day return.

2.3.3 The 'Jewish' People

A peculiar aspect of the experience of the exile, the roots of which are
definitely to be sought among the exiles and not among the
Palestinian remnant, was the emergence of the conviction of
belonging to a particular *people*. As we saw earlier, one of the features
of the times was the emphasis on *national* characteristics. A
movement which aided the development of the concept of a
specifically Jewish people had gone hand in hand with the evolution
of the notion of a specifically Jewish religion, that is, one which was
reserved for Jews. These tendencies had been initiated already prior
to the exile, at least this was the view of the circles which had created
the nationalistic ideology, namely the Deuteronomists. This attitude
was intensified under the influence of the exile, because the problem
complex had intensified in this period: one either remained a Jew, or
one became a Babylonian. The Jews lived in the midst of a foreign

population as a tiny minority. During this period the cultural influences exerted by the Babylonians were direct and immediate; moreover, they produced unquestionable results, as the lists of Jews bearing Babylonian names attest, and as is also indicated by the numerous myths of Babylonian origin which were assimilated into the Old Testament literature.

A reaction against these foreign influences is most apparent in the Priestly stratum of the Pentateuch. Such precautionary measures are starkly obvious in such things as the revised understanding of the covenant as presented in Genesis 17 (P). Where the earlier depiction of the covenant between Abraham and Yahweh in ch. 15 mainly concentrates on the motif of promise and predicts that Abraham's descendants will survive their '400 years' of exile and return to their own country as a numerous people, the Priestly notion of the covenant in ch. 17 is concerned to emphasize the observance of some concrete cultic injunctions. These do not have to do with ethical matters, but with one purely external feature which the Priestly author felt was the basis for the maintenance of the covenant: circumcision of the males. The custom of circumcision is admittedly very ancient in the Israelite-Jewish society, and it is also attested elsewhere in the ancient Near East, even before Israel came into existence. It is nevertheless significant that this particular custom became especially important at this time, that is, when the Jews in Babylon lived in the midst of a people who did not practise circumcision. Thus, the question as to whether one was circumcised or not became decisive in determining whether one was a member of the society of Jewish exiles, a Babylonian, or a Jew who had *become* a Babylonian.

The result of this cultural influence was an internal immigration among the Jewish mini-societies scattered throughout Mesopotamia, with an attendant delimitation with respect to the surrounding Babylonian world. In their daily life the Jews were obliged to live in a symbiotic relationship with the peoples around them. In this connection it became important to be able to preserve the tradition of the Jewish religion, and that the message about sin, apostasy, and retribution be preached to Jewish congregations, which perhaps did not identify themselves with the Deuteronomistic view of history, without more ado.

3. *The Post-exilic Period*

3.1 *The End of the Exile and the Return*
3.1.1 *The Persian Conquest of Babylon and the Edict of Cyrus*
Throughout the 540s BCE new signals began to reach the Jewish
congregations who lived in Babylon; these suggested that the days of
the Babylonian empire were numbered, a new ruler would permit
Israel to return to her homeland, and the state of Israel and the
temple would be resurrected in all their former glory. The
responsibility for the renewed hope among the Palestinian exiles is to
be assigned to Deutero-Isaiah, whose work is the main source for
reconstructing these ideas among the exiles. Deutero-Isaiah un-
ambiguously associated these hopes with the Persian king Cyrus. He
is the 'eagle' who is called from the east (Isa. 46.11); he is 'the
anointed of Yahweh' (Isa. 45.1); and he is the 'shepherd of Yahweh'
(Isa. 44.28), who fulfils Yahweh's will.

In order to understand the background of this renewal of hope for
future restoration of the Jewish society it will be necessary briefly to
review the historical course of events since the fall of Jerusalem. The
Neo-Babylonian empire had been more or less created by two men.
Nabopolassar and his son and successor, Nebuchadnezzar. The
empire was formed as the result of a 'national' movement in the
southern part of Mesopotamia which had opposed itself to Assyrian
overlordship. In other words, this movement was of a piece with the
general tendency of the age towards national revival. However, its
power base was anything but solid. True, the Assyrian yoke had been
cast off and the Assyrian empire was no more, but the Babylonians
had only managed to achieve this through a coalition with the
neighbouring kingdoms to the east and north, that is, those of the
Medes and Lydians.

The Neo-Babylonian empire collapsed every bit as quickly as the
Assyrian empire before it had done. As long as Nebuchadnezzar
lived, there were no serious problems. However, after his death in
562 BCE a number of events occurred in the Median empire which
were to have drastic consequences for the history of the entire
ancient Orient. At the time in question, large segments of the
population of the Median empire were organized in tribal units.
Many of these were hardy groups of nomads, including the
inhabitants of the provinces of *Fars* (= Pars = Persia). Cyrus, who
had previously been an officer of the Median king, sought and
secured the aid of the tribally organized population from whose

ranks he himself had come in order to remove the Median dynasty and become the first king of the *Persian empire*. It was Cyrus' great accomplishment that he succeeded in neutralizing the usual rivalries among the tribes and instead directed their energies against the rest of the world. As a result, during the decade which preceded the fall of Babylon Cyrus made himself master of all of modern Iran, most of what is now Pakistan, and all Asia Minor; he was also able to push forward towards India, and subsequently to turn against Mesopotamia and the Levant.

Observers in Babylon had followed these developments, and they must have recognized their implications for their own future. At the time Babylon's foreign policy was characterized by inaction, while the domestic scene was marred by conflicts between the king and the Babylonian priesthood. The last Babylonian king, Nabonidus, had deposed the powerful priestly class in the capital city in favour of the cult of a local god, Sin, the moon-god. At all events, this is the account which is most usually offered of the history of the period. There is naturally some question, however, as to whether it would have made any difference if the conflicts in question had not weakened the leadership class of the Neo-Babylonian empire. They would probably not have been able to resist the tidal wave from the east anyway. But this is imponderable; what we do know is the result: when Cyrus turned against Babylon in 540/539 BCE, the empire dropped into his palm like a ripe fruit. The 'fall' of the capital is symptomatic of the mood of the times, as it surrendered without bloodshed. Only the royal citadel attempted to resist, and it was duly defeated and obliterated. The fall of Babylon opened the way west for the Persians, who merely took over the Babylonian provinces and maintained the Babylonian provincial administration *en place*, with the single addition of Persian governors, or *satraps*. A few years later the Persians campaigned in Egypt, which was subdued by Cyrus' successor, and a few decades later they invaded Greece, when the new empire suffered its first serious defeat (490 BCE and 480/479 BCE).

If we take the information in the Old Testament at face value, then in the book of Ezra (1.2-4) we find an *edict* which is supposed to represent the Persian measures towards the Jewish society. Cyrus' occupation of Babylon was apparently followed by permission for those who wished to do so to return to Palestine. This edict has long been regarded as an indication of a supposedly new and tolerant attitude on the part of the Persians. In this connection the permission to rebuild the temple in Jerusalem has been particularly seen as an example of the 'liberal' Persian attitude towards religious matters, not least when we consider that the Persians themselves were devotees of the first 'modern' religion (with the exception of early Judaism) in the Near East, *Zoroastrianism*, in which ethical matters were emphasized at the expense of the earlier fertility religion.

It is very likely that the Persians were considerate of religions other than their own, and that the Jews enjoyed the fruits of this policy. On the other hand, it would be a mistake to underplay Cyrus' real-political intentions in liberating the Jews in Babylon. By allowing élite groups of the Jewish society to return to their homeland, which few or none of them had ever seen, the king created a bond of personal loyalty between his regime and this Jewish group, whom he therefore could count on to help him govern his far-flung empire. Yet it should also be observed that a new feature came about with the appearance of the Persian empire, since the Persians either abandoned the practice of deportation or limited it severely. In actual practice, the Persians utilized a new approach, the goal of which was to strengthen the national (or, perhaps better, the *local*) units in order to win their support, and with the minimum possible effort on the part of the Persians themselves. The means employed to this end, that is, towards maintaining peace by preventing the various 'nation states' from making war on the Persian great king or on each other, consisted of ensuring the local populations better living conditions than previously and striking instantaneously if a rebellion nevertheless broke out.

This policy was only partly successful. Rebellions took place frequently and in many locations, This may have been the case in Palestine; we possess no information about any local revolt, but the destruction layers in a number of Palestinian towns seem to indicate that the Persian period was not entirely a peaceful one. But as long as external enemies were not sufficiently strong and organized to provide a serious threat, the empire remained intact. On the other hand, 200 years later the empire tumbled into the dust in the face of the Macedonian attack under Alexander the Great, who subsequently abandoned the Persian administrative model and attempted to weld his empire together in a new way (i.e. through assimilation between conquerors and conquered).

3.1.2 The Dilemma of the Jew in Exile: Why Return?

As far as the return of the exiled Jews from Babylon is concerned, it is known today that the programme was hardly the 'standing room only' success that Deutero-Isaiah had expected. The Babylonian sources which mention the presence of Jews in Mesopotamia do not suddenly cease to speak of them after 538 BCE, the official year of the return. To the contrary, these sources continue to speak of the presence of Jews in the region for centuries under Persian rule. Nor does the Old Testament itself attempt to conceal the fact that Jewish population groups continued to live in the kingdoms to the east, first in Mesopotamia, and subsequently in Persia itself. It might even be appropriate to say that the Persian empire created a climate which favoured trade and communication and thereby internationalized the Orient, which provided the possibility for the establishment of Jewish settlements throughout the empire. In other words, the ground had been laid for the emergence of a Jewish Diaspora throughout the Middle East.

To be quite candid, there was not really very much for the exiles to return to. Compared with Mesopotamia, the Palestine of this period was the remotest conceivable province; it was a poor and under-developed region in which, as if to add insult to injury, the possessions which the deportees had once owned had in all likelihood been given to others. At the very least, a lengthy rebuilding period would be necessary if the Jews were to re-emerge as a nationally organized society in the highlands of Judaea. Therefore, only compelling arguments would suffice to convince the Jews who lived in Mesopotamia to return to their ancient homeland. Thus, the utopian account in Deutero-Isaiah of the delights of the return is not to be understood as some sort of ecstatic dream about the future; rather, it also served as propaganda aimed at those exiles who were only too content with their situation in exile.

There was clearly a need for some psychologically founded argumentation in favour of a return to Palestine. In this connection the Deuteronomistic and Priestly messages, according to which Jerusalem was *the place which Yahweh had chosen*, that is, the place where Yahweh's temple would stand and from which a new Davidic kingdom would emerge, were well suited. At least some of the exiled Jews responded positively and returned under the leadership of Sheshbazzar, who bore the title 'prince of Judah' (Ezra 1.8). They brought with them the vessels which had been removed from the temple by the Babylonians. After their arrival in Jerusalem, this group apparently began to rebuild the temple, although the project proved to require more than twenty years.

3.1.3 *The Zerubbabel Crisis and the Rebuilding of the Temple*
The first phase of the return is extremely indistinct because we do not have precise information as to who this Sheshbazzar was. The title 'prince of Judah' might seem to suggest that he was of royal descent. Thus scholars have alternately identified him with Jehoiachin's grandson Zerubbabel, with Zerubbabel's father, or with one or another son of Jehoiachin. There is no possibility of certainty in the matter, as the title could just as easily refer to the function which Sheshbazzar's Persian masters had planned for him, that is, as a local administrator or governor. It is not until around 520 BCE that we have some slightly more precise information as to the situation in Jerusalem. This information, however, is mainly connected with Zerubbabel and his collaboration with Joshua, the designated high priest of the temple, and in this connection, too, virtually all the data are concerned with the question of the re-erection of the temple.

To simplify matters a bit, it is sufficient to note that the temple was in fact rebuilt in spite of internal contradictions within the Jewish population of Jerusalem, and, further, in spite of open hostility on the part of the governors of the sometime northern kingdom, Samaria. The antipathy between Judah and Samaria was to continue in the succeeding centuries, and it eventually had religious consequences via the emergence of a distinctively Samaritan Judaism and a Samaritan temple on Mt Garizim, near ancient Shechem. This cult had clearly declared its independence of official Judaism, which of course was based on the temple in Jerusalem.

Zerubbabel was the last heir of the Davidic dynasty about whom we possess concrete information. The question of what happened to him has teased the imaginations of scholars for many years. Researchers have frequently pointed to the not inconsiderable hopes and expectations which the returnees had pinned on this figure, who, or so they hoped, would be the new king and restorer of the Davidic empire.

Around 529 BCE it is possible that the international situation could have provided an—admittedly unrealistic—basis for such expectations, since the Persian empire was then affected by a serious institutional crisis following the death of its second king, Cambyses (d. 522 BCE).

The situation was unstable for a number of years while various factions within the royal family struggled for power, and order was only finally re-established after the accession a couple of years later of Darius I to the throne. If Zerubbabel had been involved in these affairs, or even if he was merely the centre of expectations which created local unrest, it is conceivable that the Persians would have removed him by force, although it should be admitted that we have no evidence whatsoever pertaining to the issue.

3.1.4 '*Judaea*'

Nor, for that matter, do we have any information as to the conditions in the country of Judaea during the period following the rededication of the temple in 516 BCE and extending to the middle of the following century. All we can conclude as to the state of affairs in this period is that Jerusalem had by no means regained her former glory; rather, the city was entirely without the protection which strong walls could offer it and its inhabitants. And in reality there was not much reason to rebuild Jerusalem into a capital once more, since there was no longer very much for the city to be the capital of. Although it is of course impossible to be precise as to the dimensions of the Judaean territory at this time, we would probably not be completely off the mark in assuming that the province was of very limited area indeed, perhaps not more than about two thousand square kilometres (from Beth-Zur, a few kilometres north of Hebron, in the south, to Jerusalem, in the north, i.e. about 30-40 km, and from Jerusalem in the east to the western border of the Judaean mountains in the west, which is hardly more than 30-40 km). The book of Ezra contains a listing of the families which had returned from Babylon, being in all about 50,000 persons. As an actual figure for the returnees, this is unrealistic, but the figure itself may have been based on an official census of the Judaean population, the result of which was then projected back to the time of the end of the exile. One reason for such a procedure is that the official post-exilic view of history, as expressed in the books of Chronicles, maintained that all the inhabitants of the kingdom of Judah had been carried off to Babylon in connection with Nebuchadnezzar's conquest of Jerusalem.

The northern administrative district, Samaria, was considerably larger, as was the western district of Ashdod. Finally, the region south of Beth-Zur remained in Edomite hands, so that in later (hellenistic) times it became known as *Idumaea*. Edomite pressure against the Judaean population seems to have been continuous, although three hundred years had still to elapse before the Idumaeans could put a 'Jewish' king on the throne in Jerusalem (Herod).

If later sources are to be believed, however, the demarcation problem was only problematic for the religious leadership in Jerusalem. The inhabitants of the province do not seem to have regarded the Judaean borders as in any way exclusive; rather, they maintained contacts which extended to both the west and the north. This is apparent when we consider the problems which arose at the beginning of the fourth century BCE in connection with the so-called mixed marriages, that it, the marital connections which had arisen between Jews and women who came from the neighbouring regions.

3.2 *Judaea in the Fifth and Fourth Centuries* BCE
3.2.1 *Nehemiah, the Governor*
As is characteristic for our sources, by far the main part of our information about the post-exilic period concerns two individuals, Ezra, 'the scribe', and Nehemiah, 'the governor'. Considered as individuals, however, these figure are not particularly interesting, just as the events with which they are associated (Nehemiah: the construction of a wall; Ezra: a reform of marriage customs) seem somewhat banal in relation to the interest which has accrued to them in Jewish tradition. However, they become far more interesting when we consider these figures as representatives of particular attitudes, since their activities then tell us something about the situation of the Jews who lived in Palestine in the fifth-fourth centuries BCE, and about that of the then-contemporary Jews of the Diaspora.

It is characteristic of the way history was written at the time in question that the two people have been to some extent interchanged, or rather, their actions have been asigned to the opposite number, as though both figures had been present in Jerusalem at the same time. Naturally enough, modern scholarship has been mainly concerned with the attempt to unravel the threads and so to discover who came first. A sort of consensus has been arrived at in recent times, according to which Nehemiah was the first to arrive in Jerusalem, while Ezra only came onto the scene some forty years later. Nehemiah's arrival is usually dated to the middle of the fifth century BCE, and Ezra's to the beginning of the fourth century BCE. Both were Diaspora Jews who had enjoyed high position within the

Persian administration, for which reason both were able to exercise considerable authority, having, as they did, the legitimating prestige of the great king behind them. It is accordingly of lesser importance that their position was not quite so solid as the source materials seem superficially to suggest.

When Nehemiah arrived in Jerusalem around 445 BCE, according to the Old Testament book which bears his name, and of which some sections may very well ultimately derive from the individual himself, there was very little for the returnees to rejoice about. The city was still partially in ruins and also unfortified; the mores were, at least in Nehemiah's opinion, disintegrating; and the society itself was characterized by internal social disparities between the haves and the have-nots, above all, because the old system of debt-slavery for those peasants who were unable to pay their debts had been revived in the post-exilic society.

The book of Nehemiah describes how Nehemiah corrected these problems, rebuilt the walls of Jerusalem, and imported portions of the rural populace in order to repopulate the city in spite of the open opposition of the governors of Samaria and of the neighbouring provinces to the east and west. There was also opposition from some parts of the leadership stratum in Judaea, who were presumably wealthy landowners with business contacts, to the governors of the neighbouring regions. Indeed, this group of established 'haves' had every conceivable reason to oppose this representative of the Persian king, since Nehemiah quite clearly intended to carry out a social reform. Or, to say it as it actually was, following ancient Mesopotamian custom, Nehemiah issued an edict of debt-remission according to which outstanding debts were abolished and confiscated property was returned to the rural population.

3.2.2 *Ezra, the Scribe*

The book of Nehemiah is also concerned to relate how various cultic and religious reforms were carried out in Jerusalem. However, there is some uncertainty as to Nehemiah's success in this respect, since the features in question had by no means been regulated when Ezra arrived around fifty years later, in 398 BCE, equipped with new plenipotentiary powers from the great king.

Ezra's activity was mainly concentrated on the *national Jewish ideology*. Nehemiah had already attended to the political presuppositions for the growth of the Jewish society in Judaea. Thus, Ezra's task was a different one, and the point which he chose to attack was the problem of mixed marriages. This practice had apparently extended this time so as to include members of the Jerusalemite élite, and even some members of the temple priesthood. Ezra simply compelled the dissolution of these marriages, while at the same time effectuating a standardization of the cult and of the ethical principles which were so prominent a feature of Jewish religion, and which the people of Judah and Jerusalem were in future to be obliged to observe.

The events which took place in the intervals between Nehemiah and Ezra, and again after Ezra's activities, are not illuminated by documentary sources. It appears that Nehemiah introduced order into the society by strengthening the internal administration of the province, which was based on the capital, and by means of his social reforms, which attempted to correct any overly large discrepancies between the rich and the poor. Of course, such inequalities did not disappear when Nehemiah's edict appeared, but the reformer had at least managed to establish a precedent which would show how to manage such problems in future. Ezra's reform provided Nehemiah's efforts with an ideological legitimation, in that Ezra intensified the solidarity of Jewish society by *isolating* it both *religiously* and *physically* with respect to the neighbouring provinces. Considerable sections of the Priestly legislation in the Pentateuch and, not least, the rules regulating the observance of the Jubilee (Leviticus 25) may be understood in the light of this reformatory activity. Among other things, this legislation argues that fellow-countrymen are brothers in the same religion; they are one people, and, moreover, the chosen people; and that they are above all a *pure* people, cleansed of all foreign elements. Thus in future, to be a Jew was to be something more than merely someone who confessed to the right religion; he had also to derive from the right—and legitimate—origins. It is hardly remarkable that this policy led to a break with the population residing in Samaria. The attitude towards the dwellers in the north had already been settled in the Deuteronomistic literature (2 Kgs 17.24-34), and it became firmly established in the post-exilic period as an active and significant ideology which eventually led to the schism between Jews and Samaritans.

3.2.3 *The Relationship between Judaea and the Jews of the Diaspora*

Finally, the examples of Ezra and Nehemiah tell us something about where the ideology about the Jewish nation which they created actually came from: from the Diaspora in Mesopotamia and Persia. The tradition from the period of the exile continued into the post-exilic period. Admittedly, the Diaspora societies had lost some blood during the years following Cyrus's conquest of Babylon, but the loss was hardly so severe that it threatened their existence. The same questions about the nature and extent of relations with a non-Jewish society in which one lived persisted in the following centuries. They were not vitiated by the presence of a Persian religion which in many ways must have been more dangerous for Judaism than the ancient and ritually ossified Babylonian religion had been. As was already the case in Judah under Assyrian rule, the confrontation between the Persian and Jewish cultures led to both assimilation of some features and to rejection of others, not because the Persians attempted to force their religion onto anyone, but precisely because they did not attempt to do so. It was thus inappropriate to gather around some 'national' Jewish symbol in active battle against the foreign influence; there was no obvious enemy to combat, because the enemy himself had no desire to fight. For this reason, the way leading to preservation of Jewish identity led not to confrontation, but to isolation centred around the observation of the right religion. In a national sense the exilic Jews became exemplars in the proclamation of the right Jewish religion, and for the right Jewish identity. This circumstance may conceivably be reflected in the names in use in the Diaspora in this period, as scholars have pointed out the frequent occurrence of the divine name Yahweh among then-contemporary Diaspora Jews.

Back in Palestine there was a Jewish society which continued to exist also after the official end of the exile; but the majority of this society's members had not themselves ever been exiled. The destruction of Jerusalem and the dissolution of the state of Judah had no doubt been a shock to these people. Nevertheless, when the exiles began to trickle back, these people had in any case managed to survive for fifty years and accordingly were probably not in a state of social or religious crisis, as the Old Testament tradition, which has been strongly influenced by the exile, would have us believe. To the contrary, the sources for the post-exilic period allow the impression to emerge that there were multifaceted and latent contradictions between the Jews of the exile and the population which was resident in Palestine. These contradictions were ideological, but in the period after the exile the problems in question intensified because of the social discrepancies and inequalities. Nehemiah eliminated most of these difficulties, so that the path had been paved for Ezra's activity. This reinforced the internal solidarity of a society which, from now on, was to live under the guidance of the national ideology of the Diaspora, and of Jews who lived outside of Palestine.

The pure teaching came from without, but its contents centred around the temple in Jerusalem and the old country from which it had emanated. A notice in the book of Ezra further suggests that the wealthy Diaspora Jew was in future to be morally obliged to see to the financial welfare of the poor of Jewish Palestine society (Ezra 7.16). This laid the basis for a custom among exiled Jewry which is still relevant in our own times.

Chapter 6

ISRAELITE RELIGION

1. *Presuppositions for Writing a History of Israelite Religion*

Any scholarly description of the history of Israelite religion must follow the reconstruction of Israel's 'profane history' which the researcher in question proposes. This has also been the case with earlier studies of this kind. Since scholars have usually felt that the basic outlines of the history of Israel corresponded to the presentation offered by the Old Testament, they have also tended to follow the Old Testament's understanding of Israelite religious origins and character. For this reason, religion-historical examinations have to a high dgree concentrated on distinguishing what was held to be *genuinely Israelite* and, in the second rank, they have concentrated on the confrontation between *Israelite* and *Canaanite* religion. Following this procedure, the history of Israel's religion became an account of the battle between Yahweh and Ba'al—or, in reality, a struggle between good and evil.

As will be evident, an entirely different understanding of the history of Israel forms the basis of this work. It is therefore necessary to describe the development of the religion in a way that is congruent with the historical account. It is accordingly impossible to follow the Old Testament model. We have to reconstruct the course of the development of the religion in a way which is just as independent of the biblical picture as was the case with the political and social history. This conclusion leads to a drastic re-evaluation of the task of the historian of religion, since it is essential to acknowledge that we now possess considerably fewer sources on Israelite religion in the pre-national period and at the beginning of the monarchy than was the case with the profane history.

It is with Amos and Hosea that we have the first contemporary sources which offer an account of the religion which the prophets in

question held to be Israelite and of the one which they held was
Canaanite. As we shall note below, these two prophets (and their
later colleagues) were by no means witnesses to the truth; rather, the
account of so-called Canaanite religion which they offer is strongly
tendentious and presumably presents a distorted picture of that
religion. There are many indications that the contradictory relationship between Yahwism and Canaanite religion for which these
prophets argue was not generally acknowledged in their own time.
Thus, such a conception is not to be used as the basis of one's
analysis of the evolution of the religion—it could at most be the
consequence of one's examination.

In this section a somewhat different approach has been employed
than in the preceding chapters. First, a description of *Canaanite*
religion is offered, since it should be allowed to speak for itself. The
Israelite religion is considered subsequently. Here, too, the sources
are allowed to speak with their own clear voice. Since, as mentioned
previously, these source materials are quite late, I have chosen to
characterize the antithesis of Canaanite religion first: the *Israelite
legalistic religion of the post-exilic period*. Only subsequently will an
attempt be made to describe pre-exilic Israelite religion and its
transformation into the post-exilic type. In this way it should be
easier to note the differences between the religion which the
redactors who were responsible for the contents of the Old
Testament regarded as their own, and the religion which they saw as
the antithesis of their own. This procedure will hopefully also permit
us to get behind the Old Testament description of the history of
Israelite religion, because it should enable us to depict the
developmental course of the redactors' religion, and to depict the
religion from which that system of belief emerged.

2. West Semitic Religion in the Second Half of the Second Millennium BCE

2.1 The Finds at Ugarit and the Old Testament
Thanks to the discovery of a sizable corpus of religious texts, and
especially myths, from ancient Ugarit (*Ras Shamra*) in northern
Syria in this century, we now know a fair amount about certain sides
of north West Semitic religion in the Late Bronze Age. Before this
discovery, scholarship had had to attempt to reconstruct the contents
of Canaanite religion on the basis of the polemical account of it in the

Old Testament and on the basis of the (generally) even later Phoenician and Punic inscriptions from Tyre, Sidon, North Africa, and the western region of the Mediterranean Basin. One could also seek assistance in very late classical sources, particularly in Hellenistic sources, which had a more than doubtful tradition history behind them.

The understanding of West Semitic religion which was mainly based on the Old Testament has, however, strongly influenced the evaluation of the Ugaritic source materials, since these became available to us in the 1930s. Even though it had suddenly become possible to read mythological texts which derived directly from a society which was older than the historical Israel, scholars tended to force the Old Testament understanding of Canaanite cult and religious practice onto these materials. There has been perhaps too little effort made to study these sources without presuppositions. Thus the very violent events which are mentioned in the mythological literature from Ugarit have often been directly connected by scholars with the rejection of fertility religion in the Old Testament. In this vein pietistic Bible scholars, like the well-known American archeologist and orientalist, W.F. Albright, were able to conclude that Canaanite religion was probably the most disgusting phenomenon humanity has ever known. The possibility that there may have been other sides to Canaanite religion than sex orgies seems to have escaped many scholars who have concerned themselves with that religion, just as these aspects were once 'overlooked' by the circles within ancient Israel who regarded this form of religion as their main opponent.

A more useful approach would consist in the demonstration of a number of features in the Ugaritic source materials which point towards religious conditions in first-millennium Israel. Unfortunately, however, such features have usually been regarded as remnants of a Canaanite religion which was still influential upon the pure Israelite religion after the settlement of the Israelite tribes in Palestine. But one could with equal justice regard such features as indications of the basis upon which Israelite religion evolved. The features in question might be such things as types of sacrifices which we encounter in the Ugaritic texts, or the religious metaphorical language which underlies many parts of the Old Testament poetic and Wisdom literatures. It is more or less possible to write 'commentary' on the whole of this religious tradition with the aid of a study of ancient Near Eastern pictorial art. This also applies to the general understanding of the world, as expressed in Ugaritic and Israelite culture: the understanding of the creation of the world, or of the course of the year; it might also apply to fundamental ethical attitudes which were common to Ugarit and Israel, including above all social ethics, the concern to care for the needs of the poor and the worst situated in society.

2.2 Ugaritic Religion
2.2.1 Ugarit
Canaanite religion in Palestine may on no account be regarded as simply identical with the Ugaritic religious tradition. Ugarit was a trade metropolis situated on the Mediterranean in northern Syria. Since the town was a trade centre, representatives from the entire West Asiatic world met in it; they came from the then-contemporary empire in Asia Minor, that of the Hittites (to which Ugarit for some time was tributary), from the Egyptian empire to the south, from Mesopotamia to the east, and also from the Mycenaean realm in the Aegean. The population did not consist of Semitic elements only, and especially not in the capital, where a Hurrian-speaking element lived alongside people of the most diverse origins, who mainly resided there in conjunction with their respective trading activities. Thus, as is the case with many other aspects of Ugaritic social life, Ugaritic religion may well have been influenced by foreign practices and beliefs. Accordingly, it would be helpful for any religion-historical analysis of the region if we also discovered a corpus of religious texts from points further south, in Phoenicia or, better still, in Palestine; but as of yet the materials from these areas are scarce indeed. They are confined to material remains such as temple structures and graphic depictions of deities, and to such things as the names which were employed in these areas, in which the names of various deities comprise the theophoric elements.

Having acknowledged these difficulties, it is nevertheless possible to depict Ugaritic religion as just one of the many varieties of West Semitic religion, and the Ugaritic religious materials remain greatly significant, since many of the elements found in Ugaritic religion are in fact represented in the Old Testament sources.

2.2.2 The Ba'al Poems
The Ugaritic sources consist mainly of a number of mythological texts which are especially concerned with *Ba'al* and his fortunes. They consist, in part, of a cycle of texts which, taken together, make

up a lengthy epic about *Ba'al*, and, in part, of some isolated texts and fragments which also contribute to our understanding of this deity. There are far fewer texts about other deities, and most references to them are to be found in the Ba'al poems. There are, however, some other independent mythological texts concerned with other deities. There is also some information about the Ugaritic gods in two epic texts which deal with Ugaritic kingship and depict its mythological origin; these are the poems about *Aqhat* and *Kereth*. Finally, in addition to the epics we possess some lists of the various Ugaritic deities.

A thumbnail characterization of the Ba'al poems reveals that they apparently have to do with the fortunes of this god throughout the annual cycle. It is difficult to say just where they begin and where they end since, logically, they may not end at all, but merely point to a re-beginning. Ba'al is a somewhat 'unstable' deity; in one period he is dead; in another he is the king. Both periods are introduced by a divine conflict. In the first of these Ba'al combats *Mot* ('death') and loses; he is annihilated and buried. In the second he struggles with two sea monsters, *Yam* ('the sea') and *Nahar* ('the stream' or 'the flood'). Between the two battles, that is, during the period when Ba'al no longer exists, the land languishes; it *dies*, while Ba'al's sister *Anath* searches the land in an attempt to find him and revivify him. While this is going on, other gods attempt in vain to take over Ba'al's rôle as king. A single isolated text also reveals the sexual relations between Ba'al and Anath, represented as the coupling of a young bull with a heifer.

2.2.3 *Ba'al and Anath*

Historians of religion have had no difficulty in characterizing Ba'al as a god of *vegetation* and *fertility*, who was represented by the seasonal rains. If one considers the course of the seasons in the Levant, one will recognize a number of features which, in a manner of speaking, are mythically described in the Ba'al texts: the cessation of the rains in the spring months, the dying of the vegetation in summer, the recurrence of the rains in the autumn, and the vegetation which flourishes anew.

It is to be noted that Ba'al's death is every bit as essential as his resurrection. If Ba'al does not die, it will continue to rain also in the months in which the grain reaches maturity. The sun, which causes ripening, and the earth will not be fertilized so that no new grain can be sown and nourished. Therefore, the central theme in the Ba'al poems is the maintenance of the natural order, that is, the *cosmos*, and this theme recurs in the battles between the gods. Mot kills Ba'al in order to stop the rains; Anath kills Mot in order to harvest the corn (Mot's death is in fact depicted with terms borrowed from the harvest vocabulary); Ba'al combats the sea creatures so that the rains which are to come will provide fertile moisture for the earth (i.e. fresh water), rather than a sterile flood (the salt sea), which would be synonymous with the cessation of *cosmos* and the initiation of *chaos*. The battles between the gods are accordingly frequently described with the term 'chaos battle'. Finally, it is easy to see that the myth of the coupling of Ba'al and Anath supplements the larger epic picture: the topic is not the ripening and harvesting of the grain, but the ability of the animals to reproduce.

Anath has other functions than that of being Ba'al's saviour. In many respects she represents the typical female deity of the entire Mediterranean area. She is at once virginal and yet the mother of all life, just as she is also love, but simultaneously the blood-thirsty goddess of war who rejoices most when she bathes in the blood of her slain. She is the strong woman who seizes the initiative when men recoil or are seized by fear, and is accordingly the protector of all life, the surrogate who carries the day when the other gods, from El, the lord of the pantheon, on down to the last of the gods, do not dare to challenge Death in order to recover the vanished Ba'al.

2.2.4 'The Cultic Drama'
It should be obvious that this religion of Ba'al and Anath must have been popular in an agrarian society like that of Ugarit, and particularly outside of the capital, although even the incomes of the élite were mainly dependent on the maintenance of the natural cycle. Many scholars have accordingly understood the Ba'al poems as a sort of 'libretto' of a *cultic drama* which, or so they have asserted, was enacted in connection with the decisive crisis in the annual cycle, that is, at the time when the arrival of the rains was crucial to the sowing of seed. In other words, it made it possible for people to face the future with hope. The Old Testament materials had already revealed that the New Year festival took place in the autumn, and scholars had therefore—largely thanks to the insights of the Norwegian Old Testament scholar, Sigmund Mowinckel—already arrived at a number of hypotheses about the existence of such a

cultic drama during the era of the Israelite monarchy. For this reason it was easy—perhaps entirely too easy—to transfer these theories, which, after all, were only conjectural, onto the Ugaritic materials and then to see in them the confirmation of Mowinckel's hypotheses. It is correct that if the Ba'al epic was directly utilized in a cultic context, then this must have been part of the New Year ceremonials. But, to be completely candid, we have no idea as to what function the epic could have had in the event.

A comparable epic work from another culture is the sprawling Babylonian epic known as *Enuma Elish*, which we know was employed in the Babylonian New Year celebration. The poem itself recounts the story of Marduk's (in the Neo-Babylonian period Bel's, i.e. Ba'al's) battle with the forces of chaos under the leadership of *Tiamat* (the salt sea), the creation of the world, and the elevation of Marduk as king of the gods. However, we happen to know that it was not used in the context of a dramatic presentation of the myth; it was instead read aloud by a priest. This Babylonian epic, which has been strongly influenced by West Semitic religion, and which may have been composed when a West Semitic dynasty reigned in Babylon during the first part of the second millennium BCE, is admirably suited, by reason of its contents, to the New Year festival. By way of contrast, only parts of the Ba'al poems are appropriate to this time of year, while other parts would seem better suited to different seasons of the year. It is therefore likely that, as they stand, the Ba'al poems make up a literary composition whose author had worked together the various myths which were associated with the entire cultic annual cycle.

2.2.5 El

As mentioned previously, a number of gods play fairly remote rôles in the Ba'al poems; one such is the god *El*, who behaves strangely passively and ineffectually in these texts. However, El cannot defend his behaviour in the epics, since there are no texts from Ugarit dealing with him which are comparable to those which deal with Ba'al. On the other hand, the lists of deities, Ugaritic personal names, and references to El in the rest of the West Semitic region imply that El must have been extremely important in Ugarit. His very titulature (which, however, has not been found in Ugarit) as 'creator of heaven and earth' tells much about his position. As the creator and therefore the maintainer of the created world, El was generally acknowledged to be the supreme god, but unfortunately we possess no epic works which describe the creation of the world from the vantage-point of Ugaritic religion. It is, however, inconceivable that this region should not have had some form of creation myth. And in fact, we do encounter creation mythology outside of Ugarit: in Israel, the Hittite empire, and in Mesopotamia, where the creation of the world was combined with Marduk's battle with the sea; and, of course, in Egypt where several versions existed, of which some were probably of West Semitic origin.

2.2.6 *Other Gods of the Ugaritic Pantheon*

Some of the other Ugaritic deities are also worthy of mention. Ba'al is called 'son of *Dagan*' ('the grain') in the poems. This is all that we learn of Dagan in the Ugaritic epic texts. However, the West Semitic onomastica suggest that he was one of the most important gods, and we happen to know that he was worshipped in great temples in Ugarit and elsewhere; indeed, in Ugarit the temple of Dagan may well have been the largest single religious complex.

Another god who is not mentioned in the great Ba'al epic, but who figures frequently elsewhere, is the *storm-god*, a deity who was worshipped everywhere in the ancient Near East under a variety of names. Among the Hurrians he was known as Teshub; among the Hittites, as Tarhunt; and among the Semitic-speaking peoples as *Hadad*, under which name he recurs in the Ugaritic texts, where, however, he is identified with Ba'al. This provides us with yet another reason for the conclusion that Ugaritic religion cannot be regarded as normative for all West Semitic religion, but only as a manifestation of the religious type that was dominant in the Levant.

There were also female deities alongside the previously mentioned Anath; of these, only one will be mentioned here. Just as Ba'al had a female counterpart in the form of Anath, so, too, El had one in the form of *Ashera*. Her function in Ugarit is not well illuminated, except that in addition to being El's consort she must also have been regarded as the queen of the gods. Her rôle in the Ba'al poems is quite peculiar, as she there figures as a decided opponent of Ba'al. Ashera will be mentioned again later in connection with Israelite religion, in which she (or rather, her cult symbol) was regarded as a major enemy by adherents of the pure Yahwistic religion.

2.2.7 *Religious Praxis at Ugarit*

We possess some information about the actual conduct of religion in Ugarit thanks to, among other things, some ritual texts which were discovered there. We are informed that there were several sizable temple complexes dedicated to the more important deities, in particular for Ba'al and Dagan. It also appears that Ugarit had a *sacrificial cult* which included several categories of sacrifices: animal and vegetable sacrifices, partial-sacrifices (in which only a part of the sacrificial animal was dedicated to the god, while the rest was consumed by the congregation; in Israel sometimes called a 'peace offering'), whole-offerings (in which the entire animal belonged to the deity), grain offerings, and so forth. A *priesthood* was employed to maintain the sacrifices and the temple cult in general, under the leadership of a chief priest. The priesthood was subdivided into a number of categories, dependent on cultic function. As elsewhere in the Middle East during the second millennium BCE, we may assume that *temple prophets* were also employed in Ugarit in conjunction with the services, just as there was probably a regular practice of divination via the interpretation of *omina*, and for which a specialized priesthood was necessary.

2.2.8 *The King*

The king has often been held to have been the leader of the Ugaritic cult, and it is a fact that we possess a few administrative texts which refer not only to the king's but also to the queen's functions within the cult. Thus, many scholars have been prone to regard Ugaritic kingship as sacral, which is to say that the king was held to be divine or as the medium through which contact with the divine realm was achieved. It is also claimed that this contact with the divine legitimated the king's position in society. In this connection, scholars have attempted to work out cultic interpretations of the two epic poems referred to previously, that is, those concerned with the mythical origins of the dynasty, and these poems have sometimes been regarded as religious texts which reflect dramatic cultic rituals which were interconnected with the deeper significance of the monarchy. Some scholars have even gone so far as to maintain that the king and queen were the principal *dramatis personae* in the cult drama about Ba'al and Anath. They have accordingly claimed that the high point of the ceremony in question took the form of the ritual copulation of the king and queen.

This interpretation is not without its problems, although it has considerable popularity. There is surely a world of difference between the picture of the monarchy which emerges from the epic texts which deal with its origins and the picture which emerges from the hundreds of administrative documents in our possession which come the royal palace. For example, there is nothing in these documents to suggest that the king regarded himself as divine, as is obvious from his titulature, which is simply 'NN, king of Ugarit, son of NN, king of Ugarit'. Furthermore, the rôle of the king in the business life of a trading community like Ugarit is hard to reconcile with notions of the sacral significance of the monarchy which modern historians of religion have advocated.

There are a number of possible explanations for the discrepancies between the epic poems and the administrative texts. One is that the administration and populace of ancient Ugarit were entirely able to distinguish between the king *qua* administrator and the king *qua* cult leader. In other words, that people were able to keep these two spheres, the sacred and the profane, logically separate from one another. However, this conflicts with all that we otherwise happen to know about pre-classical logic (the so-called 'pensée sauvage'), which ordinarily forms a logical system in which the sacred and the profane are combined as a series of interconnected levels which reciprocally influence one another. If the king was held to be divine when he resided in the temple, one would also expect him to be regarded as such when he resided in his palace—a feature which becomes abundantly clear the moment one examines cultures in which the sacral position of the king was unquestioned, as, for example, in ancient Egypt.

Another possibility has been pointed out by the Italian assyriologist Mario Liverani. Liverani suggests that the Ugaritic poems about Aqhat and Kereth are *literary fossils*, that the understanding of kingship which they express was archaic in the late Bronze Age, a remnant of the past. It was able to survive into the Late Bronze Age because at that time kings still hoped to present themselves as mighty heroes and just judges, even though the reality was quite different.

Finally, it is also possible that the divine origin of the monarchy in Ugarit never had practical significance outside its rôle as provider of the mythic legitimation of the existing monarchy.

Naturally, these insights have profound consequences for such notions as that of the sacral marriage, which can hardly have had to do with any actual ritual usage of the late Bronze Age. A Ugaritic administrative text refers to a certain quantity of wine as 'the queen's sacrifice on the new-sown field'; but this can hardly have referred to sexual rites which took place on the field in question, but rather to the fact that the queen, as a leader of the sacrificial cult, represented the women of her society in the same way as the king represented the men. In other words, the king was the highest instance in the administration of the cult because the cult organization was part of the palace system. Similarly, the priests in Ugarit belonged to the social class called 'the king's men', meaning that they were merely part of the personnel of the palace administration.

2.3 *The Old Testament Understanding of Canaanite Religion*
The Old Testament's description of Canaanite religion seems unambiguous. Let us look at a couple of examples. The first of these is provided by the prophet Hosea (4.13):

> They sacrifice on the mountain-tops, they burn offerings on the high places, under an oak, a poplar, a terebinth, since their shade is good, so your daughters also play the whore, and your brides commit adultery.

The second passage is from the Deuteronomistic literature (2 Kgs 17.8ff.):

> They followed the customs of those peoples whom Yahweh had driven from before the Israelites . . . and the Israelites conceived unacceptable things against Yahweh their God; they built high places for themselves in all their towns, from the watchtowers to the fortified towns; they set up pillars and Ashera-poles (?) on all the high hills and under every green tree; and they burned incense on all the high places, like the nations which Yahweh had driven away before them; and they did evil things, so that they provoked Yahweh; they worshipped idols.

The perspective in both accounts is clearly polemical, although some characteristic features may be deduced from them anyway. In Palestine, worship was not ordinarily localized around the great temple complexes, as, for example, in Ugarit, but around local sanctuaries which were much more modestly equipped. Instead of actual divine images, these sanctuaries possessed only crudely carved or even uncarved stone pillars which represented Ba'al (the

so-called *masseboth*) and wooden poles (or images which were
crudely carved in wood), which were identified with the goddess
Ashera. The sanctuaries seem to have been frequently, but not
exclusively, situated just outside of the towns, by large solitary trees
or in groves on the heights. Excavations of Bronze Age town sites in
Palestine however, have, revealed that the towns contained an
official system of worship based on permanent temple structures. In
a few passages in the Old Testament we also hear of temples,
especially in connection with Ba'al, as for example, in the context of
Jehu's purge of the cult in the northern kingdom. On this occasion,
however, the temple in question was an official sanctuary of the
Tyrian Ba'al which had been built by the previous monarchical
family.

According to Hosea's description, the cult that was practised at
these sanctuaries consisted mainly of sex orgies. Many scholars have
been of the same opinion, although they have scarcely been neutral
observers. On the contrary, they have embroidered on an understanding of Canaanite religion which was established already in
ecclesiastical tradition, and perhaps also in late Jewish tradition, but
there is considerable doubt as to whether the texts under discussion
can bear such an interpretation if one subjects them to a non-
partisan analysis. We read that the 'daughters' of Israel 'play the
whore' with 'the Ba'als' and that Israelite men have sexual congress
with 'foreign women' ('harlots'; the foreign woman, that is, another
man's wife, is by definition a potential harlot). This does not signify
that they participate in sacral prostitution in the Canaanite
sanctuaries, but rather that they commit adultery by cultivating the
Ba'als instead of their rightful god, Yahweh. One ought also to note
the fact that Hosea's criticisms have to do with *Israelites* who
worship the Ba'als in sanctuaries that were situated in *Israel*.
Canaanites are not criticized for worshipping these deities in
sanctuaries that were situated in territories inhabited by Canaanites.
In passages like the one in 2 Kings 17, the understanding of what is
Israelite and what Canaanite is completely dependent upon the
understanding of history which underlies an account of Israel's
history (i.e. the Deuteronomistic History) which we have seen to be
late and ahistorical.

3. *Monotheistic Yahwism*

3.1 *The Sources: the Legal Corpora*
3.1.1 *Did the Law or the Prophets Come First?*

Reconstructions of the history of Israel's religion usually take a *diachronic* approach, and thus begin with the period of the Judges, continue on into the era of the monarchy, and then conclude with the post-exilic period. The difficulty with all this, however, is that, in reality, we know nothing concrete about the religion of pre-national Israel. In addition to this, only a very few scholars reckon the religion of the monarchy to have been authentic, *genuinely* Israelite religion; it is held instead to have been *syncretistic*. On this view, if one would seek to find the true Israelite religion, one would have to look at the period in which all inauthentic elements had been expunged from it, which can scarcely have happened before the exilic or (particularly) post-exilic periods. Thus, the real Israelite Yahwism at its purest is to be found in the religious legislation contained in the Pentateuch, in spite of the fact that the literary framework of this legislation is, respectively, the Priestly source or redaction and the Deuteronomistic redaction. Having arrived at this conclusion, the historian of religion then projects the understanding of Israelite religion which is expressed in the cultic legislation back to the earliest times.

Already Julius Wellhausen, the most eminent representative of the study of the Old Testament in the nineteenth century, recognized that this procedure was untenable. For this reason he established as a virtually programmatic slogan that *the law is younger than the prophets*, and concluded that it is necessarily dependent on the prophetic proclamation. However, the discovery of legal corpora outside of Israel, particularly in Mesopotamia, led scholars to revise Wellhausen's understanding of the law. Scholars found this appropriate because the Mesopotamian laws were from the second millennium BCE, and in fact from the first half of this period. In doing so, however, they overlooked the main difference between the Mesopotamian and Old Testament laws, namely that the lion's share of the latter have to do with religion, whereas the former are juridical measures. Admittedly, the Mesopotamian laws are fitted into a religious context (the king announces to the gods that he has reigned justly by arriving at the judgments which the laws represent), but their contents are juridical and not religious. Only a small portion of the laws in the Old Testament, that is, laws cast as juridical cases, are

laws of this sort; they are contained in the first part of the so-called
'Book of the Covenant' (Exod. 21.2–23.16), of which corpus,
however, already the second part (Exod. 22.17–23.16) moves in a
different and predominantly religious world. The juridical materials
in the Book of the Covenant may well be very old, since there are
many points of agreement between them and the Mesopotamian
legal collections. The age of the second part, however, is imponderable,
a consideration which applies to the rest of the religious legislation in
the Old Testament.

The majority of the religious laws are contained in collections of
greater or lesser size, of which the Book of the Covenant is but one.
Others are the *Holiness Code* (Leviticus 17–26) and the Deuteronomistic legislation in the book of Deuteronomy. In addition to these
there are some short collections, such as the Ten Commandments, to
which special difficulties adhere. The occurrence of the large
collections in which many different types of legislation are contained
reveals that some individual regulations may be much older than
their present literary situation would suggest. It is therefore clear
that on this point it would be wise to modify Wellhausen's view and
to radicalize it at the same time, and thus to conclude that *it is not the
letter of the law that is later than the prophets, but its 'spirit'*. The laws
dealing with the different sorts of offerings, the priestly tasks and
vestments, cultic purity, and so forth, could well date from any
period in the history of Israel. They may even have been borrowed by
the Israelites from the societies which existed in Palestine before
Israel. In the nature of the matter, many such regulations are
completely undatable. By way of contrast, however, the spirit that
animates these laws, which is to say the emphasis which is placed on,
for example, the sacrificial laws in a given corpus, which may
concentrate more on the fact that it is the right people who make the
sacrifices than on the fact that sacrifice is made, may well derive
from the time subsequent to the prophetic proclamation.

3.1.2 *Religion in 'Historical' Dress*
An important side of that feature which has been defined as 'spirit' in
these pages consists in the characteristic *historicization* of the
religion. Virtually every component of the Israelite religion has been
worked into its present situation in a historical context. Officially, all
the laws derive from Moses, whether they are Priestly or Deuteronomistic. However, even within the great legal corpora we find that

individual laws may be historically founded. Thus, the great cultic festivals during the course of the year are not explained as the harvest festivals which they once were, but as remembrances of historical events in Israel's past: likewise, such rites as circumcision are traced back to primeval events, in this case to the circumcision of Abraham. In other words, virtually every part of Israelite religion, as expressed in the late sources, was assigned a historical or aetiological explanation. Even the sanctuaries themselves were traced back to historical individuals, and the various myths Israel adopted were reinterpreted so that in 'demythologized' form they could become part of the history of Israel (for example, the Near Eastern myth of the chaos battle was reinterpreted as the crossing of the Reed Sea, or, if you prefer, this event was reinterpreted in terms of the chaos battle). The fact that the historical explanations are secondary is evidenced already by the consideration that the events in question were frequently ahistorical, that is, they never took place. And this fact in itself shows that the religious institutions had their own prehistories before the linkage of 'myth and history' had come about.

3.2 *Religious Praxis*
3.2.1 *The Temple*
When the legal materials were incorporated into their present literary situations, the people responsible felt that Yahweh only had a single legitimate sanctuary, namely the temple in Jerusalem. We possess a number of different descriptions of the structure and organization of the temple. The main source is 1 Kings 6-7, to which, however, should be added the prophet Ezekiel's description of the future temple (chs. 40-48), which in all probability really describes the original temple. Furthermore, the description of the Tabernacle (tent of meeting) in Exodus 25-27 and 36-38 presumably also reflects the sanctuary in Jerusalem.

Judging by its measurements, the temple, which was constructed by Solomon in the tenth century BCE, was a rather modest structure; or, as is usually pointed out in Denmark, it was not much larger than an ordinary Danish village church. Its significance was based on its lavish furnishings and on the religious prestige which was associated with the site. Religion, however, was not so important to Solomon as to prevent him from making his own palace significantly larger than the house of Yahweh.

The temple complex was divided into three sections: two outer
courts, one within the other, and a temple structure consisting of
three parts: a vestibule or court, an inner hall called 'The Holy
Place', and a 'cella', 'The Holy of Holies'. A number of important
cult objects were situated in the inner courtyard, to which the
general population had access; these included the alter of burnt
offering, the Sea (for ritual ablutions), and, at the entrance to the
vestibule, the two pillars, bearing the names Jachin and Boaz. There
were ten candelabra, the showbread, and the incense altar in the
Holy Place, to which the priesthood had access; and finally, in the
Holy of Holies, the Ark of the Covenant was situated, which the
entire temple was, so to speak, constructed to house. This area was
reserved for the High Priest alone.

In the biblical literature the Ark is variously described both with
respect to form and function, for which reason it is now difficult to
say just what its original rôle was, and where it came from. But
scholars generally agree that it was used as a sort of war palladium,
as a transportable cult symbol or even image of the deity in the pre-
monarchical period, and that David brought this symbol, which had
languished for some time out of the popular awareness, to his new
capital, Jerusalem. There he established the framework for the Ark
which (re-)endowed it with significance. The discussion of the origin
of the Ark is in reality a microcosmic model of the current discussion
as to the origins of the Israelite society, although it is older. To pose
the alternative sharply: did the Ark come to Palestine from without
together with the Israelite tribes, as the Old Testament tradition
maintains, or was it a cult object which was firmly rooted in the
country, perhaps originally associated with a religion which may
very well not have been Yahwistic at all?

The question of the origin of the Ark is inseparable from the
question of its function. Was the Ark a box in which the 'tablets of
the law' were kept, or was it the throne of a deity, the armrests of
which took the form of cherubs, that is, mythological beings, thus
revealing it to be type of throne that was well known in the Near
East?

An earlier popular explanation was that the Ark was originally a
container which contained the tablets on which the Ten Commandments were inscribed. However, after its transferral to Jerusalem, it
was regarded as Yahweh's throne. Another and perhaps more
plausible possibility is that after the Ark was removed and disappeared

in connection with the destruction of the temple in 587 BCE there was no longer any place in later theology for a throne. Therefore, the ark changed its character and became the container of the Law, a transformation which corresponds well to the then contemporary emphasis on the Law as the centre of the faith.

It is conceivable that before the time of David the Ark was a local cult object, a throne which was situated in Shiloh, where it symbolized the worship of the god El, who was venerated there under the title of 'El of the Armies' (*El Sebaoth*). This throne was then lost during the Philistine wars, and was forgotten. When David realized that he needed a cult symbol which could serve as the focus of his new national sanctuary, he had the Ark brought to Jerusalem. His son Solomon then constructed a house for it and made it the most important implement in the cult of 'Yahweh of the Armies' (*Yahweh Sebaoth*). It remained in the temple in Jerusalem until 587 BCE, when it was carried off to Babylon and disappeared. In the tradition the Ark then changed its character so that it became the box in which the Law was kept, and which was thought to derive from the mobile sanctuary which Moses was supposed to have constructed. Of course, in this fashion it was ultimately possible to guarantee that the entire Law was authentically Mosaic.

3.2.2 *The Priesthood*

According to the laws the legitimate cult in the temple in Jerusalem was maintained by the legitimate and authorized priesthood who, in addition to having received practical theological education were also supposed to come from a certain line of descent. The legislation distinguishes between three groups of priests who competed for the control of the temple cult in the late pre-exilic and perhaps even in the post-exilic periods. These were the Levitical priesthood, the Aaronite priesthood, and the Zadokite priesthood. The Levitical priesthood was supposed to be the ancient and true Israelite priestly class; in the late and stereotyped lists of tribes they were reckoned to be a tribe in their own right and held to have managed the cult round the country at the local sanctuaries in the pre-national period. It is a paradoxical fact, however, that the situation of this group of priests was materially weakened by the cult centralization under Josiah, since these priests were attached to the local sanctuaries which were destroyed. Moreover, they had no rôle to play at the royal sanctuary. At the same time, however, it was required of the priests (if it had not already been the case earlier) that they be of Levitical lineage, even if they did not belong to this group.

One concrete result of this genealogical ideology manifested itself in connection with the *Aaronite* priesthood. The prehistory of this group is not easy to trace, since its name, supposedly derived from Aaron, the brother of Moses the *Levite* suggests that they had at one time done service in the Ark sanctuary (in Hebrew, *Aron* means 'Ark', while *Aharon* is the name of Moses' brother, though they are probably identical words). Other traditions, however, relate the Aaronites to the 'anti-sanctuary' in Bethel. In fact, the Deuteronomistic tradition pointedly denies that the priests of the sanctuary in Bethel were Levites at all (1 Kgs 12.31). However, the association with the bull-cult in Bethel is emphasized even in traditions which do not deny Levitic descent in connection with the story of the golden calf (Exodus 32), which may not be read without keeping an eye on the description of the founding of the cult in Bethel.

A Priestly passage like Numbers 18, however, records the Aaronites as having achieved a leading position with respect to their 'brothers', the Levites. Thus the enmity between the various priestly classes seems to have left traces behind it in the history of the tradition. Some traditions (presumably of Levitic origin, or at least with pro-Levite sympathies) directly reject the Aaronites; these, however, are counterbalanced by others in which the Aaronites are assigned the place of honour. These discrepancies would be easy to explain if the Aaronites had had an ancient connection to the Ark sanctuary in Jerusalem, since during the period of the monarchy this priesthood would then have served at the royal sanctuary, whereas the Levites served in the local sanctuaries.

The third priestly group, the *Zadokites*, are more difficult to localize. Many scholars have seen them in relation to the pre-Israelite cult in the city-state of Jerusalem. They have thus regarded their ancestor, Zadok, who became one of David's chief priests, as a member of this priesthood. The genealogies relate the Zadokites closely to the Aaronite priests, which emphasizes their association with the Jerusalem temple and with its most important priestly group.

3.2.3 *The Priestly Functions*
The priesthood exercised a number of functions in the temple. Among these were the priestly rôles as religious adviser, sacrificer,

and diviner. To take the last-mentioned function first, the task of predicting the future could take place in a number of possible forms, not all of which enjoyed the same status in the religious legislation. The most honoured were the statements which were derived through the use of the *Urim* and *Thummim*, two cultic appurtenances which were part of the priestly vestments together with the *ephod*. We have no idea what these objects were like, although most scholars hold the Urim and Thummim to have been a pair of lots through which one received answers by 'tossing heads or tails'. The practice of taking omens from the viscera of sacrificial animals, which was quite extensive in the ancient Orient, was probably known in Israel, if for no other reason than the opposition to this practice in the Law (cf. Lev. 19.26 and Deut. 18.10).

The priest's rôle of sacrificer was of at least equal importance to his rôle of diviner. The cultic laws require the individual Israelite to bring his sacrifice to Jerusalem, where the priests would then administer the sacrificial ritual. This, however, is an idealized picture of the sacrificial cult, although it may represent the way things were done in the 'second' (post-exilic) temple. But it cannot have been the case originally, since at least in principle every Israelite *pater familias* carried out the familial sacrifices. In the post-exilic period the sacrificial cult outside of Jerusalem was replaced by the synagogues, although the Samaritans continued to sacrifice in their sanctuary on Mt Garizim (as they still do today).

3.2.4 *The Sacrificial Cult*
There were a variety of types of sacrifices: private sacrifices and official sacrifices, daily sacrifices and sacrifices for special occasions, animal and non-animal sacrifices, and so forth. A common characteristic is that the sacrificial animals in question were expected to be without blemish, and they had to be selected from particular categories of animal, as the priestly sacrificial legislation was dependent on a much older tradition which distinguished between *clean* and *unclean* animals. There have been many theories as to the reasons for this distinction. In practice, however, those animals were sacrificed with which the Israelites were most familiar, and which had been domesticated in the Near East for several thousand years when the Israelite laws of sacrifice were formulated.

Each day of the temple year required its sacrifices in the form of *blood sacrifice* (a lamb) and *vegetable sacrifices* (e.g. the showbread, a type of grain offering); but in addition to these there were numerous special sacrifices which were above all paid for by private individuals. They could have any number of reasons for offering sacrifice; there were sacrifices to be offered in fulfilment of a vow which the individual had made in a time of need. There were also 'sin' offerings, 'atonement' sacrifices, self-imposed fines to be paid to the deity, and sacrifices which were imposed on the individual by the sacral legislation. Blood sacrifices, in the course of which animals were sacrificed in the temple, were completed either by the immolation of the entire animal on the altar of burnt offering (the so-called *'olah*, or 'whole-offering'), and which usually figured in connection with sin or atonement sacrifices, or the animal was shared in some fashion between the deity and the sacrificer.

The 'thank-offering' was undertaken on happier occasions when one or another event was to be celebrated, and during which one consumed the sacrificial animal together with the deity. The inedible portions, such as bones and skin which had been coated with the fat of the animal, were offered up to Yahweh, while the meat itself was distributed among the sacrificers and the priests who participated in the service.

The sacrifice of the first-fruits was a special sort of thank-offering, whether the sacrifice in question was the first of the grain or of the herd ('first-born sacrifices'). Both of these sacrifices were especially associated with particular festivals. Of course, a certain type of sacrifice of the first-born could, in the nature of things, be sacrificed as occasion arose: the sacrifices which took place in thanks for the birth of a male offspring in the family.

The Old Testament mentions a few examples of human sacrifice; thus, for example, in 2 Kings 3, king Mesha or Moab sacrifices his son in a time of dire need. The story, however, can hardly be regarded as a historical report, since it is part of the legendary Elijah-Elisha cycle. Similar considerations apply to the narrative about Jephthah's daughter (Judg. 11.34-40), who had to be sacrificed by her father in fulfilment of a 'vow' when he returned from war and she was the first to greet him on his return. The story is a fairytale, a legend which had travelled throughout the cultures in the Mediterranean region. Moreover, neither of the two narratives can be claimed to be concerned with sacrifices of the first-born; in both tales the point is quite different.

Against this, we have the narrative of Abraham's 'sacrifice' of his son Isaac (Genesis 22), which certainly deals with the notion of the sacrifice of the first-born. The point of the story, however, is that the son was not sacrificed, and that the human sacrifice was replaced with the sacrifice of an animal. Very historically orientated students of religion have accordingly held that the Israelites originally practised the barbaric custom of sacrificing the first-born, and that it was replaced by a more 'humane' practice in historical times. This is, however, unlikely, as the custom of human sacrifice was in the ancient Near East so chronologically remote that it is doubtful whether it could have influenced the Old Testament tradition. The demand for a ransom for the first-born son was not the result of the fact that one had once (one, two, or three thousand years before?) sacrificed the first-born. It is instead based on an analogy. It was impossible to avoid recognizing the tension between sacrificing the first-born of the domestic animals and the fact that people did not thank their God with a corresponding payment. It is unclear as to whether the special emphasis in the Old Testament on the custom of ransoming the first-born was related to the emergence of a custom which manifested itself particularly among the Phoenicians in the first millennium BCE in the form of infant sacrifices to 'Moloch', of which there may be some indications in Judah during the monarchical period. We know too little about the form of this sacrifice, its possible extent, distribution in the Judaean populace (the royal family or the élite of the capital) to be sure that this custom was the occasion of the general rules about substitute sacrifices in the priestly legislation.

3.2.5 *The Festivals*

The temple worship was especially intense at particular times of the year, when the great festivals were celebrated. The annual cycle contained three great festal periods, beginning with the New Year festival, *Rosh Hashshana*, which normally took place in the month of October. The 'Festival of Booths', *Succoth*, took place in direct extension of the New Year festival, as did the 'Great Day of Atonement', *Yom hakkippur*. According to the historicizing interpretation, the Festival of Booths served to remind the Israelites of their wandering in the desert, and the Great Day of Atonement was a day of national lament and penitence. On this day all the accumulated sins of the year were transferred to a scapegoat which was subsequently driven away from the society, out into the desert where 'evil' lurked (seen in the eyes of the city-dwellers). Thus, sin, that is,

evil, was expelled from society to the place where it belonged, and
society was cleansed of its sin.

The second great festal period in the Jewish religious calendar was
Passover, *pesach*, which took place in the months of spring. The
'historical' reason for celebrating this festival was the exodus from
Egypt, and the biblical text on which it was based is the so-called
'Passover Legend' in Exodus 1–15, which some scholars have gone so
far as to claim was a liturgical text designed for use during this
festival. However, this festival also contains some elements which
suggest that the Passover, too, was a variety of New Year festival,
since it coincided with the first harvest of the new year, the barley
harvest, and with the births of the animal stock. Thus, a permanent
ingredient in the Passover was the sacrifice of the first-fruits and the
first of the new-born lambs as thank-offerings to Yahweh. The New
Year aspect is further emphasized by the purgation of the old grain,
which in practice meant the bread that was left over from the
previous harvest. This was (and is) expressed through the use of
'unleavened bread' (*mazzoth*) in the meals of the Passover period.

Finally, the third of the great festivals, which, taken together, are
usually referred to as 'pilgrimage festivals', was the 'Festival of
Weeks', or Pentecost (from Greek *pentekostē*, 'fifty'), seven weeks
after Passover. This festival coincides with the wheat harvest, but the
historicizing interpretation relates it to the events on Sinai after the
Exodus from Egypt. The Festival of Weeks was therefore a
commemoration of the Law as the gift of God, for the revelation on
Sinai, and for the covenant between Yahweh and Israel.

The historian of religion has no difficulty demonstrating that the
historical clothing of all three pilgrimage festivals is secondary. Thus,
for example, the bases of the Passover and the Festival of Weeks were
celebrations for successfully completed harvests (barley and wheat),
and for the animals' fecundity. The Festival of Booths, too, points to
a harvest season, namely the harvest of fruit and grapes (for
winemaking), which take place in the autumn months and conclude
the harvest cycle of the year. In this season the peasant population
traditionally kept to the orchards and vineyards and lived in huts
constructed from the available materials (branches and leaves).
These 'booths' show just how secondary the historical interpretation
really is, for precisely the materials in question are not exactly
abundant in a desert.

As far as the Passover is concerned, most scholars have long been of the opinion that it originally consisted of two independent festivals, one which celebrated the barley harvest, and one which celebrated the birth of the young animals. As long as scholars continued to adhere to the Old Testament account of Israel's origins they had no difficulty in maintaining that the barley festival, being agrarian in nature, was originally *Canaanite*, whereas the celebration of the animal births derived from the (originally small-cattle nomadic) Israelites. It was accordingly further held that the feast of Passover was an example of syncretism between Israelite and Canaanite religion that had taken place early in the history of Israel. Of course, the account of Israel's beginnings offered in these pages suggests that such a reconstruction is unreasonable. There were never separate Israelite and Canaanite festivals for the animals and the barley, respectively. If there really were two originally discrete festivals, they must have come from different sectors within Palestinian society—one nomadic, and one agrarian. It is more likely, however, that already the Israelite villages of the pre-national period (and presumably long before the Bronze Age society) celebrated a single festival in the spring in which both elements were combined.

We have some additional information which indicates when the festival of the Passover changed its character and became a national festival, since we are told that, in connection with his cult reform, king Josiah celebrated a Passover, and, further, that 'no such passover had been kept since the days of the judges who judged Israel' (2 Kgs 23.22). There is no reason to believe that when the Deuteronomists wrote their account of Josiah's Passover they had any clear recollection of the forms of worship back in the so-called period of the Judges. The passage therefore reveals that it is first in the time of Josiah that the barley and animal festival achieved national significance as one of Israel's great *historically founded* pilgrimage festivals.

3.3 *The Religious Message*
3.3.1 *The Fundamental Theological Structure*

The information pertaining to the contents of the official religion is every bit as rich as that which pertains to the practical side of worship. In order to understand the Israelite-Jewish religion, it is important to determine just what were its specific contents at various times in its history. The following account is therefore to be read in contrast to the description of the religion during the monarchical period.

The characteristic feature of the Old Testament depiction of post-exilic religion is the receding (not to say, non-existent) rôle played by the old fertility religion. In an agrarian society like that in Palestine, one would expect that the type of worship was intensely concerned with the question of the size of the harvest of the year to come, with the fertility of animals and men, with the advent of the rains, the length of the dry season, and so forth. The fact that Israelite religion was once orientated towards the natural realm is immediately clear when we consider the fundamental connection between the festival and an agrarian way of life. Nevertheless, the Old Testament legal literature and the post-exilic traditions present us with a picture of a very different religion.

This religion may be summarily described in the following manner: one worshipped a single God, namely Yahweh, who guaranteed a single people, the Israelite-Jewish society, possession of a single country, the land of Israel, on condition that that society kept the covenant which it had made with Yahweh, and which was based on a series of laws which had to be observed.

Yahweh, the God of Israel, was the sole god; all other gods were mere idols. He was not worshipped in the form of an image, as was otherwise quite customary, but as the invisible God, who had chosen Jerusalem as his dwelling, and who was omnipresent. He was at one and the same time the creator of the world, the maintainer of life, and the god who determined the course of history. He was a jealous god who did not tolerate apostasies from the worship appropriate to him, and he was the god who, in sovereign freedom, had chosen for himself a particular people, the Israelites, when they were in an otherwise hopeless situation in the desert after their flight from the Egyptians.

Israel was the chosen people, the ones who had been selected in the dawn of time through no merit of their own to be Yahweh's people in spite of their many misdeeds. For this reason it was also decisive that Israel be a pure people who did not intermarry with other peoples and who did not assimilate their customs.

The *land* was 'the land of promise', the land of Canaan, flowing with milk and honey, which Yahweh had elected to give Israel although she had done nothing to deserve it. The land was a pure land, to the extent that its pre-Israelite inhabitants, the Canaanites, had been exterminated when the Israelites conquered the land under Joshua. Israel's task was to ensure that the land continued to be pure.

Thus it was imperative to ignore the Samaritan populace, since they were not a pure people, but a mixed one. The region of Samaria would accordingly continue to be unclean as long as its inhabitants were so, whereas Judah would be pure if the Jews purged from its society those foreign elements which had been assimilated into it in the course of time.

The *covenant* was the contract which Yahweh had intended should regulate the relationship between him and his people. It was therefore also a gift from Yahweh which assured Israel that the promise that they would be his chosen people would remain in force and that they would accordingly retain the promised land. By the same token, however, the covenant also signified that the guarantee in question had certain conditions, as Israel, too, had to commit herself to honour her part of the contract.

The *Law* was the content of the contract; it specified the rules which Israel was to follow, if she wished the certainty of the promise. But the Law had several sides to it. It was in part a teaching, a *vade mecum* describing correct behaviour with respect to one's own people and with respect to foreigners (social ethics). It likewise regulated behaviour towards the only God and towards the foreign idols (prescriptive liturgics). Finally, it consisted in part of *commandments*, since its rules had been sanctioned by God, and accordingly had to be kept to the letter. The Law as guideline is eminently expressed in the Ten Commandments, which also introduce the first legal collection in the Pentateuch, and which at once informed Israel as to the only possible form of worship and as to her relationship to her neighbours. Theoretically, the rest of the legislation consists of commentary on the Ten Commandments which develops their implications.

3.3.2. The Social Location of the Official Religion

The decisive point concerns the Sitz im Leben of this Jewish religion: to whom was it addressed? What did it proclaim? When was it proclaimed? What did its authors hope to achieve by proclaiming it?

The function of this religion during the post-exilic period suggests that it was above all a guideline, not to say, a legitimation, for the exilic circles which had returned home in the belief that they were going to reform the worship of God in their old homeland. To them the promise of the land that was to become their own peculiar property was the most important incitement to leave the fleshpots of Babylon. Moreover, to them the worship of Yahweh as the only God was a natural consequence of the cultural shock they had experienced in exile, that is, in reaction to the encounter with the hundreds of different conceptions of deity which they had made while in Babylon. To these people, the question of ethnic purity was of decisive importance for their hopes of restoration. This theology was their answer to their existence as a tiny minority, and when it was eventually realized it led to a self-chosen isolation.

The official religion had, however, less to offer for those of the Jewish population who had remained behind in Palestine. They owned the country, to the extent that individual peasants or families possessed their lands and cultivated them. Whether they worshipped Yahweh alone or together with a greater or lesser number of deities was contingent upon whether Yahweh guaranteed that they might retain their lands. Here there was a clear conflict of interest with the exiles' religion of isolation, since the central message of that religion linked the right to possess the land to the observance of the Law instead of to the observance of the various magic rites out in the fields. Furthermore, the exiles were able to threaten that if the populace did not obey the Law, what had happened to the exiles would likewise happen to them; they would lose their lands and be forced to go into exile.

Thus the worship of Yahweh as it developed during and after the exile was a religion that appealed to the élite; in the first instance to the élite among the exiles, and in the second instance to those segments of exiled Jewry who had returned home. In the third instance it was also to become the religion of the man in the street in Palestine, as the élite reserved for itself the right to legislate with respect to the contents of the official religion. Indeed, it attempted to force its will on to the populace, and to this end virtually employed terror (if one considers the implications of Ezra's reform measures). We cannot know with any degree of certainty to what extent this élitist religion was victorious in the Persian period. On the other hand, it is well known that it was by no means so thoroughly established even in Hellenistic-Roman times as the Old Testament would have us believe. There are also certain religious phenomena, such as apocalyptic conceptions, which were quite prominent during the last pre-Christian centuries, and precursors of which are to be found in the early post-exilic period. Scholars have also thought to trace the ancestry of these ideas back to the religion of the monarchical period, or indeed to the traditional West Semitic religions as a whole. It appears that the élite circles behind the official religion attempted in post-exilic times to purge the cult of these elements, or at least to reinterpret them. At the same time, they ended by creating an understanding of God, or even religion which was radically different from its pre-exilic counterpart. Therefore, in order to understand the extent of this *reinterpretation* of the religion it will be necessary to reconstruct the pre-exilic religion, to the extent that this is possible. Only then will it be possible to compare the pre- and post-exilic forms of the religion in order to describe the theological work that had gone into re-evaluating the traditions of the past which was carried out by the Jewish élite during and after the exile.

4. *Pre-exilic Israelite Religion*

4.1 *Canaanite Features in the Yahwistic Faith*

4.1.1 *The Psalms as a Source for the Understanding of Pre-exilic Religion*

The most important source for the study of official Israelite religion in the period of the monarchy is the book of the Psalms. Today the main part of the Psalms are understood as cultic poems which were intended for use in the worship in the temple in Jerusalem. However, there are also considerable problems in the use of the Psalms, since they are difficult to date. Thus it can sometimes be extremely difficult to date a given psalm to the ninth, eighth, seventh, or any other, century BCE. In addition to this is the fact that some psalms are exilic, or even post-exilic, as is, for example, Psalm 137, which recalls the situation of the Jews in exile ('By the waters of Babylon we sat and wept'). This judgment also applies to a number of 'didactic poems', such as Psalms 105, 106, and 78. Finally, there may also be some pre-exilic psalms which did not originate in Jerusalem, but possibly in the sometime northern kingdom, and which were probably brought to Judah by refugees. At least parts of Psalm 68 might well belong to this category.

Ultimately, when dealing with the collection of Psalms as a whole it would be reasonable to believe that with the few exceptions of psalms which may have originated in the north, the collection otherwise represents the official religion, that is, the Jerusalemite edition, the religion which characterized the royal Judaean sanctuary. Some scholars have held a few individual psalms to be of pre-

Israelite, Jerusalemite origin; these are psalms in which an understanding of God appears which is defined as clearly Canaanite.
However, it should be obvious that judgments as to what is Israelite
and what Canaanite depend upon pre-judgments as to the relationship
between the Israelites and the Canaanites. They also depend on
certain decisions as to the specific nature of Israelite religion and as
to the time when Israelite religion emerged as a phenomenon in its
own right. In reality, such an approach renders worthless the results
of analysis of the Psalms and of other sources for pre-exilic religion.
By this means also, other and rather diffuse information both in and
outside of the Old Testament acquires significance for the description
of the religion during the monarchical period.

Our task is accordingly, in addition to attempting to describe pre-
exilic religion in an acceptable manner, to try to determine whether
Israelite religion was Canaanite, or partially so, or whether it was
distinctively different from Canaanite religion. Before making such
decisions, however, it would be wise to recall that the oldest texts
were revised when the Israelite legalistic religion was promulgated,
so that these sources were more or less made to agree with 'orthodox'
Yahwism. This process of re-reading and expurgation becomes quite
evident when we consider, among other things, the superscriptions to
the Psalms, which to a large extent are secondary and tendentious, as
well as the presence of sections in some of the psalms which are
irrelevant to their main themes, and have clearly been pasted onto
them.

4.1.2 El, Ba'al, and Yahweh

When we consider the fact that virtually all the relevant ancient texts
have been expurgated in order to make them more acceptable, it is so
much more striking to discover, nevertheless, some sections which
have slipped through the editors' 'pruning shears', and in which an
earlier understanding of God is evident. We shall mention a few
examples from the Old Testament materials here, and supplement
them with some inscriptional material from outside the Old
Testament.

As we have seen, the most important Canaanite deities were El
and Ba'al. According to the Old Testament witness, Yahweh's
struggle against this pair, and particularly against Ba'al, overshadows
all other problems. It is, however, still appropriate to enquire as to
whether Israelite religion was at all times anti-Canaanite. The first

example of a different attitude towards Ba'al is already expressed in pre-national materials in the form of Israelite proper names. The first such instance is *Jerubba'al*, the alternative name of the judge called Gideon. In the relevant text, the name is interpreted as 'the one who battles against Ba'al', a rendering which is highly appropriate in view of Jerubba'al's destruction of a Ba'al altar (Judg. 6.25-32). However, according to the rules of Semitic namegiving, the theophorous element is never the object in a name, but the subject. The name is therefore clearly Canaanite and meant before the tendentious correction of it 'Ba'al battles (i.e. for me)'. Nor is this the only case in which Israelites bear names in which the theophorous element is the name of a Canaanite god. King Saul is frequently understood as having struggled on behalf of the true Israelite faith; but if this was really the case, then one might be tempted to wonder about the names he awarded to members of his immediate family. His oldest son was called Jonathan which in unproblematic, since here the theophorous element is an abbreviated form of the name Yahweh. Jonathan's son, however, was called *Meribba'al* ('Ba'al's champion'; the name has been tendentiously corrected in the books of Samuel to Mephibosheth, but, for not immediately obvious reasons, the correct form is cited in the books of Chronicles [1 Chron. 8.34]). Moreover, Saul's son and successor to the throne was called *Ishba'al*, 'man of Ba'al' (the correct form of the name also appears in Chronicles at 1 Chron. 8.33). Scholars have sometimes attempted to sweep the problem under the carpet by maintaining that in this connection Ba'al is only an appelative meaning 'Lord'. In reality, however, this solution only makes the problem worse, since if it was possible to identify Yahweh with Ba'al in the eleventh–tenth centuries, or if the Canaanite divine designation Ba'al could be used of Yahweh in an apparently unproblematic fashion, then what are we to make of any supposed antagonism between Yahweh and Ba'al? Similar considerations apply to the names of David's sons, and particularly to the names of those who were born in Jerusalem (2 Sam. 5.14-16), although scholars have attempted to avoid the problem caused by the fact that here El and Ba'al names occur alongside Yahweh names by maintaining that the abnormalities are the result of local Jebusite influence.

Another text which is of interest in this connection is the famous passage in the Song of Moses (Deut. 32.8-9), which in the RSV reads, 'When the Most High gave to the nations their inheritance, when he separated the sons of men, he fixed the bounds of the peoples according to the number of the sons of God'. The Danish translation reads the next phrase differently from the RSV, however, and, in this case, rightly: 'and the Lord's (Yahweh's) portion was Jacob, Israel his allotted heritage'. The Danish translators have preferred to follow the Greek version of the text here, since the Hebrew version of vv. 8b-9b reads: 'he fixed the bounds of the peoples according to the number of the sons of Israel, for the Lord's portion is his people'. In other words, the Hebrew text identifies the 'Most High' (Elyon) with Yahweh, while the Greek version apparently ranges Yahweh among the *sons* of the Most High, that is, it treats him as a member of a pantheon of gods who are subordinate to the supreme god, El Elyon. Compare, in this connection, Gen. 14.19, where this god is characterized in full as 'El Elyon, the creator of heaven and earth'. It has often been held that the Greek version of Deut. 32.8b-9a is a translation of the original Hebrew version, as it must be regarded as the *lectio difficilior*. In other words, the Greek text is the more difficult to understand from the point of view of a dogmatic Jewish vantage; it is easy to imagine an editor who corrected the Greek text to correspond to the reading in the present Hebrew Bible, but not the reverse.

All this goes to show that there is evidence in the Old Testament which not only identifies Ba'al with Yahweh (or at least neutrally places them on the same level), but there are also examples in which Yahweh is regarded as subordinate to the lord of the gods, El. The psalmic literature shows us to what extent this identification of Yahweh with gods who have traditionally been regarded as Canaanite is present in the Old Testament. However, before proceeding to examine these materials, some reference should first be made to a recently discovered inscription which was unearthed in provincial Judah (the modern Kuntillat Ajrud). The section which concerns us reads, 'I bless you by Yahweh, who protects us (or: 'from Samaria'), and by his Asherah'. The Old Testament everywhere informs us that Yahweh was a unique deity with clearly masculine characteristics; moreover, he was a deity who did not tolerate other gods beside him. Thus, the notion of a female deity at his side as the queen of a pantheon seems absurd. Accordingly, when archeologists back at the beginning of the twentieth century found a papyrus inscription from the post-exilic colony on the island of Elephantine in Egypt in which the deity *Anath-Yahu* figured (Anath being the sister-cum-consort of

Ba'al whom we meet in the Ugaritic texts), they regarded the name as either the result of a local syncretistic version of Yahwism, or as an expression of the corrupt Yahwism of the sometime northern kingdom. However, taken together, the Elephantine text and the one from *Kuntillat Ajrud* (to which we also possess a parallel from Khirbet el-Qom, near Hebron) show that the idea of a female counterpart to Yahweh was known in both pre-exilic Judah and in a post-exilic diaspora community. Moreover, it should be noted that the latter society, being situated in Egypt, must have been free of the authority and control of Mesopotamian Judaism.

4.2 *Yahweh as God in Old Testament Cultic Poetry*
4.2.1 *'The King of the Gods'*
The temple in Jerusalem was a royal institution which formed part of the same complex of structures as the palace of Solomon. A Greek philosopher is said to have remarked that, 'if cows had gods, they would look like cows', and if there is any truth to this remark one would accordingly expect that in his temple in Jerusalem Yahweh was regarded as a *king*. A thorough reading of the Psalms in fact serves to show that the notion of Yahweh as ruler is dominant in them, and, moreover, that he was not only lord of men, but of the gods. There is, for example, the hymnic section in Ps. 89 (vv. 6-19), as the conception of Yahweh as king of the gods is clearly expressed here: Yahweh 'causes terror among the holy ones'; note also: 'Who among the gods is Yahweh's equal?' In this psalm, Yahweh is clearly seen as the highest god in the pantheon, and this notion has survived. It has done so for the following reason: in the Hebrew text reference is made to 'the sons of god', where, according to Hebrew usage, 'son' designates 'member of a class'; thus the phrase really means simply 'gods'. Later Judaism, however, took the phrase 'sons of god' to mean 'angels', i.e. they were not interpreted as independent deities, but as manifestations of Yahweh's will. Thus, Yahweh is here depicted as *the king of the gods*, El Elyon (even though this title is not used here). But he is also depicted as the battler of chaos, the one who has '*pierced Rahab*' (Rahab being one of the many names of the chaos-dragon); by the same token, he is also the creator god who sits enthroned upon a basis of right conduct and righteousness.

As the king of the gods, Yahweh is the creator of the world and chaos-battler as well. If we employ our earlier description of so-called Canaanite religion in the epic literature of Ugarit as a model, it appears that several facets of this portrait of Yahweh have been borrowed from Ba'al: the concept of Yahweh as victorious over the sea, and the notion of Yahweh who becomes king as a result of this victory. This understanding of Yahweh as Ba'al is most clearly expressed in Psalm 65, in which Yahweh is lauded as the one who 'softens it (the earth) with showers, and blesses its growth' (v. 11; RSV v. 10). In this psalm we also find the motif of creation (v. 7; RSV v. 6), which is a new feature with respect to the Ba'al of the Ugaritic texts. Yahweh is at one and the same time creator and combater of chaos, where Ba'al was only the victor over the powers of chaos. Thus the figure of Yahweh combines features which are otherwise assigned to both Ba'al and El (although, as mentioned previously, the creation motif is not present in the Ugaritic texts in our possession).

Which of the two West Semitic deities, El or Ba'al, exercised the greater influence upon the understanding of Yahweh? A broad comparative study of West Semitic religion in the first millennium BCE would conceivably reveal that this is a false understanding of the situation, since the confluence of these two deities so as virtually to form only one was quite widely characteristic of the region after the transition from the Bronze Age to the Iron Age. The identification of the two was natural, since both were 'kings'. Ba'al won his throne through his victory over the sea monsters, while El possessed his kingship 'from eternity'. Thus the idea of god as king was the common feature which entailed that the differences between the respective 'kings' became obscured. However, this equation of the two gods had considerable consequences for the understanding of Yahweh in the Israel of the monarchy.

To phrase the matter differently, one might say that if the Ba'al-features achieved supremacy, the emphases on the chaos-battle and the kingship of the deity were the results. This is in reality what a considerable number of scholars, following the lines laid down by Sigmund Mowinckel, have done. They have interpreted Yahweh as a dying and rising god along the lines of Ba'al, a god who once a year, namely in connection with the New Year festival, had to rewin his position as king, an event which was celebrated in the form of the 'Enthronement Festival'. A variety of psalms have been held to have been employed in the course of this festival. Thus, for example, Psalm 93 pronounces that 'Yahweh has become king/is king', and associates the creation motif and that of the battle with the dragon (the latter in a weakened form only) with this pronouncement. The theme of the righteous king is also attested in this psalm. The related Psalm 98 contains an ovation to Yahweh, in which the very forces of chaos ('the sea' and 'the Flood') participate in the praise of the king. The theory of the accession festival of Yahweh is also based on the similarity of motives between those occurring in Yahweh-contexts and those which were probably used in conjuction with the accession of a Davidic king to the throne. This evidence, however, is not unproblematic. A central theme in these psalms is that the creator-activity of Yahweh is 'eternal'. Hence, when the combat with the dragon is coupled with the creation, the battle is in the process of changing its character into that of an event in the *Urzeit*, 'something that happened back then'; and if this is the case, then it is no longer the subject of a drama that could be replayed annually. Yahweh in Jerusalem was accordingly El (El Elyon), but in this event the creator-god had usurped characteristics which were associated with the god of vegetation.

4.2.2 *Yahweh, the Imperial God*

As the main god in the royal sanctuary of Jerusalem (of course, other gods were worshipped at this site throughout the period of the monarchy, as we read in 2 Kgs 23.1-28: Ba'al, Ashera, whom we now know to have been Yahweh's consort, Shamash, i.e. the sun, Yerach, i.e. the moon) Yahweh was the national deity of Judah. He was, therefore, the god who was held to protect the country and who determined whether the land would prosper or suffer. These themes appear in Psalm 89, where the hymnic section referred to above, after having praised Yahweh as a righteous god, celebrates 'the people who praise (Yahweh)'. However, in those parts of the psalms which surround the hymn, Yahweh appears as the god who has brought catastrophe upon his people, and above all upon his king. He is accordingly requested once again to show his great mercy towards the kingdom and its monarch. Other psalms have the same contents, as for example, Psalm 80, which could well be older than Psalm 89, and in which Yahweh is directly asked, 'O Yahweh, god of hosts, how long will your wrath persist?' Yahweh is therefore also the god who allows other peoples to attack Israel, thereby bringing her existence in danger. Yahweh is the god who determines the course of history.

This understanding of the deity is frequently held to have been something specifically Israelite. However, this is by no means the case, as the Swedish scholar, Bertil Albrektson, has demonstrated. Albrektson shows to the contrary that this understanding of the rôle of the national deity was pan-Oriental. To take only a single example from among Israel's immediate neighbours, an inscription from the Moabite king Mesha (cf. 2 Kgs 3) depicts the sufferings which Moab had experienced at the hands of Omri and Ahab. Mesha describes the cause of these tribulations in the following manner: 'Omri was Israel's king, and he oppressed Moab for many days because Chemosh was angry with his land' (trans. F.H. Cryer after B. Otzen). Moreover, Mesha also believes that he had Chemosh behind him when he successfully rebelled against Israel.

Yet a third aspect of the understanding of the deity in the Jerusalem of the monarchy was based on general Near Eastern conceptions. This was the view that Yahweh was the guardian of righteousness, the one who judged his people in justice and righteousness. Yahweh similarly guaranteed that the king's rule would be just, as the king ruled on behalf of Yahweh.

The clearest example of the concept of the just king is to be found in Psalm 72, which has often been regarded as a psalm which was employed on the occasion of the accession of a new king to the throne. In the beginning of the psalm, God is requested to endow his king with his insight and justice so that he will be able to govern the people so as to support the weak in the society against the abuses of the powerful. This theme, which is one of the central motifs in the psalm, is repeated yet again: 'For he delivers the needy when he calls, the poor and him who has no helper. He has pity on the weak and the needy, and saves the lives of the needy. From oppression and violence he redeems their life' (vv. 12-14, RSV). Here this idea is connected with that of the king as the one who ensures the fertility of the country; the thought is phrased in terms which might equally well have been used of the vegetation-god Ba'al: 'May he be like rain that falls on the mown grass, like showers that water the earth!' (v. 6, RSV).

In Psalm 72 many of the themes which are normally connected with the Jerusalemite creator-god are here connected with the king; implicitly, as Yahweh's plenipotentiary, he is the one who carries out Yahweh's will and so ensures that justice and righteousness will prevail on earth. Seen in this light, righteousness is a guarantee of the world's continued existence; it is a constitutive element in the cosmic order. Moreover, this righteousness is a 'social righteousness' which protects the weak in society from wealthy men, moneylenders, and property holders.

At the time Psalm 72 was written, this idea—for we know that it was only an idea—had a prehistory several thousand years old, as it had been an invariable feature in the official national propaganda everywhere in the ancient Near East. The cosmic understanding of righteousness according to which righteousness was congruent with the natural order played a dominant rôle in both the official and the unofficial religions, since it of course gave expression to the hopes of the less fortunate. When, in the eighth century, the prophet Isaiah described the expectations that were directed towards the coming king of the Davidic dynasty (Isa. 11.1-9), he asserted that this king would reign in harmony with Yahweh's 'spirit'; he would protect the rights of the people and persecute law-breakers. He further described this as leading to a 'Messianic kingdom', a paradise on earth. In this description, as in Psalm 72, we find a tradition whose roots stretch back into the Babylonian heritage. For example, in the eighteenth century BCE, Hammurabi (the 'law-giver') had found it possible to describe his own reign as being in conformity with this tradition: 'When Marduk commanded me to give justice to the people of the land to let (them) have (good) governance, I set forth truth and justice throughout the land (and) prospered the people' (text and trans.: G.R. Driver & J.C. Miles, *The Babylonian Laws*, II, Oxford, 1955, pp. 12-13).

4.3 *The Religious Understanding of the King*
4.3.1 *God or Man?*
The Old Testament contains several understandings of the king. The reader has already encountered the negative Deuteronomistic view according to which the kingship was a form of treason against Yahweh, the 'real' king. We have also noted the positive view expressed in Psalm 72 and in Isa. 11. 1-9, which maintains that the king rules by God's will and under God's direction. If we confine our study of this question to the Psalms, we shall see that there are basically two views of the Jerusalemite king (we have no information enabling us to make judgments about the understanding of kingship in Samaria): that the king is a *god*, or that, alternatively, he is a *man*. It was actually rare in the ancient Orient that the king was accounted divine; as a rule, this view appeared in marginal regions, above all in Egypt. In Egypt the king was reckoned to be the son of Ra, and in

some periods as the very incarnation of the sun-god himself. On the other hand, the notion of divine kingship was not really all that foreign a concept, since the kingship itself was held to be of divine origin. The Sumerian King List, for example, relates that 'Kingship came down from heaven'. There are also some examples of Mesopotamian rulers who virtually regarded themselves as divinely descended.

However, the view that the king was human (the Sumerian royal title was simple LU.GAL, 'big man') was far more extensively held, both with respect to time and to geography. As was previously mentioned, the ordinary Mesopotamian view was that the king was the stateholder and priest of the god; in the West Semitic ambit, he was 'the slave of the god'.

4.3.2 *The King as 'the Son of Yahweh'*

We find a couple of examples in the Old Testament Psalms of a different attitude towards the king. Thus, we find that one poet could allow Yahweh to proclaim, 'On Sacred mountains I have begotten you like the dew of the womb of dawn' (Ps. 110.3; Danish trans. of 1977). It is possible to recognize allusions to the names of two deities in this sentence: the Dawn (*Shachar*) and the Dew (*Tal*), both of which we know thanks to the Ugaritic pantheon. The Psalm may thus be understood as a legitimation of the Davidic king in Jerusalem, since this king is himself a god, and therefore sits 'by (Yahweh's) right side'. The notes to the Danish translation of 1977 reveal, however, that this text is rather corrupt. The reason for this is apparent: to the post-exilic worshippers of Yahweh, the text was both incomprehensible and impermissible, since the Davidic monarchy no longer existed. However, this text is not an isolated phenomenon, since yet another psalm, Psalm 2, has Yahweh announce that, 'you are my son, today I have begotten you' (v. 7). This text was allowed to survive in its present form, since it was possible to regard it as an adoption formula, until it was ultimately understood in a messianic light by post-exilic Judaism and early Christianity. In context, though, it was an unambiguous statement about the reigning king of the house of David on the throne in Jerusalem. It is conceivable that the adoption motif was functional, that is, if the king's 'divinity' were somehow regarded as actual only from the moment of his accession (and it was to the accession ceremony that the psalm must have belonged). But this may be a false conclusion, since the psalm says explicitly that the king is divine because he is the son of God, and is therefore not a man. For this reason it was of no significance whether divinity was proclaimed at the accession or at the birth of the royal heir. In practice, the designated king revealed his divinity when he ascended the throne, leaving his brothers behind him.

The conception of the Jerusalemite king as 'the son of God' was derived from the Egyptian royal ideology. We can only speculate as to how it made its way to Jerusalem, but it is to be noted that the administrative systems of David and Solomon reveal a considerable number of features in common with the Egyptian system. David's administration seems to have parroted an Egyptian model, Solomon married an Egyptian princess, and the elaboration of Solomon's temple reveals unmistakably Egyptian characteristics. David's and Solomon's use of these Egyptian motifs, including the Egyptian understanding of the king, was no doubt intentional, since their empire was virtually the heir to the Egyptian empire in the Near East. Thus, in the eyes of his subjects in Judah and Israel, but also in those of his vassals in the neighbouring countries, the king in Jerusalem was meant to appear as Pharaoh, as the divine lord of the empire.

4.3.3 *The King as a Man*
This understanding of kingship did not survive the collapse of the Davidic empire for long. This is indirectly attested by the fact that the recollection of the divinity of the Judaean king is only preserved in a few isolated fragments like the ones mentioned here, and otherwise not at all. Indeed, there are not even any signs of serious polemic against this view in the Old Testament. If it did somehow manage to survive in some way, it would at most have been in the form of an undercurrent beneath the official religion. However, the idea surfaces again when the monarchy no longer existed in the form of the post-exilic messianic expectation, that is, the hopes which accrued to a coming king of the line of David; and it surfaced even more potently in the Christian concept of the Messiah as God. On the other hand, the more prosaic West Semitic understanding of the office of king no doubt entailed that the Jerusalemite king was soon toppled from his throne of deity, and had to make do as a mortal, although one who was endowed with special powers and a special legitimation which arose from his peculiar relationship to the national god.

A good example of the king's new situation as a man is the previously mentioned Psalm 72. Of course, there are countless other texts which bear witness to the non-divine side of the king, but which at the same time imply that special ties existed which linked the deity and the king to one another. This linkage was accomplished by the 'spirit' with which Yahweh endowed the king at his accession (if not before), and which was culticly expressed through the ritual *anointment* of the king during his accession (from which we get the title 'Messiah', which is actually derived from the Greek transcription of the Hebrew word meaning 'the anointed one'). Without this, the king could not reign as the representative of Yahweh; he would not be able to maintain justice, which was the mainstay of the cosmos. If the king failed, then chaos threatened, or, rather, Yahweh might threaten to bring chaos. In this event Yahweh took his 'spirit' back into himself and gave the miscreant king a 'false spirit', as, for example, happened to Saul (1 Sam. 16.14). In short, Yahweh could retract his legitimation of the reigning king, though not necessarily of the dynasty as such. But an individual unjust king was doomed to fall, and, in fact, had to be felled. Yahweh would declare him an outlaw but, as least as far as the Davidic dynasty was concerned, this did not entail the removal of the entire line. In actual practice, during the course of Judaean history this royal ideology expressed itself in a number of palace revolts against the reigning king, after which the élite class replaced the dethroned and murdered king with one of his sons. Naturally, there remains the question of what was to become of this royal ideology when it became irrelevant, that is, when the monarchy was no more: did it disappear entirely, or did it assume new forms?

4.3.4 *The Covenant between Yahweh and the King*
Before we look at this problem, it will first be necessary to examine yet another of the specific forms which the relationship between Yahweh and the king assumed in the Old Testament. Our point of departure is once again Psalm 89, but this time not the hymn, but the framework pieces. Here Yahweh announces that, 'I have made a covenant with my chosen one, I have sworn to David my servant: I will establish your descendants for ever, and build your throne for all generations' (vv. 4-5, RSV). The Psalm returns to this theme in vv. 20ff., where, however, the question which plagues the poet is, why has Yahweh broken his covenant with David's dynasty? Why

has the monarchy been rejected? The same motif recurs elsewhere, as, for example, in Ps. 132.11-12, and it is enclosed in a historical framework in the so-called 'Promise of Nathan' (2 Sam. 7), where, however, the reference to a covenant between Yahweh and David is not to be found. Finally, we are also told in a narrative text (2 Kgs 12) how such a covenant could be concretely enacted: under the active participation of the high priest, and in the form of an agreement between Yahweh and the king and between the king and the people.

The last-mentioned text tells us about the king's rôle, and about the significance of the covenantal relationship between God and king. The king was in the centre; he was the indispensable connecting link between the population in general and the national god; he represented his people to the deity, and he represented the deity to the people. For this reason Psalms 89 and 132 make the covenant contingent upon keeping Yahweh's 'law', for only in this fashion could the dynasty survive. However, since the king was more than just the representative of the dynasty, any breach on his part of Yahweh's law affected the entire nation, so that the people as a whole would invariably suffer for sins for which only the king was directly responsible. The contents of this 'law' are unknown, but they may have corresponded to what was expected of the new king according to Psalm 72: he was to use 'God's judgments' to protect the weak of society, which is to say that he was to be the guarantor of righteousness.

4.3.5 *The Davidic and Sinaitic Covenants*

There is room for disagreement as to how old was the notion of a covenant between Yahweh and the king in Jerusalem. It has often been held to have been younger than the Sinai covenant, and in this connection scholars usually refer to the fact that no covenant is mentioned in 2 Samuel 7. Therefore, or so it is claimed, the original promise of Nathan to David was concerned with 'the eternal dynasty' alone (2 Sam. 7.16), and it was only late sources such as Psalms 89 and 132 which combined this idea with the concept of a covenant between Yahweh and the king.

This view is, of course, dependent upon a particular understanding of the age of the notion of covenant, as well as of its significance for religious life. Scholars embracing this view usually assume a priori that the idea of the covenant was a dominant feature of Yahwistic religion from its faintest beginnings and later. Thus, it is claimed, when the idea of covenant was later associated with the Davidic dynasty, this was either because the king had usurped the covenant between the Israelite people and Yahweh, or else because at a late stage in the history of the monarchy an attempt was made either under the influence of the Deuteronomistic covenantal theology, or else in reaction to it, to replace the rôle of the people with that of the king.

This reconstruction is based on the idea that the concept of the covenant dates from the pre-national period, which is to say, that it was the central theme already in the oldest version of the Sinai narrative, which is now located in Exodus 20ff. In the wake of the researches of the American scholar, G.E. Mendenhall, scholars have attempted for some time to demonstrate a Sitz im Leben for covenantal theology in the second millennium BCE. To this end, parallels have been drawn between the then frequently employed international treaties, particularly in the form which was used between the Hittite king and his vassals. On this model, the covenant between Yahweh and Israel was precisely such a 'vassal treaty', one in which Yahweh had replaced the Hittite great king, while Israel had taken the place of his Syrian vassal. However, more recent studies have destroyed the basis for dating this idea of the covenant to the second millennium BCE. Scholars have instead pointed out that vassal treaties continued to be employed after the end of the Bronze Age, as, for example, in the Neo-Assyrian Empire in the first millennium BCE. Thus it has been maintained that the formalized covenant which we meet above all in Deuteronomy is related to the Assyrian international treaties, which happened to be current at the time the Deuteronomistic theology was being formulated.

Even more recently, scholars have noted that the idea of covenant first appears in relatively late Old Testament sources. In this connection it is significant that *berit*, the Israelite word for covenant, cannot with certainty be said to appear in reference to the relationship between Yahweh and Israel in any Old Testament text which is older than the seventh century BCE. It is also maintained that only a tendentious interpretation of certain passages in the earlier prophets and early psalms will unearth covenantal references in them, that is, elements whose meaning is only clear if seen in relation to a developed theology of the covenant. On the other hand, there are certainly some features and concepts which were eventually assimilated into the Deuteronomistic covenantal theology, and which in this way naturally came to influence the form and conceptual content of that theology. To cut a long story short, many scholars are today of the opinion that we shall hardly find a covenantal theology before the age of Deuteronomism, that is, in the seventh–sixth century BCE; they also hold that this theology was the work of the Deuteronomists.

But if the idea of a formal covenant between Yahweh and David arose at a relatively late date, scholars have been able to see that the notion of a special covenant between Yahweh and David could well be older. Instead of having been borrowed from an ancient tradition about a Sinaitic covenant, the covenant in question could have been a constitutive element in the royal ideology, for example, in an age in which the king was already confined by covenantal obligations to a secular master, like the king of Assyria. Thus at the fall of the monarchy, but perhaps even earlier, Deuteronomistic reform theologians may have separated the idea of covenant from the monarchy, to which they were otherwise not deeply attached. One might say that, in agreement with their understanding of the monarchy, these theologians found the king's rôle in the covenantal relationship inappropriate, and for this reason they made 'Israel' into Yahweh's partner. In so doing, they also radicalized the idea that the king alone was responsible for the well-being of the relationship on behalf of the people; now it was the entire nation that was responsible. But by the same token, it was no longer to be the king alone who ran the risk of rejection, in which event one could simply crown a new one, but the entire people of Israel. One might say that Yahweh then had the option to choose a new people for himself, but of course the Deuteronomists never considered this idea at all, as the notion would have been entirely too extreme for then-current understandings of the world. Since Israel was the people of the creator-god, they were cosmos, and the surrounding peoples who did not know Yahweh were the forces of chaos. The god who reigned over the created world could not seek alliances with the powers of chaos, although he could negate that which had been created, so transforming it into chaos. And yet this possibility contained also the possibility for the creation of a new cosmos, in the event that the Israelites changed their attitude, and if so pleased the creator-god.

5. The Transformation of Pre-exilic Religion

5.1 The Fundamental Theological Structure

Just as it is possible to summarize the post-exilic understanding of
the relationship between God and man as a few concepts which were
united into a theological system, it is possible from the multiplicity of
pre-exilic religious phenomena to distinguish some main lines which
clearly point towards post-exilic religion.

As we have seen, as far as the pre-exilic period in Judah and Israel
is concerned—although our knowledge of the religion of the northern
kingdom is only fragmentary at best—it is nevertheless admissible to
concentrate on the figure of Yahweh. This is so because this deity
was unquestionably the national deity in Judah, and probably also in
the north as well, even though the concrete forms under which his
worship was expressed differed from the Jerusalemite version of the
Yahwistic religion. As a *type* of god, Jerusalem's Yahweh was an El-
type, and he apparently had El's consort, Ashera, at his side. As El he
was the creator of heaven and earth, as well as the maintainer of
Israel, which is to say, the cosmos. Thus, he was also the combater of
chaos, and in this capacity he embodied some of the features of
Ba'al.

As the *national deity*, that is, the main god of the state, Yahweh
was the lord of Israel, and he determined Israel's history. He led
enemies to attack the country if he was angered with it; alternatively,
he sometimes saved her. As the enemies, that is, the foreigners, by
definition represented the powers of chaos, the dominant ideology
permitted the combating of Israel's political enemies to take the form
of a virtual chaos-battle (the phenomenon is often termed the myth
of the battle against foreign nations; cf. Pss. 48.5-8; 46.6-8).

The relationship between the deity and the nation was regulated
by the connection between the national deity and the *king* in
Jerusalem. This alliance took on a number of different forms, such as
the concept of the divinity of the king, that is, as the physical son of
Yahweh, or the notion of the king as the servant of Yahweh, that is,
the one who dutifully realized Yahweh's commands. However, the
king also represented the *people*, Israel (more properly, Judah) in the
eyes of the national deity, and he was responsible for their
prosperity.

The king's *responsibility* was based on the demand that he effect
the will of Yahweh, and since the will of the deity aimed at the
maintenance of the cosmos it was accordingly the duty of the king to

ensure that the laws which regulated the world also governed his own country. The laws were defined as the judgments which Yahweh had made and which the king was supposed to enact. Their concrete realization took the form of *social justice*, so that the weak would be protected against the encroachments of the 'men of violence'.

Only a society which was in balance could survive, just as only a cosmos which is in harmony with itself can be maintained. At some point during the period of the monarchy, the relationship between Yahweh and the king was redefined so that the king served as the vassal of Yahweh, being obligated to the national deity by a treaty (a covenant), the main contents of which comprised the terms which the king had, of necessity to live up to in order to reign justly. Thus, the contents of the covenant were identical with the earlier obligation upon the king to function as the representative of the national god; but the use of the covenant form tended to formalize the relationship. The question as to the maintenance or destruction of the cosmos was dependent on whether the covenant was honoured or broken.

It will be seen that all of the fundamental elements in the post-exilic religion were present already in the pre-exilic Judaean national religion. At the same time, however, there were some differences, even if these were perhaps differences in accentuation, which characterized the religion of the post-exilic period, and this was of course a result of the demise of the monarchy.

In what follows we shall attempt to determine just which elements brought about the transformation of the proclamation of pre-exilic religion, which had affirmed, in brief, a policy of 'one God, one king, one country', into a policy of 'one God, one people, one country'. At the same time, however, it will be essential to recall that the pre-exilic religion was basically Canaanite, or perhaps, to avoid the negative connotations which usually accrue to this term, we should say that the religion of the monarchical period had been a *classical West Asiatic religion*, the basic structure of which recurs from Mesopotamia to Northern Syria and Palestine. The official religion of the post-exilic period was in certain respects a continuation of the pre-exilic religion, and so it was also a West Asiatic religion. It was, however, also a religion which had relegated those features which had to do with fertility and the annual cycle to an insignificant status. This development had to do with the change in the understanding of Yahweh as the god of history.

5.2 The Reformers: the Israelite Prophetic Movement

5.2.1 Prophetism as the Watershed in the History of Israelite Religion

As we have seen, Wellhausen held that the prophets were the real creators of Israelite religion. They made up the watershed in the course of the development of the religion, as after their efforts the choice open to the Israelites was between a Canaanite fertility religion and an Israelite legalistic religion. Following the prophets' admonitions, they chose the latter. However, the official pre-exilic worship was hardly the lasciviously sexual religion which a number of European scholars have imagined it to be. On the contrary, we have seen that it was a thoroughly rationalized and conceived theological structure which put the question of justice and the preservation of the cosmos above all else. Israelite prophetism had nevertheless an important rôle in connection with the transformation of this religion, and the honour of ensuring that those aspects of it which guaranteed the fertility of the land through cultic rites and the like were purified from the cult, was to some extent theirs. As a result, the tendency was to concentrate on justice as an ethical necessity. The traditional fertility religion was relegated to a secondary place, from which, in purified form, it was able to be re-employed by Jewish religiosity in the post-exilic period.

5.2.2 The Relationship to the Divine

The religious function of the prophet was to serve as an intermediary between the next world and this one. Causal explanations of the sort common in western civilization were either unknown or not particularly respected. Thus, ancient Israelites sought to explain a given state of affairs as the result of divine intentions towards the human realm. An event which benefitted or harmed someone was the result of forces over which the individual had no control. Israel never understood a national catastrophe as a neutral, if unfortunate, occurrence; rather, the disaster was to be seen as a reminder that the land had merited Yahweh's displeasure, just as the individual saw his own fortunes as the result of the interaction of divine forces. One might attempt actively to influence one's fate by ensuring that the relationship to the divine, that is, of the nation to the national deity, or of the individual to his tutelary spirit (or to Yahweh), was impeccable. This attitude is perhaps expressed in the following distinction in the Proverbs between good and evil people: 'When the tempest passes, the wicked is no more, but the righteous is established for ever' (10.25, RSV); 'The righteous will never be removed, but the wicked will not dwell in the land' (10.30, RSV); 'A good man obtains favour from the Lord, but a man of evil devices he condemns' (12.2, RSV).

It was therefore important to be able to control the communications which took place between the divine and the human realms. Various media were available for this purpose: including more or less specialized types of oracles; there were interpreters of omens either in the form of professional priests who were employed for the purpose; or there were unauthorized specialists like the Witch of Endor, who conjured up the ghost of Samuel from the earth in order to predict Saul's death (1 Sam. 28); and there were prophets. The Old Testament gives the impression that prophetism, as the most highly regarded, was to determine the gods' intentions towards the world, whereas other means, at least in the late official tradition, were reckoned illegitimate.

5.2.3 *Early Prophetism*

Prophetism manifested itself in a variety of forms. Some prophets were priests and did service at the royal sanctuaries, while others were solely active by virtue of such legitimation as their pronouncements provided them, and they often had to combat their 'colleagues', who had different understandings of various situations than their own (the so-called 'false prophets'). Some times not only the independent, but also the temple-employed prophets were constrained to oppose the popular expectations of their public, and it was not uncommon that they were persecuted for their pronouncements. An early example is the narrative of Micaiah ben Imla, who predicted the death of the king. This narrative has been preserved in the cycle of Elijah and Elisha legends (1 Kgs 22). At the beginning of the scene in question, Micaiah is in the royal custody while the king seeks an oracle of 400 prophets, all of whom agree with his projects. The king, however, knows that Micaiah's word alone is worth more than that of all these prophets together, so Micaiah is brought before him and agrees with the king's projects. But Ahab wants to know *what is really going to happen* and, on his urging, Micaiah predicts his death, whereupon the prophet is returned to the royal jail in gratitude while the king goes off to war and his own death. Naturally, considered as a historical report this account is not worth any more than any of the other prophetic legends in the Deuteronomistic History. But on this occasion the Deuteronomists have seized the occasion to illustrate their own favourite theme, namely that throughout history the prophets had told the truth, but no one wanted to listen to them and persecuted them instead.

Nor is Micaiah ben Imla the only prophet the Deuteronomists allow to proclaim that Israel had ignored her God's warning throughout her history. To the contrary, according to them, ever since the introduction of the monarchy, prophets from Samuel to the Deuteronomists' own figures had condemned the course of history. But in spite of this attitude, we do find yet another prophetic attitude towards the monarchy, even in the Deuteronomistic History. For example, even such a classical opponent of the monarchical authority as Elisha, the spiritual heir of Elijah, served as a sort of court prophet in Samaria.

Prophetism as such was by no means restricted to Israelite religion; rather, the Israelite variety of prophetism had its natural place in West Asiatic religion in general. Some of the most interesting parallels to Old Testament prophecy are to be found in the sources from *Mari* in upper Mesopotamia, dating from the eighteenth century BCE. These texts consist mostly of letters in which a provincial governor reports to the king in Mari that one or another temple prophet has made a proclamation containing an instruction to the king from the god of the temple in question. Such messages varied widely in content: they sometimes concern political matters and direct the king to go to war or to make peace; or, they might have a religious content and so entail that the king is to build a temple, or, alternatively, that he is not to do so. What these messages have in common, however, is that they must be seen as evidence of the gods' direction of the course of history. Another common feature of these reports of prophetic activity is the consequences of this activity: the prophet in question was detained either directly or else indirectly, that is, they took from him things which could serve to identify him and serve as control instances. In other words, the authorities behave much as Ahab did in the case of Micaiah ben Imla. The prophets were entitled to intervene in political matters because they were the voices of the gods; by the same token, one could prevent illegal prophecy from occurring, presumably by annihilating such prophets if their predictions proved to be false.

We do not have other significant collections of texts from the rest of the Near East which inform us about prophetic activity; the phenomenon was, nevertheless, extensively practised. In the eleventh century, when the Egyptian trade representative *Wen-Amon* (if his tale is a historical report and not a romance) was rejected in Byblos by the local king, a Byblian prophet 'saved' his mission by guaranteeing that Wen-Amon had been sent by the god Amon, for which reason his entreaties were to be respected. We even encounter reminiscences of this sort of prophetism in such late Roman sources as Apuleius' *The Golden Ass*, dating from the second century CE. There are accordingly good reasons to suppose that the phenomenon was common to the entire region. It was not confined to the worship of any particular deity, but existed everywhere. Thus, Israelite prophetism in all its various forms is to be regarded as a manifestation of this Near Eastern prophecy, and not as a specifically Israelite phenomenon. Which is by no means to deny that the message of Israelite prophecy contained specifically Israelite elements.

5.2.4 *The Writing Prophets*
My reason for allowing the writing prophets to introduce the reformation of pre-exilic religion is that we possess a number of texts which may be regarded as authentic quotations of the prophets in question. By the same token one should be aware that we have no other choice, since we in reality know nothing about the proclamation of the early prophets. Admittedly, we do possess a sizable corpus of narratives about Elijah and Elisha, but these stories have, for one thing, been reworked by the Deuteronomistic editors, and, for another, they consist of legends the significance of which consists more in deed than in word. The speeches and views which have been inserted into the mouths of Elijah and Elisha respectively, mainly represent the opinions of the Deuteronomistic redactors.

Scholars have often regarded Jehu's revolution as an early example of the effects of the Yahwistic reform movement; however, the actual motives behind this break with the religious policy of the Omrides were probably quite different. And this may be maintained in spite of the fact that later tradition understood Jehu's revolution in quite another light, and also in spite of the fact that Jonadab ben Rechab, the ancestor of the Rechabites, is supposed to have participated in the revolution. In actuality, Jehu's religious programme was directed against a foreign cult, namely the worship of the Tyrian Ba'al.

The oldest collection of what are at least in part authentic prophetic writings may be dated to the latter part of the eighth century BCE. It would exceed our purposes here to examine all fifteen of the prophetic writings in the Old Testament; indeed, we shall content ourselves with only a couple of examples of this literature. However, the passages in question should serve to illustrate why it has been felt appropriate to assign the responsibility for the re-evaluation of the religious life to the prophets.

The first example is from the book which bears the name of the north Israelite prophet, Hosea. By way of introduction, we are informed of the marriage of Hosea to a harlot (ch. 1). This was a *symbolic action* which was intended to characterize the relationship between Israel and Yahweh. Thus, the metaphor which Hosea used to describe the relationship between the people and God was that of marriage, and the fruits of this union, namely the children whom Hosea got together with the harlot Gomer, were given significant names which pointed to the results of the marriage between Yahweh and Israel. The first son was called *Jezreel*, presumably in recollection of the bloody origins of the Jehu dynasty, but at the same time also a pun on the name Israel. The second child, a daughter, was called 'Without Pity', a name that suggested that Yahweh would be pitiless in the end. Finally, the second son received the name 'Not My People', signifying that the Israelites would be mercilessly rejected by Yahweh.

In the next section (ch. 2) the marriage metaphor recurs. Israel was the unfaithful wife who had to be punished (and, it should be recalled, the punishment for unfaithfulness was death at the time). The prophet subsequently goes on to unveil just in what Israel's crime consisted, according to Yahweh. The people had misinterpreted Yahweh's rôle; they had understood '*the ba'als*' (note the plural) as the ones who conferred fertility on the land. They had also misused their wealth so as to use its products to fashion idols for the ba'als. The actual reference is to the official national religion in the northern kingdom, as the ba'als, which were fashioned of gold and silver, refer mainly to the golden calf in Bethel (cf. Hos. 3.15; 8.4f.; 10.5; 13.2). As with the unfaithful wife in the metaphor, so would it go with unfaithful Israel, or so the prophet maintained; but, unlike the fate of unfaithful wives in general, Israel would be given a chance to make a new beginning. Israel would be taken back into the desert, and here the relationship between Israel and Yahweh would be as it had been in ancient times. The new 'betrothal' (Hos. 2.19) would be a betrothal in justice and righteousness: Israel would become righteous, and Yahweh would then once more reveal himself to be the merciful and generous god of old.

The other example is from the preaching of the almost contemporary Judaean prophet, Isaiah, who experienced both the fall of Samaria and the siege of Jerusalem under Sennacherib. Isaiah, too, had a serious message for his fellow countrymen, as we see already in ch.1 (a chapter, which is almost a compendium of the works of this prophet). Like Hosea 2, Isaiah 1 is framed as a speech which the prophet delivered to the people. In this case, one is immediately struck by the fact that Isaiah's speech is an *accusation* which lists a number of offences of which the people are said to be guilty. Also as in Hosea 2 the introduction begins with a flourish of metaphor, although this section has no single comprehensive metaphor. The prophet's intention, however, is clear enough: the Israelites were the unnatural children who did not even know their own father. For this reason the land was punished and languished in ruin. Jerusalem alone was left. The crimes committed by Israel are specified in the next section: injustice rules amongst this people. They think to be able to buy God's approval of their actions by means of sacrifices. This, however, is in vain, for it is not the content of the worship service that is significant, but the attitude of the worshippers. Thus Israel is not to expect any improvement of her relationship to her God before the people 'learn to do good; seek justice, correct oppression; defend the fatherless, plead for the widow' (Isa. 1.17, RSV). Isaiah was also familiar with the metaphor of the unfaithful wife, but he does not employ it in the same pregnant way as does Hosea, since his targets were the unjust executors of the law, the false judges, the assaults of the mighty on the weak in the society. However, this prophet, too, held that Israel would be punished and purified of her dross. After this, the relationship would be as it once was, and justice and righteousness would reign anew. Isaiah 1 concludes on a reprimand addressed to those who worship outside of Jerusalem.

These two texts do not immediately reveal that a religious reorientation was under way. The most important concepts in them are largely the same as those we encounter in the Psalms: there is a special relationship between God, that is, Yahweh, and Israel, and this relationship manifests itself in a demand for righteousness. This righteousness is further defined as a social balance within Israelite society, a situation in which 'the widow, the orphan, and the poor' receive according to their needs. Isaiah and Hosea, as well as other contemporary and later prophets who worked independently of them, nevertheless have a different view of those who participate in the cult than the one we find in the Psalms. For them the question was: did their fellow countrymen serve Yahweh only with their lips, or with their deeds as well?

5.2.5 The Prophets' Understanding of the Correct Worship of God
In reality, what the prophets did was to radicalize attitudes which were already in existence. To begin with, they stressed the obligation to worship Yahweh in such a way that it became a demand to worship *only* Yahweh. In the second place, they denied that the right worship of God consisted in mere lip-service; they demanded that the need for righteousness be taken seriously. As far as terminology was concerned, they did not differ markedly from the terminology in the Psalms on the issue of righteousness, and for this reason their addition to the ancient tradition was unproblematic. According to this tradition, 'the widow, the orphan, and the poor' were the archetypes of the vulnerable categories of people in the ancient Orient: these were the individuals who had no power to enforce their own just demands, or else they were those who were simply crushed by the problems of everyday life.

On the other hand, the prophets differed from the tradition not only in the fact that they demanded that the ideology of righteousness should be carried out in real life—which could well be just so many pretty words—but they also noted critically that it was not carried out. In short, one of the constant themes, dating from Amos and Hosea in the eighth century to Jeremiah, at the beginning of the exile, was that the society no longer lived in accordance with that righteousness which was identical with the order of the world. The Israelites had given the powers of chaos free play, they had allied themselves with them; they had 'made a covenant with death' (Isa. 28.15).

The prophets acknowledged that Yahweh directed the course of history, that is, that he was the God who could either bring catastrophe upon Israel or save her from the hands of her enemies. Not even on this point was the prophetic proclamation anything new; but here, too, they radicalized the common view. Israel's disasters were interrelated with her crimes; but the promised punishment—in the prophets' eyes—now contained the possibility of total destruction if the people did not mend their ways. For this reason the main representatives of the writing prophets are frequently described as *prophets of doom* (i.e. judgment). Scholars have perhaps tended to underplay the prophetic predictions of a better and happier future for the 'remnant that will be left' (the symbolic name of Isaiah's son), if they repented.

5.2.6 *The Prophetic Critique of the Cult*

The prophetic critique of the cult can hardly be taken to suggest that they demanded the rejection of the temple cult as such. If this had been the case, there would hardly have been any reason to complain about worship which took place elsewhere; there would have been no reason to prefer one form of worship to another. Rather, the prophetic critique had to do with the wrong attitudes of those who sacrificed in the temple.

However, the prophets did direct particular criticism of the worship that took place at the local sanctuaries, and two prophets whose activities were in the north criticized especially the cult at the royal sanctuary of Bethel and the other great sanctuaries of the northern kingdom, like Gilgal. As previously discussed, scholars have often interpreted these criticisms, which were already voiced by the prophets of the eighth century BCE, as a break with Canaanite religion, on the theory that this religion had led the Israelites to abandon their old god in favour of lascivious religious experiences 'under every green tree'. As we have seen, however, there is some question as to whether this criticism has been correctly interpreted. It did not actually have anything to do with Canaanite gods, but with the identification of Yahweh with Ba'al. This is completely clear in the book of Hosea, since according to him the idol which the people 'kissed' was that of the calf in Bethel (Hos. 13.2), which they had made for themselves. But this calf represented Yahweh, a matter on which not even the Deuteronomists were in doubt (cf. 1 Kgs 12. 26f.). Moreover, new archeological finds suggest that this Israelite bull-cult was of ancient origin; it was nothing that was suddenly invented by Jeroboam. At any rate, the archeologists have recently found a calf-sanctuary in Manassite territory which dates from the pre-national period. When this cult was rejected, it was at the same time a rejection of the fertility religion and the vegetation cycle. In the royal temple in Jerusalem Yahweh was El, the creator-god and preserver of

248   *Ancient Israel*

the cosmos, as well as the guarantor of righteousness. Thus, it was in principle possible to accuse the inhabitants of this site that they did not live up to the ideal of righteous dealing. But one could just as easily accuse them of worshipping Yahweh in other locations, since Yahweh was perhaps understood there as a fertility god. In the northern kingdom, it is possible that Jeroboam identified Yahweh with Ba'al as a counterweight to the Jerusalemite ideology; or perhaps this identification was more ancient still. In that event, Yahweh as understood in Israel was the chaos-battler and vegetation god rather than the world-creator, and if this was the case, then there was no qualitative difference between the Israelites' worshipping at the royal sanctuary or on the 'high places', that is, in the local sanctuaries.

5.2.7 *Righteousness or Fertility*

The fertility religion had traditionally played a dominant part in Palestinian agrarian society, and this type of religion was the target of the Israelite prophets' attack on the *Israelites'* worship. The tradition on which the prophets relied, and which sustained them in their assaults on the fertility religion, were every bit as ancient a part of West Asiatic religion as the fertility cult. This was the idea that righteousness was the force which governed the world, and without which the world would cease to exist. The fertility religion satisfied the immediate need of the Palestinian populace to be able to control the forces of nature. The concept of righteousness, however, was an expression of the socio-political experiences of Palestinian society throughout the millennia. It was a sort of answer to the repression of the weak in society which had always been a danger to the existence of the individual, and which was every bit as significant as the dangers which nature presented. In the latter part of the period of the monarchy, prophetism called for a break with one major aspect of the religious life of the country, although in actual fact the consequences were no more radical than that Yahweh remained the God, who assured the country of its fertility. But the prophets placed their main emphasis on the ethical aspects of the religion. In so doing, they intensified the tendency towards a centripetal movement pointing to the one sanctuary in which they felt that this aspect of their religion was best cultivated.

5.3 *The Deuteronomistic and Exilic Reinterpretation of the Heritage of Reform Prophetism*

5.3.1 *'Canaanite' versus 'Israelite'*

That the Deuteronomists were interested in reform prophetism is attested by a number of indications. For one thing, they either reworked or else simply edited collections of prophetic writings; for another, they assimilated into their own message significant portions of the prophetic proclamation. It must be noted, however, that on a number of points they relaxed the emphasis demanded by the prophets and stressed other features instead. In a way, it might be said that the Deuteronomists created the opposition to Canaanite religion, in that they identified the fertility religion with the religion which had been present in the country prior to the Israelite immigration, while they at the same time identified the ethical religion with the worship which the Israelites had brought with them into Palestine. Much more than was the case with the writing prophets, the Deuteronomists made their religion into a servant of history, and their historical theology entailed a marked restructuring of the history of Israelite religion. By re-organizing the course of history in such a way that Israel already existed as a society before her arrival in the land of *Canaan*, it became possible to assert the concept of a pure, Israelite national religion which had existed prior to the immigration. And this entailed further that Israel's struggle against Canaan came fully to parallel Yahweh's struggle with Ba'al.

This focus on the oppositional relationship between Yahweh and Ba'al, that is, between the religion of ethical righteousness and the religion of fertility, eventually resulted to some extent in the dilution of the demand for righteousness. For the Deuteronomists the problem finally evolved into the problem of the 'physical' relationship between the two gods. Thus, on their view the Israelites had of necessity to *choose* between Yahweh and Ba'al, rather than between righteousness and fertility. Hence the external manifestation of one's relationship to Yahweh became a dominant issue. In this way, for the Deuteronomists 'to do right in the eyes of Yahweh' was no longer primarily synonymous with behaving righteously, but with rejecting other types of worship: one had to concentrate all one's piety on the worship of the national god, Yahweh.

Of course, the theology of righteousness did not disappear; it did, however, become subordinated to the demand for a strictly

monotheistic religion. The reason for this changed relationship
between the emphases on faith in righteousness and on Yahweh as its
preserver and the faith in Yahweh as the sole god had to do with the
changed socio-cultural situation in which the Deuteronomists found
themselves after the deportations to Mesopotamia. In the exilic
situation, what was required was pregnant manifestations of those
features which were *national* in character, that is, Israelite, as a result
of the confrontation with a foreign culture. Previously, of course, it
had been possible to concentrate on the evaluation of conditions
within Israel's domestic situation.

5.3.2 *View of History*

On the other hand, it is important to recognize that the Deuteronomists' understanding of history was both a systematization and a
radicalization of the prophetic view of history. In the pre-exilic
period, the prophets had regarded the course of history as evidence of
either Yahweh's wrath or of his satisfaction with Israel. By way of
contrast, the Deuteronomists utilized the prophetic sin-and-retribution
scheme in a stringently systematic manner. They interpreted the
history of Israel according to this scheme, for which reason it became
the constitutive theological structure of their reconstruction of
Israel's history. Already during their first days in the country the
Israelites had abandoned their god, and in spite of manifold warnings
and examples as to how terrible the consequences of this would be,
they persisted like disobedient children. Thus Nebuchadnezzar's
conquest of Jerusalem was the final result of the fact that the
Israelites had broken the covenant between Yahweh and Israel, a
covenant into which the Israelites had once voluntarily entered.

5.3.3 *The Exilic Theology of History*

Either intentionally or unintentionally the Deuteronomists failed to
link their theology of history to other religious conceptions; but on
this point they were not followed by all their co-religionists. During
the exilic period we find a clear example of a different religious
interpretation of history, the roots of which lay in Jerusalemite
worship in the pre-exilic period. I refer to the connection which was
drawn between history and creation theology by the anonymous
prophet whom we call Deutero-Isaiah, and whose effort in this
direction was by no means a fluke of fate. The worship of El had
entailed belief in a creation which had taken place back in the *Urzeit*,

and in the course of which cosmos had emerged from chaos. The understanding of time implicit in this concept might be called *linear*, which is to say that it is related to the modern understanding of time. This understanding of temporality differed importantly from that of the fertility religion, which was indissolubly bound to the annual cycle, for which reason it may be termed either *cyclical* or *circular*. Time 'became alive' (as the Old Testament puts it) *every year*; it was recreated every year and subsequently followed the course of the year and of nature until it was recreated anew the following year. In an agrarian society, at least in principle, every year would resemble every other; indeed, it would be a copy of the previous year. Irregularities were regarded as divergences from the ideal, which was not conceived of as an average year, but as the *optimal* year, the one in which nature, meaning the gods, showered food upon man so that all could survive.

It should be obvious that as soon as a creation theology emerges victorious over a fertility theology the consequence is a new understanding of time, as Israelite post-exilic religion clearly illustrates. However, it is also clear that above all because the Israelite religious conceptions became linked with the idea of worship of a single deity its variety of creation theology did not omit to assimilate some features of the cyclic understanding of time. The official religion in the temple in Jerusalem during the monarchical period represents this sort of syncretism, in that Yahweh, understood as El, had replaced Ba'al in his capacity as combater of chaos. When cosmos was understood to have been created out of chaos (cf. Genesis 1), the chaos-battle changed its character. It had become the 'primeval battle', and so an integrated part of the creation. In the event that Yahweh annulled his work of creation, as in fact occurred when the Flood inundated the earth, this simultaneously entailed that Yahweh had given the forces of chaos free reign so that the control of the world came into the hands of hostile powers. In post-exilic Judaism the concept of the creation of the world was counterbalanced by the notion of its destruction, when chaos would once again be in force. Therefore the battle between good and evil and their respective representatives which was supposed to come after 'Judgment Day' was really a repetition of the primeval battle between the creator god and the power of chaos. This concept was by no means the exclusive property of Israelite-Jewish religion. We encounter it in many ancient cultures in which the cyclical understanding of time had altered in such a way that the period from creation to judgment was identified with an *aeon*, a world-age. It was accordingly believed that one world-age followed another or, alternatively, that the latter was identical with the former, that is, so that all things repeated themselves.

It was Deutero-Isaiah's achievement to link the creation theology and its linear understanding of time with the Deuteronomistic reconstruction of Israel's history. This entailed the identification of the original creation battle against the forces of chaos with Israel's liberation from the 'Chaos-power', Egypt. This battle was symbolically expressed by the passage of the Sea of Reeds, so that the parting of the waters of the Sea of Reeds corresponded to Yahweh's treatment of the chaos-monster (just as Babylonian Marduk cuts Tiamat, the sea-monster, into two parts). Deutero-Isaiah was accordingly also in a position to describe Israel's expected return from Babylon as a new chaos-battle, a new creation, which would be the beginning of a new world age. According to such an understanding, the destruction of the state of Judah in 587 BCE could be identified with the destruction of the created world, that is, cosmos. In reality, this is entirely logical, since in the pre-exilic period Israel as state and society was understood as cosmos, the land of the creator-god. Israel came into being when it was liberated from chaos, that is, Egypt, and on this analogy it was delivered into the power of chaos once again with the deportation to Mesopotamia. Chaos reigned from the moment Israel had ceased to exist, because Yahweh had surrendered his control of the country which he had created for himself as cosmos.

6. The Origins of Yahwism

6.1 The Question of Method

The religio-sociological background of post-exilic religion and its socio-political consequences have already been discussed and do not require repetition. The Canaanite character of pre-exilic religion, that is, its general position among the West Asiatic religions, has also been discussed. We are left with the question of the origins of the worship of Yahweh. That this is something of a problem is evident when we consider the fact that we have no evidence of a deity called Yahweh in Palestine prior to the emergence of Israel. The worship of El and Ba'al, as well as what was represented by each figure, were familiar facts of the second millennium BCE and perhaps even earlier.

But the deity called Yahweh was a novelty; thus our question concerns where he came from and what he was.

Any answer to these questions must remain hypothetical, as the Old Testament account is historically impossible. We are accordingly forced to try to peer behind the official account of the origins of Yahwism in the Old Testament and supplement this effort, if possible, with extra-biblical information. One must seek to determine whether the various types of information have any common features; after which it will be appropriate to employ historical and tradition-historical means to try to give this deity contours and an essence.

6.2 *Yahweh's Place of Origin and his Attributes*
6.2.1 *Yahweh from Sinai*

In this connection one should be aware that some scholars have pointed to references in Egyptian sources of the second millennium BCE to the presence of the *shasu* nomads in the Sinai Peninsula. Particular interest has attached to references to what was either a group of these nomads or their territory, in the texts termed *shasu jhw'*, that is, 'Yahweh's shasu' or 'shasu from Yahweh'. Of course, this information would not be held significant if we did not already possess sources which link Yahweh with the Sinai Peninsula. The connection, however, is undeniable. What is perhaps the oldest text in the Old Testament, the *Song of Deborah*, presents Yahweh as '*the one from Sinai*' (Judg. 5.5; the expression has been left out of the RSV, as from the Danish Bible, but quite senselessly). This phrase is to be compared with Ps. 68.9, which refers to Yahweh as the 'lord of Sinai'. Many scholars hold that this psalmic fragment is almost as old as the Song of Deborah and, like it, also of north Israelite origin. But these coincidences would nevertheless be of little significance if virtually the entire Old Testament tradition did not also locate Yahweh's place of origin in the Sinai Peninsula. So it is a matter of only secondary importance whether Yahweh's sanctuary was originally located at the traditional site of *Djebel Musa* (the 'mountain of Moses') in south Sinai, or in the great oasis of '*Ein Quderat*, biblical *Kadesh Barnea* in the northern part of the peninsula. We must conclude that Yahweh was originally located in the Sinai Peninsula, and that he was 'brought' to Palestine sometime between the end of Late Bronze Age and the emergence of the Israelite monarchy. This, however, is all we can say with any degree of certainty.

6.2.2 *Who was Yahweh from Sinai?*

The next questions are, what sort of god was this Yahweh, and who imported him? These are very much tradition-historical problems, and they are inseparable from the Sinai traditions in Exodus. The present framework of the narrative emphasizes the revelation of the religious laws. Some parts of this account, as, for example, the Ten Commandments, may be very old, but the narrative nevertheless first achieved its permanent form through the Priestly redaction of the Pentateuch. Form critical investigations of this section of Exodus 19ff. have suggested that once we remove the revelation of the law the *theophany*, that is, God's self-revelation, is the central event. According to the narrative in Exodus 19, Yahweh reveals himself in thunder, smoke, and fire. Corresponding descriptions of theophanies were by no means unknown elsewhere in the ancient Orient, but they do also figure in the Old Testament. As an example, one might consider Psalm 29, in which the theophany is accompanied by thunder, fire, and earthquake. However, such external manifestations of the activity of a deity do not tell us anything decisive about his character. Nevertheless, it would not be unreasonable to suppose that a deity who was associated with thunder, lightning, and earthquakes was probably regarded as a *storm god*. In this connection it would be fitting to refer to the well-known West Asiatic storm god of many names as a parallel to the Yahweh we encounter in many of the oldest biblical sources. Yahweh may well have been the local manifestation of the storm god on Sinai and, later, in Palestine.

It is in any case interesting that the Old Testament voices clear opposition to this understanding of the deity in the narrative of Elijah's visit to Horeb (another name for Sinai). Here Yahweh reveals himself to Elijah, and the description of the theophany is very suggestive:

> And behold, the Lord passed by, and a great and strong wind which cleft the mountains and shattered the rocks went before the Lord, but the Lord was not in the earthquake. After the earthquake came fire, but the Lord was not in the fire; and after the fire was a still small voice, and when Elijah heard it he wrapped his face in his cloak (1 Kgs 19.11-13).

One might say that a religion which described Yahweh as the god who brought water for the fields had no use for a Yahweh who 'strips the bark off the trees' (Ps. 29.9) and, likewise, that a religion which praised Yahweh as the maintainer of the cosmos did not require a Yahweh who manifested himself in an earthquake. Conversely, certain characteristics of the figure of Yahweh which have been held to reflect the original and most intimate aspects of him, such as his jealousy, his wrath, his hatred of other gods, and so forth, might be taken to indicate that he was regarded at an early point in time as a storm god and a war god.

6.2.3 *The Levites and Moses*

We do not know for certain just who brought Yahweh to Palestine, except that it certainly was not 'all Israel'. Many theories have been proposed to explain the phenomenon, but it is characteristic of these theories that they can neither be confirmed nor disproved. They more or less float in the air. Scholars have pointed out that the Pentateuchal tradition regards the Levites as Yahweh's priesthood, and that these Levites are treated like foreigners, in that they are forbidden to own land. It is therefore conceivable that the Levites did not originally belong to Israel, and that they were once an ancient Yahwistic priestly group who served at a sanctuary on Sinai. This priesthood, or parts of it, could have immigrated during the pre-national period and then have settled throughout Palestine.

However, there is another and at least equally reasonable explanation for the peculiar situation of the Levites. This position maintains that their place in the traditions was not the result of their early history, but a reflection of their situation at the time the traditions about the past were systematized, that is, not in the second millennium BCE, but in the middle of the first millennium. If this was the case, then the emphasis on their monopoly of the priesthood could be understood as a counterweight to the poverty to which they were subjected when the local sanctuaries were destroyed and the cult was centralized to Jerusalem. Their lack of property could also be explained by the supposition that this was a characteristic of the priesthood in general, or, alternatively, one might suggest that it reflected the social situation of the rural Levites, or, finally, it is possibly a result of Josiah's reform, through which they lost their holdings.

There are still many scholars who maintain that *Moses* was behind the introduction of Yahweh into Israel. This idea has frequently been combined with the notions of an exodus from Egypt and an immigration into the land. Thus it has been claimed that it was not 'all Israel' which participated in these events, but only a small group, a *Moses-band*. When we consider the position that Moses now enjoys in the tradition, this view is alluring. Nevertheless, it is imperative to ask whether his position within the history of Israelite religion had always been so eminent. As late as the transition from the eighth to the seventh century BCE king Hezekiah undertook to remove from the temple in Jerusalem a cult symbol which Moses was supposed to have made (2 Kgs 18.4). In other words, we do not know just who and what this Moses was before the late sources elevated him to the status of founder of the religion. We only know what the tradition made him into. It is important to acknowledge this, because the figure of Moses is frequently cited as the last bastion of the Old Testament account of the history of Israel and her religion. One sometimes even hears the remark that 'if Moses didn't exist, one would have had to invent him'. To which we may reply, with Mario Liverani, that they *did* in fact invent him! Or, as Martin Noth once expressed it, all that ancient Israel actually knew about Moses was that he was supposed to have been buried in the region east of the Jordan, and that no one knew where!

7. *Concluding Remarks*

This quite negative final conclusion confirms the view which underlies this entire study, namely that the Old Testament is a very poor source if pre-national Israelite society and its religion are the objects of enquiry. All that we can be sure of is that the Israelite conception of Yahweh during the period of the monarchy did not contain features which distinguished his worship from other types of religion in western Asia. When the Jewish religion evolved in the late monarchy, during the exile, and in the post-exilic period, it signified a novelty with respect to the earlier form of the religion. However, it was not something definitively new, but only a new way of organizing the already existing religious conceptions of the Israelites. The historical development of the religion of Israel took place in such a way that it generally followed the profane history of the land and people. During the period of the monarchy an impartial observer would scarcely have noted any differences between the states of Israel or Judah and any of the other kingdoms in the region, such as Moab, Ammon, or the Aramaic petty-states in Syria. In a corresponding way, such an observer would hardly have seen any special features in the Israelite form of worship which might have convinced him that what he was seeing was different from phenomena he had perhaps observed among Israel's neighbours. It was first with their experiences during the exile that the Israelites emerged as a distinct and special people, that is, as the Jews; and for this reason their future secular and religious history was to represent something exceptional.

A GUIDE TO RELEVANT LITERATURE

Bibliographical Notes
Traditionally a book like this includes a bibliography at the end, or else bibliographical excurses are dispersed at various points in the text. It is the intention of such a bibliography to list the most important studies which form the basis of the book itself, and at the same time, to present the reader with a starting point for further study. It is, however, my intention here to replace the bibliographical listing with a continuous bibliographical commentary. In this commentary first of all monographs are listed which contain new ideas. Secondly, works are included which are more or less directly in opposition to my own opinion. The list only includes books in English and an occasional article or two.

It is not difficult to obtain traditional bibliographies in order to supplement my rather short list of titles here. Most of the monographs mentioned here should provide such information. Among the better sources of bibliographical information are John H. Hayes and J. Maxwell Miller, *Israelite and Judaean History* (London, 1977), J. Alberto Soggin, *A History of Israel* (London, 1985), and Norman K. Gottwald, *The Hebrew Bible* (Philadelphia, 1985). Finally, I shall not omit to mention the bibliographical notes in such a general reference work as *The Interpreter's Dictionary of the Bible* I-IV (Nashville, 1962), Supplementary Volume (Nashville, 1976).

General Works
Israel was a part of the ancient Near East. Therefore, it is mandatory to obtain a basic knowledge of the ancient world in order to appreciate the history and culture of Israel. I shall in this section mention only one outstanding work, I.E.S. Edwards, C.J. Gadd and N.G.L. Hammond, *The Cambridge Ancient History*, 3rd edn, Vols. 1,i-ii, and 2,i-ii (Cambridge, 1970-1975). The new edition only covers the period before 1000 BCE, but a revision of the remaining volumes is in preparation. It is important to note that works of this kind are

normally written by highly esteemed scholars who have most of their career behind them. Thus, the scholarly position of a work like the *Cambridge Ancient History* is generally a statement of the 'current opinion', and it does not point forward to new horizons. A work like the *Cambridge Ancient History* cannot therefore be quite up to date, and necessarily always contains a series of outdated opinions.

Several histories of ancient Israel are presently available. They are mainly exponents of what was until the last decade the common opinion on the historical development of Israel. Only seldom are we presented with the necessary question as to the most important problem, the relationship between textual evidence and the events which the written sources narrate. To be included here are the histories of John Bright, *A History of Israel* (3rd edn; Philadelphia, 1981), and Martin Noth, *The History of Israel* (2nd edn; London, 1959). The newer histories by Siegfried Herrmann, *A History of Israel in Old Testament Times* (2nd edn; London, 1981), and Hendrik Jagersma, *A History of Israel in the Old Testament Period* (London, 1982) hardly go beyond the boundaries laid down by Noth and Bright. A growing new orientation is manifesting itself in John H. Hayes and J. Maxwell Miller, *Israelite and Judaean History* (London, 1977), and especially in J. Alberto Soggin, *A History of Israel* (London, 1985).

The amount of non-biblical texts from the ancient Near East has been rapidly growing during the last hundred years. To be included among them are texts from Western Asia as well as cuneiform writings from Mesopotamia and hieroglyphic inscriptions and papyri from Egypt. The West Semitic inscriptions of the first millennium BCE have been collected by J.C.L. Gibson, *Textbook of Syrian Semitic Inscriptions I-III* (Oxford, 1971-1982), and a selection of texts from the region as a whole is translated in James B. Pritchard, *Ancient Near Eastern Texts Relating to the Old Testament* (3rd edn; Princeton, 1969). A much smaller but easily available collection of texts has been edited by Walter Beyerlin, *Near Eastern Religious Texts Relating to the Old Testament* (London, 1978).

Chapter 1. Geography, Demography, Economy
There are at present several student atlases of the Bible which may be readily available; among the best is Herbert G. May, *Oxford Bible Atlas* (London, 1961). None of them is absolutely satisfying, since they are mostly too simplified for serious studies. The best manual is

without doubt that of H.T. Frank, J. Monson *et al.*, *Student Map Manual. Historical Geography of the Bible Lands* (Jerusalem, 1979 [repr. 1983]), although the arrangement of the maps is unusual. Sooner or later a proper map of Israel will be indispensable and the best available today is that of Ernst Höhne, *Palästina. Historisch-archäologische Karte* (Göttingen, 1981). It comprises two detailed maps of Palestine in the scale 1:300,000.

A general survey of the geography of Palestine is presented by Denis Baly, *The Geography of the Bible* (2nd edn; New York, 1974), and a modern description of the geographical conditions is found in Yehuda Karmon, *Israel. A Regional Geography* (London, 1971). A historical geography was published by Yohanan Aharoni, *The Land of the Bible* (2nd edn; Philadelphia, 1979).

Two important works on the living conditions and culture of ancient Israel should also be included in this list, although both of them are somewhat dated: Johannes Pedersen, *Israel. Its Life and Culture,*. I-II (London, 1926-1940) and Roland de Vaux, *Ancient Israel*, I-II (New York, 1961). Both works contain an extraordinary amount of insight and knowledge, but also an evident disregard for the importance of a scientifically oriented social-anthropological approach to the subject. As an introduction to a modern study of the living conditions and social structure of ancient Israel it is advisable to obtain such sociological knowledge. A well-known and respected introduction to this field is Ian M. Lewis, *Social Anthropology in Perspective* (Harmondsworth, 1976). A fine example of the possibilities of a scientifically oriented study of the living conditions is David C. Hopkins, *The Highlands of Canaan* (Sheffield, 1985). Although this monograph is devoted to the study of the agricultural sector in the early Iron Age it is also relevant to more than 90% of the population in Palestine during all of its history before 1948 CE.

Chapter 2. Text and History
There are, at present, several general introductions to the OT literature, popular ones as well as scholarly books. I shall only mention a small selection of the newest. J. Alberto Soggin, *Introduction to the Old Testament* (2nd edn; London, 1980) belongs to the last-mentioned category. As representing the first category we may refer to Rolf Rendtorff, *The Old Testament. An Introduction* (London, 1985), and the rather unconventional 'sociological' introduction by Norman K. Gottwald, *The Hebrew Bible. A Socio-Literary Intro-*

duction (Philadelphia, 1985). Rendtorff's book is a mixture of a traditional interpretation of the history and religion of Israel and some important new views on the development of the Israelite literature, especially as represented by the Pentateuch. Thus, it may be considered a preamble to a proper re-evaluation of Israel's political, religious and literary history, although Rendtorff himself does not seem prepared to abandon his traditional standpoint. Gottwald's *The Hebrew Bible* represents such a break with the classical understanding of Israel's history, but it is at the same time totally dependent on the same author's massive *The Tribes of Yahweh* (New York, 1979). Therefore, it combines an exceedingly traditional understanding of the age and milieu of the OT literature with a radical reassessment of especially the earliest history of Israel. We may say that Gottwald has been caught by the same trap as Rendtorff in that he does not provide a natural synthesis of his concept of Israelite history and his reconstruction of Israel's literary history.

Pertinent to the question of the OT as a source of historical knowledge is John Van Seters, *In Search of History* (New Haven, 1983). This monograph contains a radical reassessment of the age and character of Israelite history writing for which I have a great deal of sympathy, however, I would not overlook its apparent weaknesses in terms of methodological stringency. A short, but valuable monograph on historical method and the OT has been presented by J. Maxwell Miller, *The Old Testament and the Historian* (Philadelphia, 1976), and an excellent survey of the various aspects of the literary study of the OT has been written by John Barton, *Reading the Old Testament* (London, 1984).

Finally, this section should not omit references to the archeological evidence. I shall mention first and foremost the authoritative statement of Kathleen M. Kenyon, *Archaeology in the Holy Land* (4th edn; London, 1979). Another important book on this subject is Yohanan Aharoni, *The Archaeology of the Land of Israel* (London, 1982). Easily accessible even to the general reader is the archeological dictionary edited by Michael Avi-Yonah and Ephraim Stern, *Encyclopedia of Archaeological Excavations in the Holy Land*, I-IV (Oxford and Jerusalem, 1976-1978).

Chapter 3. Premonarchical Israel
The reconstruction of Israel's prehistory in this chapter is based on

Niels Peter Lemche, *Early Israel. Anthropological and Historical Studies on Israelite Society in Pre-Monarchical Times* (Leiden, 1985). This monograph should be seen in the light of the earlier discussion between the supporters of the OT version of the Israelite conquest of Palestine on one hand and the scholars who are highly critical of this notion on the other. The classical conflict between the supporters of the conquest theory and its alternative, the idea of a peaceful settlement of Israelite small-cattle nomads is represented by John Bright, *A History of Israel*, not in its 3rd edition (Philadelphia, 1981), but in its first (London, 1959), and Martin Noth, *The History of Israel* (2nd edn; London, 1959). A third explanatory model was presented by George E. Mendenhall, *The Hebrew Conquest of Palestine* (The Biblical Archaeologist Reader III; New York, 1970), pp. 100-120 (it originally appeared in 1962), according to which Israel originated via a peasants' rebellion in Palestine. This idea of a peasants' rebellion also forms the subject of Norman K. Gottwald, *The Tribes of Yahweh* (New York, 1979). See now also in this tradition the collection of articles edited by David N. Freedman and David F. Graf, *Palestine in Transition* (Sheffield, 1983).

Pre-Israelite Palestinian history (the little we know) is surveyed in *The Cambridge Ancient History*, I-II (3rd edn). The administrative system in a Western Asiatic state (Ugarit) is described by Michail Heltzer, *The International Organization of the Kingdom of Ugarit* (Wiesbaden, 1982). See also the same author's *The Rural Community of the Kingdom of Ugarit* (Wiesbaden, 1976). Giovanni Buccellati, *Cities and Nations of Ancient Syria* (Rome, 1967), deals with the question of the national state compared to the territorial state. His study must, however, be used with caution because of its somewhat unreflective application of the OT evidence.

The focal problem of the Hebrews (the *habiru*) has been the subject of several studies. The relevant sources have (until 1955) been collected and translated by Moshe Greenberg, *The Hab/piru* (New Haven, 1955). A reasonable survey of the problem, although perhaps not quite up to date, is included in Manfred Weippert, *The Settlement of the Israelite Tribes* (London, 1971), and in George E. Mendenhall, *The Tenth Generation* (Baltimore, 1973).

The social structure of Israelite tribal society has been examined by Niels Peter Lemche, *Early Israel* (Leiden, 1985); this study by and large presents a more complicated but also more accurate picture than the pertinent chapters in Norman K. Gottwald, *The Tribes of Yahweh* (New York, 1979).

The exposition of the earliest history of Israel here expressly disagrees with the one by Roland de Vaux, *The Earliest History of Israel*, I-II (London, 1978) which is only a fragment of what was intended to be the most voluminous history of Israel which has ever appeared in print. Of course it is also a departure from the model laid down by such scholars as John Bright and Martin Noth. My explanatory model may, on the other hand, draw support from monographic studies like A.D.H. Mayes, *Israel in the Period of the Judges* (London, 1974) (I published a monograph in Danish on the same subject and with the same title in 1972) and C.H.J. de Geus, *The Tribes of Israel* (Assen, 1976) (on the period of the Judges), or Thomas L. Thompson and Dorothy Irvin, 'The Joseph and Moses Narratives', in John H. Hayes and J. Maxwell Miller, *Israelite and Judaean History* (London, 1977), pp. 149-212, which may be evaluated as a conscious counterweight to studies like that of Siegfried Herrmann, *Israel in Egypt* (London, 1973). The study of the patriarchs has been totally changed since the publication of Thomas L. Thompson, *The Historicity of the Patriarchal Narratives* (Berlin, 1974), and John Van Seters, *Abraham in History and Tradition* (New Haven, 1975). Cautious endeavours to modify the theses of these authors have not been too successful (an example is William McKane, *Studies in the Patriarchal Narratives* [Edinburgh, 1979]).

Chapter 4. The Monarchy
It is characteristic of the modern study of the history of Israel that we possess a long series of important monographs about the pre-monarchical period, whereas only rather few studies have been devoted to the period of the Monarchy. This situation reflects the general attitude of scholars towards the Hebrew Monarchy. Most scholars actually adopt the OT view on the kings and their era. On this view, the monarchical period did not contribute to the development of the Israelite tradition, it only diluted it. Especially the religious development during the monarchy is interpreted as a departure from the pure Yahwistic faith.

The only newer monograph which is totally devoted to this period is, on the other hand, intended to be read by the general public, E.W. Heaton, *The Hebrew Kingdoms* (Oxford, 1968), but even here more than half of the space is occupied by a discussion of the religion and prophecy. The evolution which led to the establishment of the kingdom and later on to its dissolution into two independent states has been described by the later German scholar Albrecht Alt in two splendid articles, 'The Formation of the Israelite State in Palestine', and 'The Monarchy in the Kingdom of Israel and Judah', both of which appeared in an English translation in his *Essays on Old Testament History and Religion* (Oxford, 1966). Of course, the basic approach is quite different from the one presented in this book. Recently, the subject of the formation of the Israelite state has attracted the attention of several scholars, among whom Franck S. Frick, *The Formation of the State in Ancient Israel* (Sheffield, 1985) but see also the journal *Semeia*, 37 (1986): *Social Scientific Criticism of the Hebrew Bible and Its Social World: The Israelite Monarchy*, ed. Norman K. Gottwald.

A lively debate is presently concentrated on the subject of the most important source of Israelite monarchical history, the Deuteronomistic History. The foundation of this debate was laid as early as WW II, by Martin Noth in a study which has recently appeared in English translation in two parts as Martin Noth, *The Deuteronomistic History* (Sheffield, 1981) and *The Chronicler's History* (Sheffield, 1987). Of the modern studies I shall mention only a few, thus Richard D. Nelson, *The Double Redaction of the Deuteronomistic History* (Sheffield, 1981) and A.D.H. Mayes, *The Story of Israel between Settlement and Exile* (London, 1983). John Van Seters, *In Search of History* (New Haven, 1983) also contains an important contribution to this discussion. We must, however, not forget the monograph by Moshe Weinfeld, *Deuteronomy and the Deuteronomistic School* (Oxford, 1972) although he approaches the problem of Deuteronomism from another angle.

Israelite monarchical society has been described by Roland de Vaux, *Ancient Israel*, I (New York, 1961), although his treatment is a little antiquated now. The economic structure has been the subject of study by a professional economist, Morris Silver, *Prophets and Markets. The Political Economy of Ancient Israel* (Boston, 1983). The royal administration has been analyzed by Tryggve N.D. Mettinger, *Solomonic State Officials. A Study of the Civil Government Officials of the Israelite Monarchy* (Lund, 1971), while Gösta W. Ahlström has recently tried to explain the relationship between the royal administration and the official religion in his *Royal Administration and National Religion in Ancient Israel* (Leiden, 1982). Keith W. Whitelam, *The Just King* (Sheffield, 1979), defines on the other hand the juridical aspect of the Hebrew kingdom.

The concept of a 'reserve ideology' which is referred to above forms the theme of an important article by the American social anthropologist Philip C. Salzman, 'Ideology and Change in Middle Eastern Tribal Societies', *Man* n.s. (1978), pp. 618-37.

Shorter but (in the absence of more comprehensive monographs) important surveys of the political history are present in John H. Hayes and J. Maxwell Miller, *Israelite and Judaean History* (London, 1977), pp. 332-488 (by J. Alberto Soggin, Herbert Donner and Bustaney Oded). Among the monographic literature dealing with the formation of the state we may select Baruch Halpern, *The Constitution of the Monarchy in Israel* (Chico, 1981), and the traditions about Saul and David have been reviewed by David M. Gunn, *The Story of King David* (Sheffield, 1978) and *The Fate of King Saul* (Sheffield, 1980) (although mainly from a literary point of view).

On the religion in the period of the Monarchy, cf. Chapter 6.

Chapter 5. The Exilic and Post-Exilic Periods
The scholarly interest in the Exile and the Post-Exilic period is somewhat different from the lack of interest in the political history of the Israelite kingdoms. But, generally, the study of the political history during these 'dark' centuries has not awakened much response, whereas the intellectual development is a matter of much attention today. Only a few comprehensive monographical studies have been devoted to the period in general, among which Peter R. Ackroyd, *Exile and Restoration. A Study of Hebrew Thought of the Sixth Century BC* (London, 1968) is perhaps one of the most important (but see also his popular book, *Israel under Babylon and Persia* [Oxford, 1970]). Not to be forgotten are the contributions by Bustaney Oded and Geo Widengren, in John H. Hayes and J. Maxwell Miller, *Israelite and Judaean History* (London, 1977), pp. 435-539, and on the Babylonian exile James D. Newsome, *By the Waters of Babylon* (Edinburgh, 1980). An interesting study on the Jews in Mesopotamia in this period is Ran Zadok, *The Jews in Babylonia during the Chaldean and Achaemenian Periods according to the Babylonian Sources* (Haifa, 1979), a monograph especially devoted to the Jewish personal names in cuneiform sources. The living conditions in Palestine in the period have been expertly surveyed by Ephraim Stern, *The Material Culture in the Land of the*

Bible in the Persian Period, 538-332 BC (Jerusalem, 1982). Among other studies, especially on the intellectual response to the Exile and to the Persian and Hellenistic foreign regimes are Ralph W. Klein, *Israel in Exile* (Philadelphia, 1979), W.S. McCullough, *The History and Literature of the Palestinian Jews from Cyrus to Herod* (Toronto, 1976), and finally Morton Smith, *Palestinian Parties and Politics which Shaped the Old Testament* (New York, 1971). The content of these monographs and other studies shows, however, that my delimitation of my history to the period before Alexander the Great is an arbitrary one. The development of Jewish society did not, of course, stop in 332 BCE.

Chapter 6. Israelite religion
As was to be expected, the problem in this section is not to find relevant titles but to limit the number of books to be included here. Necessarily the bibliography must concentrate on the themes of this chapter. There are accordingly several aspects of Israelite religion which I do not even touch on, such as the very important question of how the Israelite and Jewish religion also produced the apocalyptic and messianic current of early Judaism. Here I may only refer to the recent synthesis by Benedikt Otzen, *Judaism in Antiquity* (Sheffield [in preparation]).

As a rule, the monographs listed below do not consider Israelite religion to be problematic. The account of the development of the Israelite religion thus usually follows the current opinion of Israel's historical development. We may here refer to the general histories of Israelite religion where this attitude is exposed in a pronounced way, as in Georg Fohrer, *History of Israelite Religion* (London, 1973), or in the perhaps more reliable synthesis, by Helmer Ringgren, *Israelite Religion* (2nd edn; London, 1969). My approach is based here as elsewhere on the fundamental question of the relationship between text and history, which in the context of religious history may be translated as the relationship between ideology and reality. To put the matter briefly, this is the question of myths. On this subject I can refer to Benedikt Otzen, Hans Gottlieb and Knud Jeppesen, *Myths in the Old Testament* (London, 1980), a book which irrespective of its pedagogical qualities leaves out rather important aspects of the modern study of myths, especially the structuralist view. More about this is included in the study by John Rogerson, *Myths in Old Testament Interpretation* (Berlin, 1974).

A short but clear characterization of West-Semitic religion is
included in John C.L. Gibson, *Canaanite Myths and Legends* (2nd
edn; Edinburgh, 1978). Here we also find the most important
Ugaritic texts transcribed and translated; the book also includes a
short but concise bibliography. Gibson's account of Canaanite
religion may be supplemented by the popular introduction in Helmer
Ringgren, *Religions of the Ancient Near East* (London, 1976). Among
the studies which have appeared since the publication of Gibson's
volume we may mention C.E. L'Heureux, *Rank among the Canaanite
Gods* (Missoula, 1979), as well as the extensive study of the Baal epos
from Ugarit by Baruch Margalit, *A Matter of 'Life' and 'Death'*
(Neukirchen, 1980). The monarchy in Western Asia has generally
been considered as 'sacral', e.g. by Ivan Engnell, *Studies in Divine
Kingship in the Ancient Near East* (Uppsala, 1943), although I am not
able to subscribe to his opinions. As a counterbalance, I may also call
attention to the monumental study by Henri Frankfort, *Kingship and
the Gods* (Chicago, 1948). An up-to-date account of the West-Semitic
view of kingship has yet to appear.

The problem of the appearance of the 'monotheistic Yahweh-
religion' is in fact the central theme already in Julius Wellhausen,
Prolegomena to the History of Ancient Israel, which appeared in 1878,
and which is perhaps the most famous study ever written in the field
of OT studies. An English translation is available with a preface by
W. Robertson Smith (reprint, New York, 1965). In many respects,
this is an account of the religious developments in ancient Israel to
which the present author is more able to subscribe than is the case
with most modern histories of religion. The question of monotheism
in Israel is, however, also the topic of OT theology. There are several
OT theologies presently available, but irrespective of their Christian
origin and basis they normally present a better description of what is
here defined as post-exilic religion than the histories of religion
contain. I shall mention the principal OT theology of the post-war
period, that by Gerhard von Rad, *Old Testament Theology*, I-II
(Edinburgh, 1962-1965), and also the recent synthesis by Ronald E.
Clements, *Old Testament Theology* (Atlanta, 1979). An interesting
study devoted to the temple and its priesthood has been written by
Moshe Haran, *Temples and Temple-Service in Ancient Israel* (Oxford,
1978), whereas Aelred Cody, *A History of Old Testament Priesthood*
(Rome, 1969) is totally at the mercy of the traditional view of
Israelite history.

Pre-exilic Israelite religion is often described as the outcome of the struggle between Israel and Canaan or of the struggle between Yahweh and Baal. Such studies normally contain a section on certain aspects of Canaanite religion, but they concentrate on its impact on Israelite religious development during the Monarchy. A clear exponent of this approach is William F. Albright, *Yahweh and the Gods of Canaan* (London, 1968) and Frank M. Cross, *Canaanite Myth and Hebrew Epic. Essays in the History of the religion of Israel* (Cambridge, Mass., 1973). Among the mass of studies along these lines, I may mention Patrick D. Miller, *The Divine Warrior in Early Israel* (Cambridge, Mass., 1973), E. Theodore Mullen, *The Assembly of the Gods (The Divine Council in Canaanite and Early Hebrew Literature)* (Chico, 1980) and the recent monograph by John Day, *God's Conflict with the Dragon and the Sea. Echoes of a Canaanite Myth in the Old Testament* (Cambridge, 1985).

Among the more specific aspects of pre-exilic religion we may mention a couple of studies on the character of Hebrew kingship, first and foremost Tryggve N.D. Mettinger, *King and Messiah. The Civil and Sacral Legitimation of the Israelite Kings* (Lund, 1976), a study by a Scandinavian scholar who has, however, departed from the previous Scandinavian, and also Anglo-Saxon speculations about the sacral position of the kings. See also Audry R. Johnson, *Sacral Kingship in Ancient Israel* (2nd edn; Cardiff, 1967).

In order to study the problem of the transformation of Israelite religion it is mandatory to obtain a general knowledge of modern scholarship devoted to prophecy in ancient Israel, although the central and classical major study on this is still Johannes Lindblom, *Prophecy in Ancient Israel* (Oxford, 1962), which is based on a Swedish original which appeared as early as 1934. Lindblom's chapter on the religio phenomenological aspects of prophecy may be supplemented by Ian M. Lewis, *Ecstatic Religion. An Anthropological Study of Spirit Possession and Shamanism* (London, 1978). More traditional views on prophecy are present in the books of Ronald E. Clements, *Prophecy and Covenant* (London, 1965), and *Prophecy and Tradition* (Oxford, 1975). The question of cultic prophecy has been considered by Audry R. Johnson, *The Cultic Prophet in Ancient Israel* (Cardiff, 1962). See also his more recent book, *The Cultic Prophet in Israel's Psalmody* (Cardiff, 1979). Newer views on the place of the prophet in his society and on the psychological and sociological aspects are expressed by Robert P. Carroll, *When*

Prophecy Failed (London, 1979), by Robert R. Wilson, *Prophecy and Society in Ancient Israel* (Philadelphia, 1982), and by David L. Petersen, *The Role of Israel's Prophets* (Sheffield, 1981).

A special problem is the age of the idea of the covenant in the OT. Unfortunately, the fundamental study on this by Lothar Perlitt, *Bundestheologie im Alten Testament* (Neukirchen, 1969), has not been translated into English. We may, however, recommend the survey by Denis J. McCarthy, *Old Testament Covenant. A Survey of Current Opinions* (Oxford, 1973) (a general introduction to the subject), and by the same author *Treaty and Covenant* (2nd edn; Rome, 1978). Also the survey of previous research by Ernest W. Nicholson, *Exodus and Sinai in History and Tradition* (Oxford, 1973), may be of interest. An exciting new essay on the re-evaluation of the concept of God during the Exile and in the early post-Exilic period has been published by Tryggve N.D. Mettinger, *The Dethronement of Sabaoth* (Lund, 1982).

It is important to understand that the deuteronomistic view of history was not their free invention, as it was rooted in a concept of the gods which was the common property of all Near Eastern religions. This subject has been studied especially by Bertil Albrektson, *History and the Gods. An Essay on the Idea of Historical Events as Divine Manifestations in the Ancient Near East and in Israel* (Lund, 1967). See also H.W.F. Saggs, *The Encounter with the Divine in Mesopotamia and Israel* (London, 1978), especially part III: 'The Divine in History', pp. 93-124.

Finally, the origin of the Yahwistic faith: The current opinion is duly transmitted by almost every study, whether a general introduction or a more specialized monograph. A classical exponent is George Fohrer, *History of Israelite Religion* (London, 1973). The most famous defence of the historicity of the Mosaic tradition is William F. Albright, *From the Stone Age to Christianity. Monotheism and the Historical Process* (2nd edn; New York, 1957). We may say that the approach of this last-mentioned book is the antithesis of my own interpretation.

INDEX

INDEX OF BIBLICAL REFERENCES

Genesis
1-11   36, 62, 166
1   61, 251
2   61
4   59
4.23-24   62
6-9   41, 61
11   59
11.28-31   31
12-36   36
12.6-7   59, 65
14.19   226
15   185
17   185
22   217
22.19-28   117
26.12ff.   16
28ff.   117
28   59, 62
29-30   20
29.31-30.24 98, 110
33.18-20   59, 65
34   65
36   62
37-50   36, 162
37.12-17   20
49   38

Exodus
1-15   36, 218
14   109
16-18   36
19-24   36, 254
19   254
20ff.   236
21.2-23.16 35, 71, 210
21.2-11   93, 94
21.2   85, 88
22.17-23.16 210
25-27   211
32   214
36-38   211

Leviticus
17-26   37, 210
19.26   215
25   37, 194

Numbers
1.1-47   97
1.48-54   97
3.14-39   97
10-36   36
18   214
21.4-9   166
23-24   38
26   103
26.29   103

Deuteronomy
11.26-32   65
12   64
18.10   215
27   65
32.8-9   225
34   36

Joshua
1-12   37
2-6   110, 111
6   71
7   91
8   59, 111
9   111
11.10   83
13-21   37, 89
23   62
24   65

Judges
1-12   37, 62
1   113
2   62
4   38
5   38, 103

5.5   253
6-8   107
6.25-32   225
9   65, 100, 134f., 162
9.8-15   135
10.1-5   107
11.34-40   216
12.7-15   107
13-16   37

1 Samuel
4   133
4.6, 9   133
8-12   120
8   120
8.11-17   152
9.1-10.16   120, 121
10.17-27   91, 121
11   121
12   121
12.25   121
13-14   133
13.3   133
16-2 Sam. 6 37, 52, 54
            119
16.14   234
28   241

2 Samuel
5.3   137
5.14-16   225
7-1 Kgs 2   37, 119
7   235
7.16   235
20.1   138

1 Kings
4   139
4.1-6   143
4.7-19   143

1 Kings (cont.)
6-7   140, 143, 211
7.13-40   155
9.10-14   142
9.15-25   139
9.15   71
10.1-13   143
11   126, 143
11.14-40   142
11.26   157
12   65, 143
12.16   138
12.26ff.   247
12.31   214
13   17, 163
14.29   58
15.7   58
15.27   157
15.31   58
15.33   58
16-2 Kgs 9   37
16   147
16.5   58
16.24   72
16.29   58
17-2 Kgs 13   157
18.2-6   153
19.11-13   254
21   151
22   241

2 Kings
2.23-24   17
3   216, 230
9   157
9.2   157
10.15-17   158
12   235
12.20-21   126
14.5   126
14.8-14   123
14.19-21   126
16.7   128
17   208
17.3-6, 24   128
17.8ff.   207
17.24-34   194
18-20   49
18-19   70
18.1-8   166
18.4   256

19.35-36   70
21.1-18   166
23.1-28   229
23.15-20   163
23.22   219
24.14, 16   180
25.12   177

1 Chronicles
8.33   225
8.34   225

Ezra
1.2-4   187
1.8   189
7.16   196

Psalms
1   38
2   168, 232
2.7   232
15   66
24   66
29   254
29.9   254
36   38
44.17   183
46.6-8   238
48.5-8   238
51   47
65   228
68   223
68.9   253
72   47, 230f., 234f.
72.1   47
78   223
80   124, 229
89   183, 229, 234f.
89.4-5   234
89.6-19   227
89.20ff.   234
93   228
98   229
104-106   38
105   223
106   223
110   168
110.3   232
132   235

132.11-12   235
137   38, 223

Proverbs
7   62
10ff.   62
10.25   241
10.30   241
12.2   241

Isaiah
1-39   45
1   245
1.17   245
5.1-7   63
7   50
11.1-9   231
28.15   246
36-39   49
40-55   45, 174
44.28   186
45.1   186
46.11   186
55-66   45, 174

Jeremiah
32   152
35   158
39.10   177
41.1-3   176

Ezekiel
14.14, 20   46
40-48   211

Amos
4.4   162
5.5   161
7.10-17   161

Hosea
1   244
2   244f.
2.19   244
3.15   244
4.13   207
4.15   161f.
8.4f.   244
8.5f.   161
9.15   162
10.5   244

Hosea (cont.)		12.12	162	Zechariah	
12	116	12.13	117	1–6	174
12.4-5	117	13.2	161, 244, 247		

INDEX OF AUTHORS

Ackroyd, P.R. 266
Aharoni, Y. 261f.
Ahlström, G. 265
Albrektson, B. 230, 270
Albright, W.F. 199, 269f.
Alt, A. 147, 265
Avi-Yonah, M. 262

Baly, D. 261
Barton, J. 262
Beyerlin, W. 260
Bright, J. 260, 263f.
Bucellati, G. 263

Carroll, R.P. 269
Clements, R.E. 268f.
Cross, F.M. 269

Day, J. 269

Edwards, I.E.S. 259
Engnell, I. 268

Fohrer, G. 267, 270
Frank, H.T. 261
Frankfort, H. 268
Freedman, D.N. 263
Frick, F.S. 265

Gadd, C.J. 259
Geus, C.H.J. de 264
Gibson, J.C.L. 260, 268
Gottlieb, H. 267
Gottwald, N.K. 259, 261ff., 265
Graf, D.F. 263
Greenberg, M. 263
Gunn, D.M. 266

Halpern, B. 266
Hammond, N.G.L. 259
Haran, M. 268
Hayes, J. 259f., 264, 266
Heaton, E.W. 264
Heltzer, M. 263
Herrmann, S. 260, 264
Höhne, E. 261
Hopkins, D.C. 261

Irvin, D. 264

Jagersma, H. 260
Jeppesen, K. 267
Johnson, A.R. 269

Karmon, Y. 261
Kenyon, K. 111, 262
Klein, R.W. 267

Lemche, N.P. 263f.
Lewis, I.M. 261, 269
L'Heureux, C.E. 268
Lindblom, J. 269
Liverani, M. 206, 256

McCarthy, D.J. 270
McCullough, W.S. 267
McKane, W. 264
Margalit, B. 268
May, H.G. 260
Mayes, A.D.H. 264f.
Mendenhall, G.E. 236, 263
Mettinger, T.N.D. 265, 269f.
Miller, J.M. 259f., 262, 264, 266
Miller, P.D. 269
Monson, J. 261
Mowinckel, S. 202f., 228
Mullen, E.T. 269

Nelson, R.D. 265
Nicholson, E.W. 270
Noth, M. 105ff., 256, 260, 263ff.

Oded, B. 266
Otzen, B. 267

Pedersen, J. 261
Petersen, D.L. 270
Perlitt, L. 270
Pritchard, J.B. 260

Rad, G. von 268
Rendtorff, R. 64f., 261f.
Ringgren, H. 267f.
Robertson Smith, W. 268
Rogerson, J. 267

Saggs, H.W.F. 270
Salzman, P.C. 266
Silver, M. 265
Smith, M. 267
Soggin, J.A. 259ff., 266
Stern, E. 262, 266

Thompson, T.L. 115f., 264

Van Seters, J. 115f., 262, 264f.

Vaux, R. de 261, 264f.

Weinfeld, M. 171, 265
Weippert, M. 263
Wellhausen, J. 209f., 240, 268
Whitelam, K. 265
Widengren, G. 266
Wilson, R.R. 270

Zadok, R. 266